Democracies and Foreign Policy

Bernard C. Cohen

Democracies and Foreign Policy

Public Participation in the United States and the Netherlands

The University of Wisconsin Press

The University of Wisconsin Press
114 North Murray Street
Madison, Wisconsin 53715

3 Henrietta Street
London WC2E 8LU, England

Printed in the United States of America

Library of Congress Cataloging-in-Publication Data

Cohen, Bernard Cecil, 1926–
    Democracies and foreign policy: public participation in the
United States and the Netherlands / Bernard C. Cohen.
       200 p.   cm.
    Includes bibliographical references and index.
    ISBN 0-299-14640-5 (cl.).   ISBN 0-299-14644-8 (pbk.)
    1. United States—Foreign relations—1945–1989—Citizen participation.
    2. Netherlands—Foreign relations—1948–1989—Citizen participation.
    I. Title.
    E840.C64   1995
    327.73—dc20   94-38501

For Sara
with love

Contents

Preface

This book is the result of more than a decade and a half of comparative study of democratic foreign-policy making. More specifically, it is a comparison of the public side of foreign-policy formulation in two Western democratic political systems, the United States and the Netherlands, during much of the Cold War. By the "public side of foreign-policy formulation," I mean all the manifestations of political activity in the foreign-policy arena that take place outside the institutions officially responsible for foreign policy and that have some impact on that policy. Despite a certain amount of skepticism, recurrently expressed, that any outside agencies can have any impact whatever on foreign policy, it is difficult to imagine a modern democratic system in which there is none.[1]

The course of my research on public participation in the foreign-policy making of these two countries has been marked, however, by more persistent questioning of a different sort, from a gallery of observers in both countries: Why the Netherlands? Why the United States and the Netherlands? Why do you need a comparison? What are you looking for? Why compare public participation, rather than foreign policies themselves? How do you compare these things? These are all legitimate—and provocative—questions, and they are deserving of answers here at the very beginning, although not necessarily in the order as above. One further question—what did you actually discover about public participation by this comparative inquiry?—will be addressed in all of the succeeding chapters.

To begin with, why a comparison? What am I looking for? These questions can be answered in part with a little bit of personal intellectual history. Throughout my professional life I have been concerned

---

1. See, e.g., Bernard C. Cohen, *The Public's Impact on Foreign Policy* (Boston: Little, Brown and Co., 1973).

with the foreign-policy-making process in the United States and particularly with the impact on foreign-policy making of what we can call
"public-opinion institutions," such as the press, interest groups,
citizen-education groups, and even the mass public. There were strong
historical-cultural reasons for that research focus, beginning as it did
only a few years after the end of the Second World War. A major public-
policy concern at that time was the capacity of the American democracy
to sustain an active foreign policy committed to the defense of Western
values and institutions. My governing assumption—shared by many
other scholars of my generation—was that this problem of public opinion and public participation was essentially an American problem.
There were two very persuasive reasons for that assumption: first, the
American democracy was believed to be especially vulnerable to frequent shifts in public mood and commitment in foreign-policy matters.[2] The interwar history of American isolationism was a recent and
evocative reminder of the possibilities of significant change in public
mood, and the constitutional role in foreign policy accorded to the U.S.
Congress was the major device by which that mood could be translated
into a dominant political force.[3] Second, given the leadership role of the
United States at that time in the defense of the West, the stability and
continuity of American foreign policy took on an extraordinary importance throughout the Western world. The belief that the American democracy functioned differently from all other democracies insofar as
foreign policy was concerned was a justification for an exclusive focus
on it, rather than an incentive to a comparative analysis.[4]

Much has been learned through this research focus, both substantively and theoretically, over the past half century. There is no question
that we have a better understanding today than we did a generation
ago of the structure of American foreign-policy attitudes and belief systems and of the ways that they become institutionally significant and
politically relevant—even though the circumstances shaping the "governing assumption" have changed over this time period.[5] But the en-

2. Lester Markel et al., *Public Opinion and Foreign Policy* (New York: Harper and Brothers, 1949); Gabriel A. Almond, *The American People and Foreign Policy* (New York: Harcourt, Brace and Co., 1950).

3. Robert A. Dahl, *Congress and Foreign Policy* (New York: Harcourt, Brace and Co.,
1950); Daniel S. Cheever and H. Field Haviland, Jr., *American Foreign Policy and the Separation of Powers* (Cambridge: Harvard University Press, 1952).

4. Perhaps I should say "a *further* justification," beyond the ordinary interest of scholars in their own political system. Cf. V. O. Key, Jr., *Public Opinion and American Democracy*
(New York: A. A. Knopf, 1961).

5. Out of an enormous literature, the reader might consult Barry B. Hughes, *The Domestic Context of American Foreign Policy* (San Francisco: W. H. Freeman, 1978); Bernard C.

largement of our knowledge, understanding, and perspective over these years has revealed the limitations of an exclusive focus on American public-opinion structures, institutions, and foreign-policy processes even for an understanding of the American situation. As James N. Rosenau has so effectively pointed out, one can draw only limited conclusions about the ultimate significance of public-opinion factors in foreign-policy decision making in the absence of comparable knowledge about all the other factors that may be involved in national decision making on those issues.[6] Public-opinion factors need to be set in the context of other relevant variables, in the same framework of analysis, before their impact can be adequately assessed. That by itself is an enormous—and therefore enormously daunting—task.

Furthermore, the relative significance of public opinion and other variables may differ from country to country, not only because countries are differently situated with respect to the international political system but also because their foreign-policy decision making takes place within the confines—the operative rules and procedures—of independent national political systems. It is this latter aspect of the problem that I am pursuing in this book: one's capacity to understand the interplay of domestic actors and institutions on foreign-policy matters in the United States (as anywhere else) requires sensitivity to the constraining effects of the political system—a sensitivity that is greatly enhanced through the comparative analysis of the public dimensions of foreign-policy making in more than one political system. Our attention is drawn, of course, to democratic political systems, since that is the kind we live in and the context in which public-opinion institutions have their greatest play, but even democratic political systems differ one from another in very important and sometimes very subtle ways.

Despite a widespread acknowledgement that we need to move in this direction if we are to enlarge our knowledge about democratic foreign-policy making, not much progress has so far been made. Students of foreign-policy process tend almost everywhere to specialize in single countries. Students of "comparative politics," who also specialize in single countries, tend almost everywhere not to be very inter-

---

Cohen, *The Press and Foreign Policy* (Princeton: Princeton University Press, 1963); Cohen, *Public's Impact* (1973); John E. Mueller, *War, Presidents, and Public Opinion* (New York: John Wiley and Sons, 1973).

6. Much of Rosenau's work has reflected this perspective, which was initially elaborated in his "Pre-Theories and Theories of Foreign Policy," in R. Barry Farrell, ed., *Approaches to Comparative and International Politics* (Evanston, Ill.: Northwestern University Press, 1966), pp. 27–92.

ested in foreign-policy processes. And students of general politics who do engage in cross-national comparison also tend to ignore the foreign-policy component of their subject.[7] As a consequence, the literature of foreign-policy making is generally set in single countries; it is idiographic in its treatment of decision-making variables and haphazard and often implicit in its treatment of political systems—even where the system bears directly on the performance of specific public-opinion institutions. Even the few attempts at comparative research into democratic foreign-policy making manage only occasionally and briefly to escape these limitations.[8] I hope that this book demonstrates both the possibilities and the advantages of the comparative study of foreign-policy making.

All right, a comparative study of foreign-policy making. But why the United States and the Netherlands? I start with the United States because it remains an area of practical as well as intellectual interest to me. I am concerned not only with how democratic political systems make foreign policy but also with how *this* democratic system makes foreign policy. Even after a professional lifetime of research in the public aspects of American foreign-policy making, I am still struck by the uncertainties in our understanding, which I have sketched in the foregoing paragraphs. Oddly enough, however, no one has ever asked me, "Why the United States?" But in both the United States and the Netherlands, I have repeatedly been asked, "Why the Netherlands?" As a parsimonious and not really facetious answer: Why *not* the Netherlands? I have not found the literature of the comparative method to be of much help in answering this question—or even in justifying my choice, since, truth to tell, I made it on a number of grounds. The methodological arguments about most-different-systems design versus most-similar-systems design[9] seem to me to evade the central ques-

7. See, e.g., Norman H. Nie and Sidney Verba, "Political Participation," in Fred I. Greenstein and Nelson W. Polsby, eds., *Handbook of Political Science*, vol. 4 (Reading, Mass.: Addison-Wesley Publishing Co., 1975), pp. 1–74. Nie and Verba include the Netherlands in some of their comparisons, but they focus on electoral activities and participation within local communities. Even more disappointing is Samuel Eldersveld, Jan Kooiman, and Theo van der Tak, *Elite Images of Dutch Politics* (Ann Arbor: University of Michigan Press, 1981); the authors leave the Foreign Ministry and Defense Ministry out of their sample of bureaucrats and foreign and defense questions out of their substantive purview.

8. See, e.g., William Wallace and W. E. Paterson, eds., *Foreign Policy Making in Western Europe: A Comparative Approach* (New York: Praeger Publishers, 1978), esp. the chapters by Ib Faurby on Scandinavia and by Jan Deboutte and Alfred van Staden on the Low Countries.

9. For the first, see Adam Przeworski and Henry Teune, *The Logic of Comparative Social Inquiry* (New York: John Wiley and Sons, 1970), and for the second, Arend Lijphart,

tions: until one has studied all of them fully, how does one know which "systems," "cases," or "countries" are most different and which most similar? A priori judgments about differences and similarities are superficial and unconvincing.[10] Similar or different in what respects or along what dimensions? to what degrees? to what effects? Even *after* having completed this comparison of the Netherlands and the United States, I am still at a loss as to how it should be classified. In some ways the two systems and countries are very much alike, as we shall see, but in other ways they are very different. And I am as much interested in the similarities as in the differences, for both tell us something about foreign-policy institutions in democratic systems. But these are findings or conclusions, rather than grounds for the initial selection of what countries to compare. The common thread—the comparable case—was "democratic political systems," but the question of *which* democratic systems to study was decided on other grounds.

For one thing, the Netherlands offered a *sense of contrast* to the United States—not really a *catalogue of differences*, because I did not know to begin with which differences were apparent and which real, which significant and which not. But from our complex superpower perspective, the Netherlands is a smaller power with simpler problems, suggesting large possibilities for instructive comparison[11] (and at the same time, I confess, offering the illusion of easy intellectual mastery!). It is also a parliamentary system, a multiparty system, and a society which traditionally had well-differentiated political, economic, social, and religious institutions to represent the interests of culturally distinct groupings in the population.[12]

"Comparative Politics and the Comparative Method," *American Political Science Review* 65 (3): 682–93 (September 1971). Ib Faurby has employed the most-similar-systems design in his essay "Foreign Policy Making in Scandinavia," in Wallace and Paterson, eds., *Foreign Policy Making*, pp. 106–34. Donald Granberg and Soren Holmberg have chosen the most-different-system design in *The Political System Matters: Social Psychology and Voting Behavior in Sweden and the United States* (New York: Cambridge University Press, 1988).

10. Granberg and Holmberg, (*The Political System Matters*) briefly point out some "quite pronounced" differences, mostly structural and institutional, between the American and the Swedish political systems (pp. 6–7) but provide no systematic discussion of those differences as a basis for their research design.

11. See, e.g., Peter R. Baehr, "The Foreign Policy of the Netherlands," in J. H. Leurdijk, ed., *The Foreign Policy of the Netherlands* (Alphen aan den Rijn: Sijthoff en Noordhoff, 1978).

12. This "pillarization" (*verzuiling*) of Dutch society and polity and its subsequent transformation may be traced in successive editions of Arend Lijphart, *The Politics of Accommodation: Pluralism and Democracy in the Netherlands*, 1st and 2nd eds. (Berkeley and Los Angeles: University of California Press, 1968, 1975), and in the more frequently re-

Furthermore, the Netherlands offered a personal challenge—something completely new to me, from the language up. I had done no prior research on the country, and prior to the fall of 1975, when I began this study with a Fulbright Research Award at the University of Amsterdam, I had spent no more than one weekend there. And by no means the least important reason for me was the presence in the Netherlands of a group of Dutch scholars with an active interest in the formulation of Dutch foreign policy and the role of domestic factors in it—areas in which there had been up to that point no systematic scholarly research.[13] Indeed, why *not* the Netherlands? What better place?

Since the comparative study of public participation in foreign-policy making is not ordinarily the centerpiece of what is variously known as "comparative foreign policy" or the "comparative analysis of foreign policy,"[14] I should say more than I already have about public participation. In particular, why compare public participation, rather than other aspects of foreign policy? Comparative foreign policy as a subfield is concerned mostly with measuring the relationships between interstate, state, or political-system variables and foreign-policy behavior; the dependent variable is foreign policy itself, measured in the discrete bits of events-data, with quantitative skill and sophistica-

---

worked editions of the Dutch version, *Verzuiling, pacificatie en kentering in de Nederlandse politiek* (Pillarization, pacification, and change in the politics of the Netherlands) (Haarlem: H. J. W. Becht, 1986, most recent revision). See also Eldersveld, Kooiman, and Van der Tak, *Elite Images.*

A word about my decision rules for translations: when books and articles are written in Dutch, I have used the Dutch titles and followed the first mention with an English translation in parentheses. When they are written by Dutch authors in English, I have used only the English title. When I have quoted from Dutch sources, I have translated into English. (Since virtually all Dutch political scientists can read English, I have not bothered to translate titles from English to Dutch.)

13. See Philip P. Everts, "Een onderzoek naar binnenlandse invloeden op het buitenlands beleid—een theoretische verantwoording" (An inquiry into domestic influences on foreign policy—a theoretical justification), in Peter R. Baehr et al., *Elite en buitenlandse politiek in Nederland* (Elite and foreign policy in the Netherlands) (The Hague: Staatsuitgeverij, 1978). This volume represented the first fruits of a continuing interuniversity collaboration in the Netherlands; subsequent volumes are Philip P. Everts, ed., *Controversies at Home: Domestic Factors in the Foreign Policy of the Netherlands* (Dordrecht: Martinus Nijhoff, 1985); and Philip P. Everts and Guido Walraven, eds., *The Politics of Persuasion: Foreign Policy Implementation by the Netherlands* (Brookfield, Vt.: Gower Publishing Co., 1989). It was a privilege for me to have participated on an ad hoc basis in some of the early work of this group.

14. See James N. Rosenau, "Comparative Foreign Policy: One-Time Fad, Realized Fantasy, and Normal Field," *The Scientific Study of Foreign Policy,* 2d ed. (New York: Nichols Publishing Co., 1980).

tion. On this subject I share the view of Howard Lentner, who wrote, in a review of such a study: "The book under review is surely among the best that the subfield of scientific analysis of foreign policy has produced. Yet it tells us nothing about the people, the institutions, or the problems that it purports to explain."[15] But it is precisely "the people, the institutions, . . . the problems"—the political contexts of foreign-policy decision making—that I have the greatest interest in, an interest that is rooted in democratic theory and in the nature of democratic society. Verba and Nie have written that "if democracy is interpreted as rule by the people, then the question of who participates in political decisions becomes the question of the nature of democracy in a society."[16] Democratic societies may even be defined by the extent, the character, and the quality of citizen participation in decision making—by the relationship of public-opinion institutions to policy-making institutions. When people are not happy with the conditions of their lives and with the decisions that produce those conditions, they sometimes seek to change the patterns of participation in the relevant decision-making process. And although foreign policy is not generally the stuff of which revolutions are made, once a revolution is in progress (as we saw in eastern Europe) foreign policy and international politics are not sheltered from the winds of change.

There are very substantial normative dimensions to the problem of public participation in foreign-policy making, which are themselves worth at least a book. Is it good or bad? Is it advantageous or disadvantageous? For whom? And how much is enough, or too much? It is in the nature of politics and public policy, even foreign policy, in a democratic country that when some participants win, others may lose. Claims about "the national interest" in foreign policy, like claims about "the public interest" in domestic policy, do not obscure the fact that there are often legitimate differences of interest and of opinion on foreign-policy issues. And to the extent that public participation in foreign policy has policy consequences (rather than merely psychological ones), that means that some points of view are adopted—some people win—and others lose out.

The participants in these contests no doubt have their own evaluation of whether the process was good or bad and how much was enough. But we are apart from any particular contest, independent of any fray, and our interest is of a different kind. Our interest is inescap-

15. Howard Lentner, *American Political Science Review* 75(3): 757 (September 1981).
16. Sidney Verba and Norman H. Nie, *Participation in America: Political Democracy and Social Equality* (New York: Harper and Row, 1972), p. 1.

ably normative, even though it may appear instrumental; it is strengthening what Verba and Nie call the crudely defined heart of the matter about democracy: "The more participation there is in decisions, the more democracy there is."[17] Governments in democratic societies can continue to function only so long as there is a sense of shared purpose between leaders and led. That may be a vague and even ritualistic statement, but the Vietnam experience in the United States and the peace movement of the early 1980s in the Netherlands bring very specific referents to it. And the changes in eastern Europe at the end of the 1980s suggest that it is not only in democratic societies that shared purpose is at some point necessary if governments are to function. "Rational foreign policy" cannot be defined apart from the values for which it is in service. And if those values are very actively opposed by the citizens in a democratic society, the policy cannot long be maintained. There may well be the seeds of ultimate and inescapable conflict here between the values of democracy and the values of national autonomy or independence, but unless or until that point is unequivocally reached, we have—and should have—no choice, I believe, but to cultivate the sense of shared purpose between leaders and led.[18]

There is reason enough in all this for us to look closely at "the people, the institutions, . . . the problems" in both the United States and the Netherlands—to seek by comparative study to enlarge our understanding of the interrelationships between the structure of a national political system and the patterns of public participation in foreign-policy making in that system. On the practical level, I will compare the different impacts, in the two countries, that political parties and party competition, national legislative bodies, the media of communication, mass opinion and its modes of expression or articulation (public-opinion polls, demonstrations, etc.), organized interest and action groups, and specialized advisory bodies have on the thinking and behavior of foreign-policy officials, both in the permanent bureaucracy and on the political (ministerial) level. The differences in the public-opinion institutions of these two countries, taken together with the differences in the two political systems, are very instructive; they are

---

17. Ibid. James N. Rosenau summarizes a number of conceptions of "participation" in *Citizenship Between Elections: An Inquiry into the Mobilizable American* (New York: Free Press, 1974), pp. 92–94.

18. Nie and Verba have a more practical justification for encouraging citizen participation: "The moral of the story is not that less participation is better, even though participation can have antiegalitarian consequences. Rather, the moral is not to leave political activity to the other fellow—for it will be his or her preferences that leaders will hear and to which they will respond" ("Political Participation," p. 70).

also extremely useful in forcing a reassessment even of well-known aspects of American foreign-policy-making processes. How does public participation manifest itself, for example—what forms does it take in the two countries? To what extent is participation of various kinds rooted in the political culture—welcomed, supported, even facilitated by certain elites by virtue of the mores as well as the structure of the system? To what extent are these forms of participation a function of the way political power is organized in a political system? And what is the impact of these relationships on such routine but important things as the public-affairs activities of foreign-affairs bureaucracies or the everyday practices of journalists who cover foreign affairs? These are the kinds of questions I will explore in the chapters that follow. The answers they yield will speak not only to the characteristics of the foreign-policy-making processes in the two countries but also to larger issues such as the measure of democratization that has been achieved in those processes over time and the consequences for international relations that lie in different capacities to cope with public demands and to establish and maintain international commitments.

A few words, finally, on the question of how one compares these things. I am making a qualitative comparison, although quantitative measures of particular phenomena will be introduced from time to time. I have studied the roles and functions of institutions in foreign-policy making by examining the perceptions and behavior of individuals actively involved in these institutions in both countries. If all this lacks the illusion of firm reality that is sometimes suggested by hard data, that is a reflection of the subject itself, which is inescapably a matter of interpretation and judgment at key points. Precision in the comparison of imprecise things is even harder to achieve when the very shapes of the phenomena differ in the two countries.

The field of "comparative politics" has wrestled inconclusively for a generation with the problem of appropriate analytic categories for the comparison of political systems, although the language I have been using here suggests how thoroughly the concepts of structuralism and functionalism have invaded our thinking.[19] It is testimony both to the complexity of the subject matter and to the conceptual anarchy of the discipline, however, that no single perspective or overarching construct really dominates or even lends itself to many purposes other than that in which it had its origins. Most typologies or sets of catego-

19. See Gabriel A. Almond and James S. Coleman, eds., *The Politics of the Developing Areas* (Princeton: Princeton University Press, 1960), for the initial application of these sociological concepts to comparative politics.

ries end up being used "rather more as outlines of the arrangement of their material . . . than as guides to research or self-conscious contribution to theory."[20]

A further problem, however, lies at the very heart of the matter of cross-national comparisons: the problem of finding a desirable and appropriate balance between the analytical and theoretical rigor needed to maximize comparability and the accompanying risk that such rigor will affect our perceptions of reality and impose a false identity on the phenomena under study. The search for a general science of politics in Western-oriented countries in the postwar years has led to a rather substantial internationalization of political science; and since American political science has been the largest single source of this modern literature, the use of categories of analysis developed from the study of American politics and political institutions is both explicit and extensive in other countries, including the Netherlands.[21] One needs always to be on guard to make sure that theories and constructs used for comparative purposes do not become instruments of selective perception. This is not an argument for casual and undisciplined comparison but rather a caution against becoming the prisoner of rigid models.[22]

It should be very clear from much of what I have already said that I believe the political system to be of central importance in structuring the opportunities, incentives, constraints, channels, and mechanisms that are available to nongovernmental actors to participate in foreign-policy making. And if my reasons for so believing are not now either obvious or clear, they should become so in the first chapter. One implication of that position, however, is that the variable of "size," so hard to overlook in any comparison of the United States and the Netherlands, is not obviously a key determinant of these things, and I have so argued elsewhere.[23] "Size," in fact, has so many different components—the

20. Robert H. Salisbury, "Interest Groups," in Fred I. Greenstein and Nelson W. Polsby, eds., *Handbook of Political Science*, vol. 4 (Reading, Mass.: Addison-Wesley Publishing Co., 1975), p. 182.

21. Some examples from the Dutch literature relevant to this study are Everts, "Een onderzoek"; G. van Benthem van den Bergh, "Over de democratisering van de buitenlandse politiek" (On the democratization of foreign policy), *Internationale Spectator* 24(1): 49–66 (1970); and J. J. de Jong et al., *Pressiegroepen: De invloed der georganiseerde groepen op het maatschappelijk en politiek leven* (Pressure groups: The influence of organized groups on social and political life) (Utrecht: Uitgeverij Het Spectrum, 1959).

22. For a general discussion of this problem, as well as an argument for "borrowing" heuristic models, see Gabriel A. Almond, with Laura Roselle, "Model Fitting in Communism Studies," in Thomas F. Remington, ed., *Politics and the Soviet System* (New York: St. Martin's Press, 1989).

23. Bernard C. Cohen, "Political Systems, Public Opinion, and Foreign Policy: The United States and the Netherlands," *International Journal* 33(1): 195–216 (Winter 1977–78).

main ones being geographical area, population, GNP or other indicators of the level of economic activity, and relative military power—that it is misleading if not useless to treat it as a single variable. With an eye to these different components, members of the Dutch "foreign-policy elite" are themselves rather sharply divided on the question whether the Netherlands is properly described as a "small" country in international politics, with nearly 40 percent of an elite sample rejecting that description. The differences in the responses to this question among the various subgroups in that sample strongly suggest that they are responding to different dimensions of the concept of "small."[24] Ronald P. Barston's attempt some years ago to generalize about the foreign policies and foreign-policy capabilities of "small states" suggests some of the difficulties involved.[25] Some of the specific variables that are wrapped up in the notion of "size" are relevant to a political system, however, and may even be said to be a part of it. The size of the population, for example, interacts with social and political factors and thus has a bearing on the actual size of the pool of potential participants in foreign-policy activities. Aspects of "size" that do have relevance of this kind in both countries will be discussed in the appropriate contexts in the chapters that follow.

Time is a very useful companion in a research endeavor like this, which has been incubating for over fifteen years. Time lends a valuable perspective to events, allowing one to distinguish between genuine changes in political relationships and mere swings of the pendulum. Where the pendulum swings, we can recognize a passing event for what it is, and we can have greater confidence in our generalizations over time. But where changes are real and substantial, one must be doubly cautious in generalizing from the lessons of one time period to the issues of another, and the limits of those political eras must be noted. For this reason, I have limited my time frame to a single generation and to the domestic political systems and foreign-policy processes

---

24. For example, 56 percent of the top-level Foreign Ministry officials in the sample and an equal proportion of the political party leaders viewed the Netherlands as a small country in international politics, whereas 88 percent of the business leaders in the sample shared that view. See Alfred van Staden, "Voorstellingen omtrent Netherlands invloed: hun samenhang met opvattingen over macht en beleidsvoorkeuren" (Propositions concerning Dutch influence: Their connection with conceptions of power and policy preference), in Baehr et al., *Elite en buitenlandse politiek*, p. 71. A. de Swaan, however, argues that in world trade the Netherlands is a great power ("Nederland als wereldmacht" [The Netherlands as a world power], *NRC-Handelsblad, Weekeditie*, Dec. 8, 1981, p. 8).

25. Ronald P. Barston, "Introduction," in Ronald P. Barston, ed., *The Other Powers: Studies in the Foreign Policies of Small Countries* (London: Geo. Allen and Unwin, 1973).

that marked it—the period of a stable Cold War relationship between East and West, from the late 1950s to the end of the 1980s—and I have paid only the most passing attention to interesting events and cases, both early and late, that fall outside this period. The erosion of Soviet military power and the disintegration of the Soviet empire in eastern Europe mark the coda to the international relations of the past half century. The environment that has helped to shape both Dutch and American foreign policy in the post–World War II period is changing, although with what consequences it is too soon to know. But one may surely regard 1990 as a historical watershed and a fitting point at which to round off this comparison.

Finally, a word about a few of the designations I use in this book: the people who inhabit the United States are known everywhere as Americans, and those who inhabit the Netherlands are known everywhere as Dutch, and I shall so call them here. These are also valid adjectives to apply to all manner of things, in addition to people, within these countries. It is a different matter with the countries themselves, however: Americans often refer to the Netherlands as "Holland," which is more a tourist designation than an official one. North Holland and South Holland are provinces in the Netherlands, and they comprise important parts of the country. But the country is the Netherlands, and I shall call it by that name. The Dutch, on the other hand, generally refer to the United States as "America"—a designation that has patriotic currency here but no official standing. Thus, I refer to this country always as the United States.

A book of this kind may find readers in both the United States and the Netherlands. Although Dutch readers are likely to be more familiar with the American political system than Americans with the Dutch system, it is in the nature of the case that readers on each side (as well as those in other countries) will be uninformed on some matters that are important to a proper understanding of the other. For this reason I shall have to say a bit more about both countries than I would want or have to say were I addressing informed readers in only one of them. Although I hope that I shall always have something new to tell someone even about his or her own political processes, I know I can count on informed readers everywhere to skip judiciously when the terrain gets very familiar.

Acknowledgments

It is a pleasure to acknowledge the obligations I have incurred to others in the course of my work. I would like, first of all, to express my thanks to those institutions whose generosity has made this study possible: the Fulbright-Hayes Commission; the Netherlands-America Commission (the joint Fulbright organization in the Netherlands), under the masterful leadership then of Wobbina Kwast; the John Simon Guggenheim Memorial Foundation; and the Research Committee of the Graduate School at the University of Wisconsin—Madison. I am grateful also to the University of Amsterdam, which had considerably more than its (or any university's) share of troubles in the 1970s but which nonetheless welcomed yet another American international-relations scholar.

Among individuals on the Dutch side, my special thanks go to Peter R. Baehr and Cees van der Eijk. Peter, now Professor of International Relations at Leiden and director of the Netherlands Institute of Human Rights at Utrecht, was my Fulbright sponsor at the University of Amsterdam and my point of entry to the Dutch foreign-policy community, both academic and "real-world"; Cees, now Professor of Political Science (*Algemene Politicologie*) at Amsterdam, was my mentor in Dutch politics and political behavior. Both were generous beyond accounting in spending time on my education, providing office space for me on my several visits to the Netherlands, and helping me with access to libraries. Both read the draft of this book and supplied necessary correctives. And both of them and their wives, Malie Baehr and Kitty Ketchum–van der Eijk, welcomed me and my wife into their homes and their families.

Alfred van Staden and Philip P. Everts were exceedingly helpful at all stages, including reading and commenting on the manuscript. Others who were especially helpful in many ways over these years were C. Paulien van den Tempel, J. Henk Leurdijk, Rob Mokken, J. L. Heldring, Henk Houweling, Jan Siccama, Frans Roschar, Arend Lijphart, Hans

Daalder, and Hans Daudt. I also learned a great deal about the Netherlands from Steven B. Wolinetz of the Memorial University of Newfoundland, Canada. Although I can't mention them by name, there are more than two dozen members of the Dutch Foreign Ministry, the lower house of the Parliament, and the press corps who extended themselves in lengthy interviews, sometimes in their homes, and in additional helpful gestures.

A special word of thanks and of affection to Els and Rob Goudsmit and to their sons, Maarten, Michiel, and Joost. They are all friends in the special Dutch meaning of that word, and theirs has been a home away from home for me and for members of my family. They opened a window to Dutch life, culture, and history that has not only informed my understanding of the Dutch political system but has also made this long effort such an enormous personal pleasure. In his remarkable study of Dutch culture in the seventeenth and eighteenth centuries, Simon Schama pleads the same excuse as an English traveler, Peter Mundy, concerning his stay in Holland in 1640: "I have bin the longer aboutt the discription of this place etts., because there are soe many particularities wherein it differs (and in some excells) allsoe beeing myself somewhat affectionated and enclined to the Manner of the Country."[1] I share their sentiments entirely, although my excuses must be different!

I want especially to thank two friends and colleagues on the American side who have read my draft manuscript and who have been extraordinarily helpful critics: Leon D. Epstein and Charles O. Jones. While my Dutch associates have been helping me become a "comparativist," Leon and Chuck have been making me a better Americanist. David Nixon also helped me with a superb essay on American interest groups.

Needless to add, none of these people bears any responsibility for what I have written. I suspect I have failed to satisfy some of them on a key methodological issue, the structure of comparison—what is included for one country but not the other. What accounts for the way a country develops its foreign policy is a difficult question at best; to ask it of two countries at the same time does not make it easier. I have tried to be systematic and parallel; where I have failed, I hope that I have at least been stimulating and provocative.

I am grateful to the editors of *International Journal* for permission to

1. Simon Schama, *The Embarrassment of Riches* (Berkeley and Los Angeles: The University of California Press, 1988), p. xi.

revise and extend portions of my article "Political Systems, Public Opinion, and Foreign Policy: The United States and the Netherlands" (33[1]: 195–216 [Winter 1977–78]), and to the editors of *Acta Politica* for permission to make similar use of "Political Parties and Foreign Policy in the United States and the Netherlands" (25[4]: 451–66 [October 1990]).

Democracies and Foreign Policy

1

The Political Systems of the Netherlands and the United States

The Organization of Political Power

Anyone who has ever wandered down the proper shelves in a good library or bookstore will recognize the presumption in the titles of this and the next chapter. Quite obviously, it is beyond the limits of the possible adequately to describe the political systems of the United States and the Netherlands even in the framework of two chapters. Such is not my intention. My goal, rather, is to set forth those features of their political systems that seem to me best to explain the circumstances or conditions that govern public participation in foreign-policy making in both countries. In the selection of these features—necessarily subjective or interpretive on my part—lies the first key to the structure of the comparison I shall be making and, hence, to the specific matters discussed for each country. I will pay attention only to a part of these political systems—mostly the governmental part—to understand better the nongovernmental parts. As a necessary first step, however, let me place these two countries in an international-system context, so that we have a sense of the international perspectives that have energized their foreign-policy processes through the "Cold War" years.

The discrepancy in international power and position between these two countries is so great and so obvious that one hardly has to make the point. Similarly, the potential divergence in their foreign policies—exemplified in the early 1980s in the concept of "Hollanditis"

3

as the disease of Dutch neutralism—has been well advertised.[1] The danger is that we might put too much emphasis on these two kinds of differences and overlook some fundamental similarities in their international histories and contemporary perspectives.[2]

Until World War II, the dominant feature in the landscape of both countries was neutrality—on and off for over two centuries for the Dutch[3] and for about one and a quarter for the Americans—with respect to the power struggles in Europe. Although neutrality was easier for the U.S., given its geographical location, in both cases it was feasible during the last century of its existence because it suited the political interests of Great Britain, then the world's dominant power. The independence and neutrality of the Low Countries were for Britain the measure of an acceptable European balance of power, while the Monroe Doctrine was as much a British interest—and a charge for the British Navy—as it was an American one. This common experience had remarkably similar consequences in both the Netherlands and the United States. Not only did it produce a long-term political affinity for the British;[4] it was also responsible for an attitude of moral superiority toward the practitioners of "power politics" elsewhere.[5]

1. Walter Z. Laqueur, "Hollanditis: A New State in European Neutralism," *Commentary* 72(2): 19–26 (August 1981). This article created a great stir in the Netherlands when it first appeared; it was immediately read and discussed by all members of the Dutch foreign-policy community, and within six weeks it provided (characteristically) the title for an Amsterdam nightclub revue!

2. See Alfred van Staden, "American-Dutch Political Relations since 1945: What Has Changed and Why?" in J. W. Schulte Nordholt and Robert P. Swierenga, eds., *A Bilateral Bicentennial: A History of Dutch-American Relations, 1782–1982* (Amsterdam: Meulenhoff International, 1982).

3. Because the Netherlands has slid into and out of several alliances and wars since the end of its days as a Great Power in 1713, Dutch scholars disagree among themselves on how to characterize the history of their foreign policy, making distinctions such as neutrality, abstentionism, and neutralist abstentionism to describe different periods. C. B. Wels, *Aloofness and Neutrality: Studies on Dutch Foreign Relations and Policy-Making Institutions* (Utrecht: HES Publishers, 1982), says that abstentionism "took on a permanent character" after the Treaty of Utrecht in 1713 and lasted until 1940 (p. 17). Jan G. Siccama, "The Netherlands Depillarized: Security Policy in a New Domestic Context," in Gregory Flynn, ed., *NATO's Northern Allies: The National Security Policies of Belgium, Denmark, the Netherlands, and Norway* (Totowa, N.J.: Rowman and Allanheld, 1985) reserves the phrase "neutralist abstentionism" for the period 1839–1940 (p. 115). Joris J. C. Voorhoeve, *Peace, Profits, and Principles: A Study of Dutch Foreign Policy* (The Hague: Martinus Nijhoff, 1979), discerns five different phases in Dutch neutralist abstentionism, beginning in 1648. See his chapter 3, pp. 42–54.

4. Not universally, of course: in both countries there had been strong pro-German sympathies at various times in the twentieth century.

5. Walter Lippmann, *U.S. Foreign Policy: Shield of the Republic* (Boston: Atlantic–Little, Brown, 1943); J. L. Heldring, "De invloed van de openbare mening op het buitenlands

World War II put an end to the policy of neutrality in both countries and led to a policy of alignment and commitment. For the United States, the change was the greater: after generations of moral condemnation of balance-of-power politics, we became a central player in the international balance, the world's leading military power, ultimately committed to the defense of many other countries as the means of protecting ourselves. "Realism" won out over "idealism."[6] The Dutch, too, came down off the fence, becoming a "faithful ally" in NATO.[7] But the tendency to moralize about and in foreign policy has had a harder time dying in the Netherlands, perhaps because, as several Dutch observers have put it, the alliance became the protector of Dutch independence, allowing the Dutch people, if not their leaders, their traditional luxury of substantially ignoring the balance of international power.[8]

Of greater significance than the fact of commitment, however, is the perceived degree of each country's autonomy as an actor in international politics, and on this dimension the two countries seem to have come closer together from positions that were once substantially divergent. There are some constraints on the actual freedom of choice available to American officials in any period, given the basic commitments of that period—commitments to allies and to enemies both. And additional constraints flow from the new conditions of "interdependence"

---

beleid" (The influence of public opinion on foreign policy), *Internationale Spectator* 24(1): 24–34 (8 January 1970); C. L. Patijn, "Het Nederlandse buitenlandse beleid" (The foreign policy of the Netherlands), *Internationale Spectator* 24(1): 14–23 (8 January 1970); Voorhoeve, *Peace, Profits, and Principles*. See also Peter R. Baehr, "The Foreign Policy of the Netherlands," in J. H. Leurdijk, ed., *The Foreign Policy of the Netherlands* (Alphen aan den Rijn: Sijthoff en Noordhoff, 1978). Wels, *Aloofness and Neutrality*, notes that the Swiss as well as the Dutch and Americans "thought they had a mission" in foreign policy (p. 21).

6. See, e.g., Hans J. Morgenthau, *In Defense of the National Interest: A Critical Examination of American Foreign Policy* (New York: A. A. Knopf, 1951); and George F. Kennan, *American Diplomacy, 1900–1950* (Chicago: University of Chicago Press, 1953).

7. Alfred van Staden, *Een trouwe bondgenoot: Nederland en het Atlantisch Bondgenootschap, 1960–1971* (A faithful ally: The Netherlands and the Atlantic Alliance) (Baarn: Athos, 1974).

8. See, e.g., Heldring, "De invloed van de openbare mening"; Patijn, "Het Nederlandse buitenlandse beleid"; and Voorhoeve, *Peace, Profits, and Principles*. Siccama points out that the concept of "national interest" has no place in Dutch foreign-policy thinking ("Netherlands Depillarized," p. 117). In March 1992, however, after the Indonesian Government threw the Dutch development-assistance program out of the country, "hardnosed" reappraisals of Dutch interests in foreign policy began to appear in the press: see W. Wansink, "Het benarde vaderland" (The fatherland in peril), *Elsevier*, 4 April 1992; and Joris J. C. Voorhoeve, "Nederland is niet te klein voor rol in de wereld" (The Netherlands is not too small for a role in the world), *NRC-Handelsblad, Weekeditie*, 21 April 1992.

which have bound the American economy so closely to aspects of the world economy and to the economies of particular countries. But the prevailing *perception* in American foreign-policy circles has been one of substantial autonomy over time—reflected in wide-ranging debates about changes in security policy, foreign policy, and foreign-economic policy.

In the Netherlands, there was for many years a perception of severely *limited* international autonomy as a consequence of the Dutch international position.[9] In the words of a Foreign Office official in the 1970s, "The margins of choice for Dutch foreign policy are very, very restricted by outside factors beyond our control." These factors, generally understood as the NATO alliance and membership in the European Community,[10] were not greatly different from those that impinged on American autonomy or that of other members of the Western community (including France). They were certainly not different *in kind*. By the 1980s, however, it was no longer so widely believed in the Netherlands that policy with respect to some of these institutions was beyond national control. If public debate about the direction of future policy can be taken as the reflection of prevailing perceptions in the Netherlands, as in the United States, then one has to conclude that freedom of choice seemed to many Dutch to have expanded well before the drastic changes in East-West relations that began in 1989.[11]

Europe in the 1990s will be a very different place from the Europe of the four and a half decades preceding. In the absence of the Warsaw Pact, the structure of the NATO alliance may well be so loosened that

9. In the second wave of a panel study of Dutch voters in 1973, respondents were asked, "Who makes or make the decisions, in your opinion, on the foreign affairs of Holland—Holland or the big powers?" Sixty-five percent responded, "The big powers," and 21 percent, "Holland itself." See L. P. J. de Bruyn and J. W. Foppen, *The Dutch Voter, 1972–73*, vol. 2 (Nijmegen: Institute for Political Science, 1974), question 68.

10. Baehr, "Foreign Policy of the Netherlands." Decolonization may also have been important in the development of Dutch feelings of lack of autonomy—but the Dutch were not the only power to have experienced decolonization in these years.

11. For an extended discussion of Dutch autonomy in foreign policy, see Philip P. Everts, ed., *Controversies at Home: Domestic Factors in the Foreign Policy of the Netherlands* (Dordrecht: Martinus Nijhoff, 1985), chaps. 1, 2, 16, and passim; and Philip P. Everts and Guido Walraven, eds., *The Politics of Persuasion: Implementation of Foreign Policy by the Netherlands* (Brookfield, Vt.: Gower Publishing Co., 1989). Several Dutch scholars now point out that since the degree of autonomy is a matter of perception to begin with, it is a domestic political phenomenon anyway, rather than an international one, and is thus subject to political determination. See P. 't Hart, "Beslissen over buitenlands beleid" (Determining foreign policy), *Acta Politica* 21(2): 209–24 (April 1986); and Alfred van Staden, "The Changing Role of the Netherlands in the Atlantic Alliance," *West European Politics*, 12(1): 99–111 (January 1989).

issues of autonomy in that context disappear (though they may get more acute in the context of the European Community).[12] But it is quite likely that the attitudes and perceptions about autonomy that developed in the 1980s—and that encouraged still wider public participation in the Netherlands—would have pushed the Western alliance in the same direction that it was eventually pulled by the crumbling of the Eastern alliance. Even stalwarts of the foreign-policy establishment in the Netherlands, listening to their public foreign-policy debates at the beginning of the 1980s, privately acknowledged that "Holland is no longer the faithful ally it once was."

In brief, then, although the sense of international position and power may differ as between the Netherlands and the U.S.,[13] and although the specific issues that preoccupy them may differ, the two societies share a view that the international system has not taken away all their power to choose and that fundamental foreign-policy decisions may still (or again) be made. This represents a major change from the first four postwar decades in the Netherlands and is part of a larger set of changes in Dutch society and politics that have become manifest in the foreign-policy field and that made the Netherlands by the mid-1980s look and sound a bit like the divided and disputatious United States of the late 1960s.

The features of the political system that I want to address here as being especially relevant to public participation in foreign policy are structural, in a broad sense, rather than behavioral. I will be concerned in this chapter with *legal-constitutional matters,* including the organization of political power, the political-party system, the character of executive-legislative relations, and the authority of the head of government; in the following chapter I will deal with *institutional matters,* particularly the major foreign-policy-making institutions, and with *aspects of the "political culture"*—the norms that shape the way people think about these institutional and constitutional matters and think about approaching them.

The American Legal-Constitutional Structure

The legal-constitutional structure of a country forms such a closely knit fabric that it must be seen as a whole, rather than as a collection of

12. See, e.g., *Internationale Spectator* 44(11) (November 1990), special English-language issue on "Autonomy and Interdependence."

13. In the Netherlands, most knowledgeable observers of the foreign-policy scene would agree with the argument by one of their number that "We don't count for much in the world," whereas U.S. presidents keep reassuring the American people that the U.S. is and shall remain the most powerful country in the world.

threads. For that reason I shall take up the United States and the Netherlands separately, comparing whole structures rather than individual parts. That approach is particularly necessary when the structures are as dissimilar as these, one of them being a two-party presidential system and the other a multiparty parliamentary system.

In the U.S. the Founding Fathers designed a system to prevent the concentration of political power, as their way of avoiding tyranny either from the ruler above or from the mob below. One important element of this system is federalism—the division of power between the national and state governments—but since the foreign-relations power rests exclusively in the national government, federalism is not relevant to our present concern. A more important element of the American system is called the "separation of powers," but in reality it is both the sharing of powers by separate and coequal branches of government and the competition for power by different governmental institutions (and often by different political parties). Although a considerable amount of the foreign-relations power has gravitated to the president over the history of the Republic,[14] there remains a very substantial dispersion of the foreign-policy power throughout the American government in both the executive and legislative branches—reinforced in our day by the War Powers Act and other post-Vietnam assertions of congressional foreign-policy power.[15] As a result of this dispersion it is difficult to find the levers that run the foreign-policy system. Indeed, "Who makes American foreign policy?" is a historically persistent question in academic as well as public discussion of foreign policy—the focus of countless lectures, courses, and books. This difficulty exists for participants in the system as well as for observers on the outside. The literature on "bureaucratic politics" in American foreign-policy making testifies to the inability even of highly placed officials to exercise tight control over the formulation and execution of foreign policy within their own branch of government.[16]

In the process of separating branches, if not powers, the Consti-

14. For a historical account of this development, see Arthur M. Schlesinger, Jr., *The Imperial Presidency* (Boston: Houghton Mifflin, 1973).

15. See Cecil V. Crabb, Jr., and Pat M. Holt, *Invitation to Struggle: Congress, the President, and Foreign Policy* (Washington, D. C.: Congressional Quarterly Press, 1980).

16. This literature is well sampled in Morton H. Halperin and Arnold Kanter, eds., *Readings in American Foreign Policy: A Bureaucratic Perspective* (Boston: Little, Brown and Co., 1973). For other examples, see Morton H. Halperin, *Bureaucratic Politics and Foreign Policy* (Washington, D.C.: The Brookings Institution, 1974); Robert Gallucci, *Neither Peace nor Honor: The Politics of American Military Policy in Vietnam* (Baltimore: Johns Hopkins University Press, 1975); and Edmund Beard, *Developing the ICBM: A Study in Bureaucratic Politics* (New York: Columbia University Press, 1976).

tution has explicitly vested executive authority in one individual, the president. The cabinet, being wholly in the executive domain, is responsible only to the president, who appoints its members (subject to confirmation by the Senate) and who may request their resignations, individually or (as President Nixon once did) collectively, entirely on his own authority. Cabinet members may or may not have important ties to organizations or institutions in the country, but such ties do not in any event create mutual responsibility or collective responsibility.[17] In particular, the secretary of state and the secretary of defense have, in modern times, had no significant political power base independent of the president, and thus they have no *public*-representation functions to perform in the making of foreign policy. Their representative functions within the American government are limited to the not-so-simple institutional tasks of speaking to their departments on behalf of the president even as they speak to the president on behalf of their departments and to the Congress and the public on behalf of both.[18] These officials are not necessarily identified with the political party of the president who has chosen them; there is a long tradition of nonpartisan public service associated with these two positions, even though the incumbents have, in modern times at least, never survived a change in the party in the White House.[19] But even when there *is* a clear partisan identification (as for example with Muskie or Baker at the State Department[20] or Cheney at the Defense Department), there is in practice no overt partisan political activity in those offices.[21] The long-standing and widespread conviction that politics ought to "stop at the water's edge," although it has certainly not kept foreign policy out of American politics, has contributed to the substantial depoliticization of these two cabinet positions and thus to a certain muting of partisan

17. No one seems inclined to displace last generation's definitive study: Richard F. Fenno, Jr., *The President's Cabinet* (Cambridge: Harvard University Press, 1959).

18. This is in sharp contrast to the *eigen verantwoordelijkheid*—"one's *own* responsibility"—of the Dutch ministers; see pp. 21–22.

19. With respect to the tradition of nonpartisan public service, see, e.g., David Halberstam, *The Best and the Brightest* (New York: Random House, 1972); Walter Isaacson and Evan Thomas, *The Wise Men: Six Friends and the World They Made* (New York: Simon and Schuster, 1986).

20. One is tempted to add Kissinger, but Kissinger is known to have offered to serve Democratic as well as Republican candidates and administrations.

21. In 1992, Secretary of State Baker left the State Department to work on President Bush's reelection campaign. And when an official in the State Department was found to have used the Passport Office files for partisan political purposes, she was immediately fired.

debate on foreign policy. It has also contributed to strengthening the hand of the president in the making of foreign policy.

The U.S. Constitution also provides fixed terms of office for all elected officials—terms of different lengths, which overlap so that the entire executive and legislative branches can never be renewed or removed at the same time. These provisions ensure some continuity of government at the elected level, but they also serve in some degree to insulate the government not only from the gusts of passion that may sweep an uninformed electorate but also from their well-considered preferences with respect to policy questions.

In brief, then, political power in the United States is so parceled that it is not easy for the government to respond swiftly and collectively to public preferences, especially when they are diverse. Preferences need to be very powerful and unambiguous (as they were, for example, in the case of humanitarian help for Kurdish refugees fleeing Iraq in 1991) to overcome the "noise," the inertia, and the network of existing commitments within the system, and foreign policy in particular very rarely creates public preferences of such clarity and strength. The Vietnam War experience is very instructive in this regard. Assuming that the American government was responding chiefly to public preferences in disengaging from that war, it still took many years and several elections for that disengagement to be accomplished.

The organization of political power in the United States has some self-evident implications for public-opinion institutions and for public participation in foreign-policy making, but to appreciate fully its significance, one must see it in the context of the American political-party system. The dispersion of the foreign-policy power, which has its roots and finds its nourishment in a system of separated, shared, and often competing powers, would be of limited practical significance if there were a political-party system in the U.S. that was able to provide overriding policy direction and control within and across the legislative and executive branches of government. The actual situation, however, is quite the contrary. The two national parties are more or less "umbrella" organizations, covering tremendous diversity among the state and local party organizations that call themselves by the same names. Power in these political parties is very widely dispersed among the state and local organizations across the land.[22] As Leon D. Epstein points out, American political parties were built on "spoils"—on

22. See Lewis A. Dexter's comments in *How Organizations Are Represented in Washington* (Indianapolis: Bobbs-Merrill, 1969), p. 2.

patronage—and not on ideology, and they began to lose strength when reform movements reduced the scope of patronage in the public service. And they began to lose control of candidate selection early in the twentieth century, when state governments began to run direct-primary elections.[23]

The major function of national party organizations in the United States is to elect a president, not to help him govern. The platforms of the two major parties, which are drawn up and adopted at the quadrennial conventions of the parties when they choose their presidential candidates, are not unequivocally policy programs. Platforms serve a number of functions for the parties: they can be vehicles of compromise among candidates or statements of position by victorious candidates, and they are calls to the faithful and appeals to those who are looking for candidates to support.

Contemporary culture has rarely been kind to party platforms. They are generally regarded as irrelevant to policy, and they are generally ignored by voters—as well as by political scientists who study voters.[24] But they are not always ignored by politicians and hence are not ignored by political scientists who study parties: Pomper pointed out some years ago that the "fulfillment of platform pledges is common, but it is not required." And politicians, he added, "appear to take them seriously."[25] In the twenty war and postwar years (1944–1964) covered by Pomper's analysis, however, only 6 percent of the total number of foreign-policy pledges in the platforms of the two parties were in conflict (representing competing visions about the purposes and directions of foreign policy), 47 percent were bipartisan (in both party platforms), and 47 percent were one-party pledges (different promises, appealing to different and distinct groups of voters).[26]

There are further reasons to be cautious about the policy significance of national party platforms. Congressional candidates seek office

23. Leon D. Epstein, *Political Parties in the American Mold* (Madison: University of Wisconsin Press, 1986), pp. 4, 13.

24. It is worth noting that the major studies of American voting behavior, although they deal extensively with the question of voters' perception of ideological and issue differences between the parties, do not once refer to party platforms. See Angus Campbell, Philip E. Converse, Warren E. Miller, and Donald E. Stokes, *The American Voter* (New York: John Wiley and Sons, 1960); and Norman H. Nie, Sidney Verba, and John R. Petrocik, *The Changing American Voter* (Cambridge: Harvard University Press, 1976).

25. Gerald M. Pomper, *Elections in America: Control and Influence in Democratic Politics* (New York: Dodd, Mead and Co., 1968), pp. 201, 203. I am grateful to Charles O. Jones and Leon D. Epstein, who separately drew Pomper's work to my attention.

26. Ibid., pp. 193–95.

with the help of state and local parties—although they may get various sorts of assistance from the national party organizations—and each state or local party has its own ideological and political character. The two major national parties have no formal membership rosters[27] and no organized or systematic mechanisms to aggregate the preferences of their supporters. The Republican Party has an ongoing opinion-polling mechanism which provides some broad understanding of the distribution of preferences at a moment in time, but there is no comparable political or organizational mechanism to convert those preferences into programs. Political platforms in both parties develop more out of the ideologies of leading candidates or out of their recent political experiences—successes, failures, vulnerabilities, the results of midterm elections, and so forth—than out of organized policy preferences within an organized party structure.

Furthermore, the parties have no mechanisms that can ensure compliance with those platforms by legislators—or by presidents.[28] Since members of Congress draw their political power from their constituencies and their political authority from the Constitution, there are not many important ways in which even members of the president's party can be disciplined for failure to support the president's program. Usually, when a president needs support, he offers carrots to those who might help, rather than applying sticks to those who don't. Congressional leadership can deprive a wayward colleague of choice committee assignments or other advantages of office, but those are extreme penalties that are applied only very rarely and then only to the most persistent, egregious, and offensive failures to follow party leadership.

In this system, national party organizations and programmatic mandates have—and can have—only a limited role. Every four years the parties each nominate a presidential candidate, but with the rapid spread of the presidential preference primaries, the party conventions have become the *place* where party nominations are formalized, rather than the *machinery* for selecting the nominees. The party organizations help to elect the nominees, but the major effort is made by the candidates themselves, who, together with their campaign organizations, handcraft political strategies in many diverse electoral districts and construct their own electoral coalitions. These coalitions may include diverse party organizations, but they are

27. The Republican Party, however, has set a high standard of organization in recent years, maintaining "sustaining membership" lists of known Republicans as the basis for very effective fund-raising.

28. Presidents tend to follow party platforms, especially when they have been instrumental in writing them, but there are frequent deviations.

mainly built on appeals to large population blocs such as farmers, women, minorities, business, or labor.[29] And if they are successful, they subsequently reward their supporters with policies and reward faithful service to the party with appointments. But these are political and moral claims on a president, not legal claims. They may define the people to whom he listens and those whom he favors, but they in no way diminish his individual constitutional responsibility for the executive power. The party organizations help with the process of appointments, especially at the lower levels, because there are so many positions at stake in the American government, but they do not have any responsibility—or even ability—to help the new president *govern*.

A significant consequence of these characteristics of the American party system is the frequent presence of what some have called "divided government"[30] and Jones has called "the separated presidency,"[31] in which the executive branch is controlled by one political party and at least one of the two houses of Congress is controlled by the other party. Divided government may be seen as a form of coalition government,[32] although there is no design, no advance planning, no agreement—merely a need to work together at least for the minimal requirements of government. Coalitions may also exist within the Congress, where they take the form either of temporary, ad hoc arrangements among groups of legislators across party lines for the purpose of advancing specific pieces of legislation or of more enduring alliances, usually of an ideological kind and applicable across a wider spectrum of policies. In either case, however, they are informal arrangements, and their rise and fall, although they may shape the legislative output, do nothing to the continuity or structure of either the executive or the legislative branch.

These institutional limitations of the American party system reflect the hard rock of the American Constitution, which creates diverse, autonomous, yet overlapping constituencies from which individuals

29. The Dutch have observed that American election campaigns do not much concern the substance of policy, except for presidential debates. See Philip van Praag, Jr., "De verkiezingscampagne van 1986" (The election campaign of 1986), in Cees van der Eijk and Philip van Praag, Jr., *De strijd om de meerderheid: De Verkiezingen van 1986* (The struggle for a majority: The elections of 1986) (Amsterdam: CT Press, 1987), pp. 12–13.

30. E.g., James L. Sundquist, "The New Era of Coalition Government in the United States," *Political Science Quarterly* 103(4), 1988.

31. Charles O. Jones, "The Separated Presidency: Making It Work in Contemporary Politics," in Anthony S. King, ed., *The New Political System*, 2nd ed. (Washington, D.C.: American Enterprise Institute, 1990).

32. See Sundquist, "New Era."

draw their political authority independently of each other and which then distributes the powers of governance itself independent of party. This is all exposed in the sometimes fragile nature of the relations between the executive and the legislature. I noted above that members of Congress derive their political power independently from their constituencies and their political authority directly from the Constitution and that party majorities (and thus party control) may differ, as between the two houses or between Congress and the executive. The president similarly derives his political power from a national constituency and his political authority directly from the Constitution, and he possesses the executive power no matter how well or how poorly his party has fared in congressional, state, or local elections. The capacity of such a political system to function with any degree of coherence and purpose depends on a president's ability to forge unity within his own party and to be persuasive in his dealings with the public, with the opposition party in the Congress, and with his own executive departments.[33] We have seen ample evidence in modern American history that a considerable degree of success in this undertaking[34] (as well as occasional spectacular failures) can be recorded no matter which parties are found in the executive branch and the two houses of Congress.

One last implication these legal-constitutional aspects of the American political system contain for the foreign-policy process: with power—including foreign-policy power—so widely distributed in this system, there are multiple points of access to it. If it is difficult to find the levers that run the foreign-policy system, there is also opportunity to participate in the search for them, from the inside *and* the outside.

The Dutch Legal-Constitutional Structure

Only recently have people in the Netherlands bothered to ask the question "Who makes foreign policy in this country?" Only recently, perhaps, because the answer is in general rather less ambiguous: the minister of foreign affairs, joined in particularly weighty matters by the minister-president (the prime minister) and the rest of the government, makes—is responsible for—foreign policy. As in the United States, however, some of the actual business of formulating policies and carrying on activities involving other countries has in recent years been conducted by other ministers as well, not least among them the

---

33. See Richard E. Neustadt, *Presidential Power* (New York: John Wiley and Sons, 1980).
34. E.g., Republican cohesiveness was chiefly responsible for winning the budget and tax cuts in the early Reagan years.

minister of defense and the minister for development cooperation, and in other more "domestic" ministries—and as in the United States, there is some conflict among these ministries as a consequence of the intersection of their activities.[35]

Whereas the United States has a federal system, political power in the Netherlands is concentrated in the national government. It is perhaps the most centralized state among the Western European democracies.[36] The Netherlands has a parliamentary system, which further concentrates political power in cabinet government. Because the party system is crucial to the organization of political power in the Netherlands, I shall begin this discussion of the Dutch political system by looking at the parties.

The Dutch have an electoral system that is based on proportional representation. Governance is organized around the parties that are represented in the Parliament, and political authority is exercised by the parties that are represented in the cabinet. The number of electoral lists that have competed in the national elections since 1918 ranges from a low of ten to a high of fifty-four, and the number of parties winning seats has ranged from seven to fourteen. But power is more concentrated than these figures suggest: the five largest parties have won over 70 percent of the popular vote and over 75 percent of the seats in Parliament in each of those elections.[37]

There are three centers of Dutch party power. The largest comprises the party organizations themselves. The major parties have complex structures with local, regional, and national sections, strong bu-

35. See, e.g., Everts, ed., *Controversies at Home*, esp. chapter 4, "The Makers of Foreign Policy"; and Alfred van Staden, "Consistentie en beleidscoordinatie" (Consistency and policy coordination), in B. R. Bot et al., *Lijn in de buitenlandse politiek van Nederland* (Coherence in the foreign policy of the Netherlands) (The Hague: Netherlands Institute of International Relations "Clingendael", 1984).

36. See Rudy B. Andeweg, "Institutional Conservatism in the Netherlands: Proposals for and Resistance to Change," *West European Politics* 12(1): 43 (January 1989).

37. In the seven elections that were held during the 1970s and 1980s, the parties with lists competing in the elections have numbered in the twenties, and the number of parties gaining seats has ranged between nine and fifteen. A general source of data on Dutch politics and society is the *Compendium voor Politiek en Samenleving in Nederland* (Compendium for politics and society in the Netherlands) (Alphen aan den Rijn: Samsom Uitgeverij [sections continuously updated]). For the distribution of the vote over all parties winning seats in the lower house of Parliament in the parliamentary elections from 1946 to 1981, see Cees van der Eijk and Broer Niemöller, *Electoral Change in the Netherlands* (Amsterdam: CT Press, 1983), table 1.2, pp. 12–13. For a broad overview of the composition of the Dutch Parliament since 1918 and of the composition of the governments since 1848, see *Parlement en Kiezer* (Parliament and voter), published annually or biennially by Martinus Nijhoff, The Hague.

reaucracies, and equally strong traditions of internal democracy.[38] The second center, smaller in scope, comprises the party organizations— the *fracties* (fractions)—within the Second Chamber, which is the lower house of the Dutch Parliament. The third and obviously the smallest center is the party representation in the cabinet (and the ministerial council) at any given time.[39] Each of these, as we shall see, has interests and perspectives that are not always shared by the others.

The formation and proliferation of political parties in the Netherlands are encouraged by the comparative ease with which a party can gain representation in Parliament.[40] Given the size of the population (approximately fifteen million), the average turnout (approximately 86 percent of eligible voters), and the number of seats in the Second Chamber (150), proportional representation in the Netherlands means that a seat may be secured by between fifty-five thousand and sixty thousand votes. While there is a long history in the country of dissidents splitting off from large parties and forming new ones, there have in fact been as many aggregations or consolidations as there have been defections in the past twenty-five years, and the aggregations, on the whole, have had more significance for national politics.[41]

38. The party organizations control the nominating process, determining who gets on the electoral list and in what order. A good example of the significance of a party apparatus over the life of politicians was provided in the spring of 1990 when the VVD (Liberal Party) bureaucracy was instrumental in securing the resignation of the party's leader in the Second Chamber.

39. See, e.g., R. B. Andeweg, A. Hoogerwerf, and J. J. A. Thomassen, eds., *Politiek in Nederland* (Politics in the Netherlands), 3d ed. (Alphen aan den Rijn: Samsom Uitgeverij, 1989); M. P. C. M. van Schendelen, J. J. A. Thomassen, and H. Daudt, eds., *'Leden van de Staten-Generaal, . . .': Kamerleden over het werking van het Parlement* ('Members of the States-General, . . .': Members of Parliament on the workings of Parliament) (The Hague: VUGA-Uitgeverij, 1981); Rudy B. Andeweg, ed., *Ministers en Ministerraad* (Ministers and Ministerial Council) (The Hague: SDU Uitgeverij, 1990); and Rudy B. Andeweg and Galen A. Irwin, *Dutch Government and Politics* (New York: St. Martin's Press, 1993).

40. Hans Daalder points out that there were many political parties in the Netherlands prior to universal suffrage and that proportional representation "did not so much cause as consolidate the fragmentation" of the party system ("The Mould of Dutch Politics," *Western European Politics* 12[1]: 13 [June 1989]).

41. In 1966, D'66 (*Democraten '66* [Democrats '66]), now D66, was formed, followed in 1970 by DS'70 (*Democratisch Socialisten '70* [Democratic Socialists '70]). The former has done well enough at times to become a national coalition partner; the latter, however, has disappeared. In the meantime, the CDA (Christian Democratic Appeal) was created in the late 1970s by the merger of the major Catholic and Protestant parties, KVP (Catholic People's Party), ARP (Anti-Revolutionary Party), and CHU (Christian-Historical Union); a left-leaning environmental party, *Groen Links* (Green Left), was created in 1990 by the merger of PSP (Pacifist Socialist Party), PPR (Political Party Radicals), CPN (Communist Party in the Netherlands), and EVP (Evangelical People's Party). (In 1991 a PSP stalwart,

Dutch political parties have varying ties with religious and cultural streams in Dutch society and history,[42] but they are all "ideological" in the sense that their programs develop from long-debated and well-articulated principles. Prior to elections, the party programs are published individually by the parties as an appeal for votes, and later, collectively by the government as a historical record of the event. Overall, Dutch political parties offer the voters a substantial range of programmatic electoral choice; the political mythology (which is also a tautology) remains that every significant viewpoint has its representatives in Parliament.

Despite the visible importance of the parties in Dutch political life, their "hold" on the citizenry is qualified. Membership in Dutch political parties—achieved by declaration followed by the regular payment of a contribution—is small, and it has been declining steadily in recent years: from 15 percent in 1946 it dropped to 8 percent by 1967 and to 4 percent by 1986. The drop has affected all except the small orthodox parties.[43] If informal estimates that only about 1 percent of the party membership participates in discussions of foreign policy are correct, those numbers are very small: assuming an equal propensity to participate, across the parties, it means about 1,250 in the Christian Democratic Party (*Christen Democratisch Appel*—CDA), 1,000 in the Labor Party (*Partij van de Arbeid*—PvdA), 750 in the Liberal Party (*Volkspartij voor Vrijheid en Democratie*—VVD). And party preferences proved to be so unstable by the time of the 1981 national election study that the authors of that portion of the study concluded that there was no reason to use the conventionally defined notion of party identification.[44] Furthermore, the foreign-policy

---

F. van der Spek, proposed to reestablish the PSP on the ground that *Groen Links* had moved too far to the right. See *NRC-Handelsblad, Weekeditie,* 29 October 1991.) These mergers, of course, serve to diminish the number of parties competing for seats and the number actually represented in the Parliament.

42. See A. Lijphart, *Verzuiling, pacificatie en kentering in de Nederlandse politiek* (Pillarization, pacification, and change in the politics of the Netherlands) (Haarlem: H. J. W. Becht, 1988).

43. See R. A. Koole, "Political Parties Going Dutch: Party Finances in the Netherlands," *Acta Politica* 25 (1): 37–65 (1990); and Alfred van Staden, "The Changing Role of the Netherlands in the Atlantic Alliance," *Western European Politics* 12(1): 107 (January 1989). The *Dutch Parliamentary Election Study 1986,* Cees van der Eijk, Galen A. Irwin, and Broer Niemöller, eds. (Amsterdam: Steinmetz Archives, 1988), reports, however, that 8 percent of the first-wave sample claimed to be a member of a political party (p. 44).

44. Cees van der Eijk and Broer Niemöller, "Binding met partijen" (Commitment to parties), in A. Th. J. Eggen, C. van der Eijk, and B. Niemöller, eds., *Kiezen in Nederland* (Voting in the Netherlands) (Zoetemeer: Actaboek, 1981), chapter 6. For a more

voice of the parties, quite convergent to begin with,[45] is muted—and that of the foreign minister is amplified—by some fundamental elements in the Dutch political system.

Political power in the Netherlands is organized around the current standing of the parties and finds its expression in the cabinet. In the Dutch multiparty system, cabinet government is by necessity coalition government.[46] But coalitions often—some might say inescapably— stand between voters and their wishes. In effect, the political structure for carrying out the diverse preferences of the voters becomes a vehicle for sidetracking many of those preferences, and in the process the role of the parties as voices of public opinion becomes attenuated. For one thing, becoming a coalition partner does not necessarily follow from a party's electoral success. In the last quarter of a century the Dutch have developed a tradition of majority coalitions, but one can put together a coalition of parties representing a majority in the Parliament without including the largest single party—as the Labor Party discovered in 1971 and again, to its chagrin, in 1977. The process of cabinet formation is a work of art as well as of politics; it starts, after an election, with a canvass of the political judgment of senior "players"—including the leadership of the different levels of party power[47]—and it does not necessarily reflect the distribution of preferences of the electorate as reflected in their votes for the Second Chamber[48] or even the preferences

---

elaborate discussion of their "grave reservations as to the viability of this concept [of party identification] in the Dutch situation," see Van der Eijk and Niemöller, *Electoral Change*, chapter 8.

45. See Everts and Walraven, eds., *Politics of Persuasion*, p. 45.

46. For references to the rich literature on coalitions in the Netherlands, see Daalder, "Mould of Dutch Politics," n. 31, pp. 19–20.

47. See J. J. Vis, "Kabinetsformatie" (Cabinet formation), chapter 9 in Van Schendelen, Thomassen, and Daudt, eds., *'Leden van de Staten-Generaal, . . .'* See also the brief discussion prepared by the Information and Public Relations Department of the Second Chamber: *De 2de Kamer: De kabinetsformatie* (The Second Chamber: The cabinet formation) (The Hague: Staatsdrukkerij, 1981).

48. "A party may . . . 'win' the elections, but 'lose' the government formation. When the governing Social Democrats won ten seats in 1977, they ended up on the opposition benches; when they lost nine seats in 1981, they entered government again!" Andeweg, "Institutional Conservatism," p. 48. See also J. J. A. Thomassen, "Politieke strijdpunten en coalitie-voorkeuren" (Political issues and coalition preferences), in Van Schendelen, Thomassen, and Daudt, eds., *'Leden van de Staten-Generaal, . . . ,'* p. 209.

In October 1990, in a discussion in the First Chamber (the upper house of Parliament) on low voter turnout in recent Dutch elections, Hans van Mierlo, the leader of D66, explained the declining voter turnout as a consequence, not a cause, of the defective legitimacy for "The Hague" in the country. "What must the voter now think of a political system in which a governing party such as the VVD loses ten seats and yet returns to the

of voters or of party rank and file for particular coalitions.[49] However, parties have sometimes made it clear to the electorate before an election that they would rule out certain coalition partners on the basis of their election programs. Only once (in 1986) have the coalition partners gone into an election seeking the continuation of the coalition—running, in effect, on their record instead of on their election programs.[50]

The formation process itself, facilitated by intermediaries appointed by the Crown, is a bargaining process through which the parties involved hammer out a written agreement on the main lines of policy to be followed over the lifetime of the cabinet. This "governing accord"—a compromise among the coalition partners on the program they will pursue in the new government—is necessarily different from the program with which each party fought the election; thus, not only are the participating parties committed to a "different" program for the life of the government, but also the politicians who are involved are committed to a set of policies that have been accepted by their non-parliamentary parties.[51] This process, which with a few exceptions has become more specific and detailed since the 1960s, tends to rub away the hard edges of doctrinal differences among parties both in anticipa-

---

cabinet, as happened in 1986? . . . What must the voter think of a political system that systematically and consistently denies 'the last and most essential condition for democracy: You're finished with something or someone if that is what the majority wants'? That does not hold, namely, for the CDA . . . This party can't be blown out of the cabinet. Even if they lose ten seats you can bet your life that they will be back again" (*NRC-Handelsblad, Weekeditie,* 30 October 1990).

49. In the spring of 1989, after the VVD brought down the CDA-VVD cabinet, two-thirds of the CDA rank and file still expressed a preference for continued rule with the VVD. After the elections that fall, the CDA leadership formed a coalition with the PvdA, and at the very next meeting of the CDA party council, "no one—repeat, no one—of those present found it necessary even to discuss the course of events since the elections" (editorial in *NRC-Handelsblad, Weekeditie,* 26 December 1989).

50. See G. A. Irwin and J. J. M. van Holsteyn, "Towards a More Open Model of Competition," *West European Politics* 12(1) 119ff (January 1989). Efforts in the 1960s and 1970s to "transfer . . . coalition negotiations from after to before the elections" got nowhere in Parliament. Andeweg, "Institutional Conservatism," pp. 55–56.

51. The Governing Accord of the Third Lubbers Cabinet (CDA-PvdA) accepted a program of the Second Lubbers Cabinet (CDA-VVD), called "Development-Relevant Export Transactions," with which the new minister of development cooperation disagreed. When a field review of this program revealed that the program favored export promotion over the needs of developing countries, the minister told the Second Chamber, "I would never have devised it, but there it is." The newspaper account continues: "Pronk [the minister], his hands and feet bound to the governing accord between CDA and PvdA, promised the Chamber to strengthen the program further and to extend it" (*De Volkskrant,* March 30, 1990).

tion of the possibility of governing[52] and through the negotiations them-selves. It also tends to reduce a government's room for maneuver once the parties and the ministers are tied together by the governing accord. There is thus a premium on foresight and clarity in the development of the accord, since conflicts in interpretation or in jurisdiction can threaten the demise of the government.[53]

Once the cabinet is installed, its survival becomes an important value in itself, taking precedence over many issues. Except for a brief period in the early 1980s, when Dutch nuclear-weapons policy was under active political challenge, foreign-policy issues have not been deemed important enough in postwar Dutch political life to form the basis for a challenge to the government.[54] That is reinforced by the fact that the major political parties—especially the party fractions in Parliament—behave "responsibly" in foreign policy, which is to say that they share in and help to develop foreign policies that are "reason-able" enough that there is little advantage for anyone in contesting them.[55] Although it is not an iron law of Dutch politics that "you don't bring down a government on a foreign-policy issue," that is often said by politicians and ministers, and the circumstances in which that might happen are severely limited.

There is a fundamental significance in all this that has no parallel in the American experience. An important part of the bargaining in the cabinet formation involves the division of governmental positions—the ministers and the *staatssecretarissen*,[56] or under secretaries—among

52. In the elections of 1981 and 1982, e.g., the Labor Party leader rejected extreme positions on cruise missiles in order not to exclude the possibility of a coalition with the Christian Democrats. See Thomas R. Rochon, *Mobilizing for Peace: The Antinuclear Movements in Western Europe* (Princeton: Princeton University Press, 1988), p. 171, and Peter R. Baehr, "Het parlement en het buitenlands beleid" (Parliament and foreign policy), in Th. C. de Graaf, D. A. van der Hoeven, and P. J. Langenberg, eds., *Omtrent het Parlement: Opstellen over parlement en democratisch bestuur* (Concerning the Parliament: Essays on parliament and democratic control) (Utrecht: Uitgeverij Veen, 1985), pp. 212–13.

53. One of the first tasks of a new cabinet is to present to the Parliament a Government Declaration—a statement of the policies built into the accord. In 1981 the process of drafting the declaration revealed some important disagreements among the parties, and the government was kept alive only by going back to the formation process and clarifying and repairing the governing accord.

54. See Baehr, "Het parlement."

55. This is one possible definition of "consensus"; see the discussion in Chapter 3. See also n. 45 above.

56. *Staatssecretaris* is variously translated by the Dutch as minister of state, state secretary, under minister, assistant minister, assistant secretary. Since it is the second-ranking political position in a ministry, it translates best as deputy minister or under secretary; I prefer the latter.

the parties in the coalition. The choice of the prime minister may also be involved, but in recent years the premier has usually been the first name on the electoral list (*lijsttrekker*) of his party, thus narrowing the choice to the leadership of the major party or parties in the coalition. Although that may seem obvious, prior to the 1970s "elections very often had no predictive value for who would become minister-president."[57] The change has contributed significantly to the stature of the prime minister.

The division of positions usually means that otherwise competitive and even antagonistic parties share the practical responsibility for governing, even within ministries. In the Third Lubbers Cabinet, the minister and the *staatssecretaris* were from the same political party in only three ministries; they were from different parties in six ministries, and there was no *staatssecretaris* in four ministries.[58] In the Ministry of Foreign Affairs, there were two persons with the rank of minister (the minister of foreign affairs and the minister for development cooperation) who came from different parties.[59] This sharing of practical responsibility for governing also means that the prime minister can exert little direct authority over the ministers, because there is no authority relationship. In fact, the prime minister is actually minister-president, technically the first among equals in the cabinet. The ministers are constitutionally independent, although they function within the political framework of an agreed-on governing program, and they have a legally unfettered responsibility to speak their

57. J. Th. J. van den Berg, "De Minister-President: 'Aanjager van Noodzakelijk Beleid'" (The minister-president: "Booster of necessary policy"), in Andeweg, ed., *Ministers en Ministerraad*, p. 98.

58. "The *staatssecretaris* is sometimes appointed as a watchdog from one party over the minister of another. In practice the *staatssecretarissen* seem seldom to behave like a 'political mother-in-law,' but they do function as a communications channel between their department and the ministers of their party" (Rudy B. Andeweg, "Tweeerlei Ministerraad: Besluitvorming in Nederlandse kabinetten" [Two kinds of ministerial council: Decision making in Dutch cabinets"], in Andeweg, ed., *Ministers en Ministerraad*, p. 33).

59. This latter situation provides a good illustration of the problem at hand: The foreign minister (CDA) and the development minister (PvdA) were quickly and publicly at odds over the relationship between development-assistance policy and human-rights policy. Whereas the development minister controlled the only interesting budget in the foreign-affairs field, the foreign minister was more or less successful in asserting his primacy in the human-rights area—to the public unhappiness of some PvdA members. *Het Parool*, April 13, 1990, quotes a PvdA member of the European Parliament: "I have doubts now and then about whether the PvdA has a high enough profile. We have to keep the PvdA ministers on the left-hand track. We are simply in a different party from the CDA."

own mind and follow their own course.[60] Van der Beugel refers to this as a nineteenth-century governmental structure that divides policy into closed-off provinces, without hierarchy and without leadership except as it can be exercised personally by the prime minister.[61] In the absence of hierarchy, the alternatives are independence or accommodation, the delicate balancing of general or governmental interests and the interests of the ministers and the people they speak for in their own party and in Parliament.

In this structure, the responsibility and the initiative in foreign policy rest with the minister of foreign affairs and his *staatssecretaris*, who may (and in the Third Lubbers Cabinet did) come from different political parties. Even when the prime minister and the foreign minister are from the same political party, which they often are, the prime minister by tradition rarely intrudes into the foreign minister's domain.[62] Three factors in contemporary political life are creating pressures of a contradictory sort, however, pushing (and pulling) the prime minister to the fore. Two of these are general in character and create tensions in all departments. They are the impact of the media—especially television—in focusing attention on the leader of the government, and the increasing need, in a modern complex society, for a greater amount of policy coordination, which tends to force leadership to the top.[63] The third factor, the growing role of the heads of government in the European Community, is international in character and pits the prime minister specifically against the foreign minister. To interact with European colleagues on equal terms, the Dutch prime minister wants a measure of authority in foreign policy that the foreign minister is thus far unwilling to grant.[64] Even

60. This *eigen verantwoordelijkheid* is found to a greater or lesser extent throughout Dutch public life: for example, the leaders of private organizations that are supported by government funds are defended in the exercise of their own responsibility even when they use those funds in opposition to government policy. See Chapter 6.

61. E. H. van der Beugel, "Vaststellen en uitvoeren van buitenlandse politiek" (Determining and implementing foreign policy), *Internationale Spectator* 24(1): 67–75 (1970). Andeweg quotes Ed. van Thijn, former parliamentary leader of the Labor Party and longtime mayor of Amsterdam: "The Netherlands are no longer the Republic of the Seven United Provinces but now form the Republic of the Fourteen Disunited Departments" (Andeweg, "Institutional Conservatism," p. 52).

62. See Peter R. Baehr, "Democracy and Foreign Policy in the Netherlands," *Acta Politica* 18(1): 37–62 (January 1983); and Voorhoeve, *Peace, Profits, and Principles*, e.g., pp. 68, 82.

63. See Van den Berg, "De Minister-President."

64. In late 1990 the prime minister asked his cabinet colleagues for his own mandate in foreign policy, especially in relation to Europe. The minister of foreign affairs found the proposal "unacceptable." The premier, he argued, "must travel the route of a constitu-

the fact that the prime minister makes informal comments at these international meetings without ministerial "clearance" (formal positions are established in advance by the cabinet,[65] and formal speeches are written in the Foreign Ministry) is disturbing to some in the Foreign Ministry, who argue that the prime minister cannot take positions contrary to those of the Foreign Ministry. But there are others, in the ministry and elsewhere in the Netherlands, who see this as a first step in a long-overdue adjustment in the organization of national decision making.[66] Nevertheless, it potentially represents as significant and as far-reaching a political and constitutional shift in power as would a move in the direction of "responsible government" in the United States, making the executive responsible to a congressional majority.

The foreign minister, then, has three roles—as the head of the Foreign Ministry, chiefly responsible for the conduct of the country's foreign policy; as a political-party representative in the government; and as a member of the government, sharing (however tenuously) its responsibility for national policy. The role as a political-party "representative" has been strengthened since 1981 by the appointment of a "political adviser," authorized for all the ministries by the new government that year. Although this procedure may facilitate communication on policy preferences between the foreign minister and party colleagues elsewhere, it does not do much for the authority of a prime minister who is from a different party or for the freedom of maneuver of the cabinet as a whole. The prime minister, however, has two advisers (out of a total of eleven) in the Ministry of General

---

tional change and not in a sneaky way try to become *primus dominus* instead of *primus inter pares*" (*NRC-Handelsblad, Weekeditie*, November 6, 1990). For more on the general issue, see Everts and Walraven, *Politics of Persuasion*, pp. 61–62.

65. Van den Berg, "De Minister-President," p. 114.

66. E.g., Van der Beugel, "Vaststellen en uitvoeren." A high official in the Foreign Ministry indicated to me several years ago that if the Netherlands ever had two socialist foreign ministers in a row, that would cause problems within the (rather conservative) ministry that could be resolved only by having "a real cabinet around the prime minister and not the present situation."

Max van der Stoel, who served as foreign minister in the 1970s and again briefly in the 1980s, recognized that the prime minister has a larger role to play in foreign affairs and proposed that in the next cabinet formation, the incoming premier and foreign minister should explicitly enlarge the ground rules to permit the former to play that role without weaking either the position of the latter or the foreign policy of the country. See M. van der Stoel, "Grotere rol premier in buitenlands beleid" (A larger role for the premier in foreign policy), *NRC-Handelsblad, Weekeditie*, July 28, 1992.

Affairs whose portfolio is foreign affairs[67] and who accompany the prime minister at international meetings. One has to assume that their advice concerns the foreign policies of the Dutch Foreign Ministry as well as the foreign policies of other countries.[68]

In most parliamentary systems, executive and legislative powers are hard to disentangle, since cabinet ministers are also members of Parliament. In the Netherlands, however, if an individual who has just been elected to Parliament is offered a ministry, he or she must decide which of the two positions to hold, since one may not hold both at the same time.[69] That, together with coalition politics, makes for a set of executive-legislative relations that is different from most parliamentary systems and also different from the American system of "separation of powers."

The foreign-policy power of the Dutch Parliament is distinctly subordinate to that of the cabinet (and thus of the foreign minister). There is very little in the way of legislation in Dutch foreign policy— so little that the Ministry of Foreign Affairs has no legislative staff of its own and relies on the staffs of other ministries in rare cases of need.[70] The Second Chamber approves declarations of war (of which there have been few in the last three hundred years) and international treaties. International agreements that are contrary to the Constitution are constitutionally permissible but require a two-thirds majority in both chambers of Parliament. Parliament conducts an annual debate over the foreign minister's budget and a companion statement of policy; irregular debates may be held at any time on the basis of a formal paper (*nota*) provided by the minister or on the occurrence of important international events. Parliament may also hold official inquiries (*enquêtes*) on foreign-policy matters, but these are extremely infrequent. There is no formal "question hour," but members of Parliament may submit questions in writing to the foreign minister at any time. If oral rather than written answers are required, they are

67. Everts and Walraven, eds., *Politics of Persuasion*.

68. Despite the differences between the United States and the Netherlands in the relationship between the head of the government and the head of the foreign office, in both countries a certain value is placed on continuity of leadership in foreign affairs. Between 1948 and 1991, ten different individuals have served as secretary of state to nine different U.S. presidents; during this same period, only seven different individuals have served as minister of foreign affairs in the cabinets of eleven different Dutch premiers.

69. Since ministers are not members of Parliament, their participation in debate is scheduled in advance.

70. See Baehr, "Het parlement," p. 204.

scheduled for a Thursday, normally within three weeks.[71] Finally, the Foreign Policy Committee of the Second Chamber, composed of the foreign-policy specialists of the political parties in the Second Chamber, meets often with the foreign minister, in both open and closed session, and has been holding hearings (on Mondays only) with increasing frequency in recent years. But the committee's functions are consultative and informational only; it has no "gatekeeping" responsibilities and cannot keep matters from reaching the chamber for regular debate.[72]

Although the Dutch Parliament is technically independent of the government, even the most independent-minded parliamentarians recognize that the possibilities of their exercising real control over the government—over the permanent officials as well as the ministers— are very slim in the foreign-policy field. One reason is common enough: ministers tend to bring their problems to the Parliament after decisions have been made, the minister is substantially committed, and the credibility of the government abroad is at stake. Another reason is that some members of Parliament simply believe that the foreign minister *ought* to have considerable freedom vis-à-vis the Parliament. But the major constraint on the power of the Parliament derives from the inescapable fragility of a governing coalition and the burdens that imposes on the parliamentary fractions of the government parties— ordinarily a majority. Once these fractions have given their consent to the formation of the new government, the pressure on them to keep saying yes is very great. Most issues of foreign policy are widely regarded as unimportant most of the time for the Dutch electorate,[73] and thus, as several Dutch members of Parliament have expressed it, it is unlikely that the government is going to be brought down by the Parliament over an ordinary foreign-policy issue.[74] Important judgments about foreign policy rest less with the parliamentary fractions than with the parties themselves. The Labor Party (PvdA), for example, which participated in the government coalition in the fall of 1981, made it a matter of party policy that it would leave the government if the

71. For concise descriptions of the rules governing written and oral questions, interpellations, and inquiries, see the section on De Staten-Generaal (The Parliament) in *Parlement en kiezer* and H. A. H. Toornvliet, *De Staatsinrichting* (The polity), 2d ed. (Utrecht: Uitgeverij Het Spectrum, 1987), pp. 156–61.

72. See Voorhoeve's excellent discussion in *Peace, Profits, and Principles*, pp. 77–84.

73. See the more extensive discussion of this point in Chapter 3.

74. "If he [the minister of foreign affairs] is not prepared to listen and/or to adjust his policy, there is not much that the Parliament can do except force him to resign, and, as we have already said, there is no eagerness to do that" (Baehr, "Het parlement," p. 215).

cabinet decided to accept the emplacement of Pershing II rockets and cruise missiles on Dutch territory—despite the contrary view of the party's Parliamentary leader (and *lijstrekker*) going into the election.[75] Furthermore, the partisan questions that preoccupy the foreign-policy specialists of the parties in the Second Chamber preoccupy them less as members of the Foreign Affairs Committee (on which most of them sit) than as foreign-policy specialists within their parties. The committee itself has rarely demonstrated an interest in taking the initiative on issues the responsibility for which lay elsewhere. But the foreign-affairs experts in the larger party fractions (where there are enough members to specialize on such issues) can as individuals or as party spokespersons sometimes make themselves heard in the ministry.[76]

To sum up at this point: There are contradictory strains in the Dutch political system insofar as public-opinion institutions are concerned. There are extensive partisan channels, through which public participation can be directed and preferences recorded, leading both to Parliament and to the government. But Parliament and the parliamentary fractions have little formal or direct impact on the foreign-policy decisions of the government—certainly less impact than the U.S. Congress has on American foreign-policy decisions, as we shall see later.[77] Government coalitions, furthermore, are strategic creations that do not necessarily (or always) reflect the true partisan configuration of Parliament. And the government ministers themselves have a considerable degree of freedom of action since their parties and their party fractions have given their assent to the policy statements in the Governing Accord and have a big stake in the survival of the coalition. The formal link between public-opinion institutions and public preferences, on the one side, and the foreign-policy power, on the other, is therefore somewhat tenuous, despite the subjective sense of satisfaction that all political viewpoints are or could be reflected in the Parliament.

75. See n. 52 above.

76. Sometimes, but not always: in 1975 the Labor Party Congress adopted resolutions concerning the MBFR (mutual and balanced force reductions) negotiations between East and West that "were contrary to the official foreign policy line of the government and both Van der Stoel and Vredeling [respectively the foreign minister and the defense minister, both Labor Party] did not agree to them. The Foreign Minister had said in a newspaper interview before the Congress met that he would not feel bound by its decisions, while the Defense Minister was to become notorious for his statement that 'party congresses do not buy airplanes' " (J. H. Leurdijk, in Everts and Walraven, eds., *Politics of Persuasion*, p. 144).

77. See Chapter 4.

2

The Political Systems of the Netherlands and the United States

The Organization of Foreign-Policy Making

The way that foreign-policy-making institutions are organized within political systems has implications for public participation that are as consequential as the legal-constitutional arrangements. Not only may governmental foreign-policy agencies themselves be on the receiving end of public attention; the whole conception of bureaucratic politics recognizes that administrative organizations in government may need to make alliances of varying sorts with public groups in pursuit of their joint purposes.[1] I will have occasion later to discuss phenomena of that sort; my interest here is simply to point out how the organization of foreign-policy making in both countries structures the opportunities for public participation.

The Organization of American Foreign Policy

I said earlier that the foreign-policy power in the United States was widely dispersed, even within the executive branch. Among the many organizations with foreign responsibilities the State Department takes a certain precedence, if only for historical reasons: it was the first department of government to be established, and until 1947 the secretary

1. See the works cited in Chapter 1, n. 16.

of state stood second in line of succession to the presidency, behind the vice president. The Department of State is not large in Washington terms, but for an organization without many operating responsibilities it is rather substantial: it employs approximately ten thousand persons at home and an equal number abroad, in all capacities. It has a rather complex organizational structure in which priority is given to a half dozen "geographical" bureaus (e.g., Inter-American Republic Affairs, African Affairs) possessing "line" authority and doing the most important "political" work in relations with foreign countries. The remaining bureaus (e.g., Economic Affairs, Public Affairs,) are "functional," having "staff" responsibilities.[2] Any such division is necessarily arbitrary, however, since most foreign-policy questions have at a minimum both geographical and functional components—they usually concern complex substantive problems that affect one or more specific countries. For this reason, any statement of policy on such questions has to go through a process of internal clearance (approval by all offices with an interest in the matter), which, like any large-scale bargaining process, is time-consuming and offers many opportunities for both participation and obstruction. And the end product is often—predictably—not greatly different from the status quo, since that is the easiest thing for many diverse offices to agree on.[3] This circumstance, abetted by the traditional caution of diplomatists,[4] is largely responsible for the department's reputation for being, in President Kennedy's words, a "bowl of jelly" or for having, as someone else put it, "no central nervous system." The political level in the department—those people who may change with each administration and who bear the political responsibility for decision—reaches down into each of the bureaus, although it does not go far below the head of the bureau (the assistant secretary level). It clearly does not go far enough to override either the interests or the cautions of the career personnel.

At the heart of the State Department is the Foreign Service of the United States, a separate career service whose members until 1954

2. A good sketch of the department is provided in John H. Esterline and Robert B. Black, *Inside Foreign Policy: The Department of State Political System and Its Subsystems* (Palo Alto, Calif.: Mayfield Publishing Co., 1975).

3. Secretary of State Dean Rusk once complained to a congressional committee that the clearance process took at least two weeks and that he always knew how it was going to end up but that he had to go through it nonetheless.

4. Andrew Scott's classic analysis still has face validity: "The Department of State: Formal Organization and Informal Culture," *International Studies Quarterly* 13(1): 1–18 (March 1969). See also John Ensor Harr, *The Professional Diplomat* (Princeton: Princeton University Press, 1969), esp. chapter 6, and Robert Pringle, "Creeping Irrelevance at Foggy Bottom," *Foreign Policy* 29:128–39 (Winter 1977–78).

spent most of their working lives abroad. Reforms then enlarged the Foreign Service—by absorbing members of the Civil Service who were then working for the department in specialized capacities—and made all of its staff, new and old, liable for service both at home and abroad. There are now approximately four thousand career Foreign Service Officers, and they are disproportionately responsible for the "political" work of the department, which is the most highly valued kind of work. Despite the 1954 reforms and subsequent efforts to change the nature of the organization,[5] the Foreign Service has not lost its reputation as a conservative, elite group of "generalists."[6]

The department as a whole has been remarkably open to the public since World War II, when the Bureau of Public Affairs was established to help provide a basis for popular understanding of the developing postwar political arrangements. (The president and the secretary of state were intent on averting the kind of "return to normalcy" that had sent an isolationist [Republican] administration to the White House in 1920.) The bureau continues to serve as a contact point (although not the only one) between the department and nongovernmental groups, and it maintains rather comfortable work space for the many journalists who cover the department. It has been only since the civil disturbances of the Vietnam War years that getting into the building requires an appointment with someone in the department; prior to that time, one could simply walk in and knock on any door.

The State Department had few important functions (and limited personnel) until World War II, and thus it had few important competitors. Since then, however, its position has been challenged as a consequence of three fundamental developments in American foreign policy: (1) The postwar abandonment of isolationism and the acceptance of an active role in international affairs meant a continuing important role for the military establishment and for the burgeoning intelligence agencies. (2) The worldwide conflict with the Soviet Union inspired a "new diplomacy," an expansion of the range of

5. See, for example, the report of the Committee on Foreign Affairs Personnel (The Herter Committee): *Personnel for the New Diplomacy* (Washington, D.C.: Carnegie Endowment for International Peace, 1962); *Diplomacy For the '70s: A Program of Management Reforms for the Department of State* (Washington, D.C.: U.S. Government Printing Office, 1970); *Commission on the Organization of the Government for the Conduct of Foreign Policy, Report* (Washington, D.C.: U.S. Government Printing Office, 1975), esp. chapter 4. See also William I. Bacchus, *Foreign Policy and the Bureaucratic Process: The State Department's Country Director System* (Princeton: Princeton University Press, 1974).

6. See Barry Rubin, *Secrets of State: The State Department and the Struggle over U.S. Foreign Policy* (New York: Oxford University Press, 1985).

American interests abroad—particularly in Third World countries—
beyond the traditional political boundaries to include also economic,
social, cultural, scientific, and technological as well as military matters. This expansion broadened the range of competencies thought
to be necessary for effective representation abroad,[7] as well as the
range of agencies and institutions, public and private, that were
willing and eager to supply those competencies. (3) The grudging
acceptance in the 1970s of "interdependence" meant that activities
and interests, as well as agencies, not previously thought to be part
of foreign policy—for example, those relating to energy, grains, or
interest rates—were suddenly internationalized, so to speak.[8]

These vast changes in the character of American foreign policy,
none of which appears likely to be reversed or even substantially
altered as a result of the collapse of Communist regimes around the
world, have been reflected in lines of cleavage among the organizations involved in contemporary foreign affairs and in the opportunities that situation has provided for still other interested parties to
join the fray. Some specific problem areas of conflict and competition
are worth noting:

(1) The State Department and the Defense Department (including the military services and the Joint Chiefs of Staff) have periodically been at odds since Defense was created as a unified department
in 1947. The conflicts have sometimes had the character of personal
animosities between the secretaries—for example, Acheson and Johnson, Kissinger and Schlesinger, Haig and Weinberger. In many instances of policy disagreements between the two departments, the
State Department has, for reasons of policy commitments abroad,
often been on the "hawkish" side, while the Department of Defense,
on which any military burden falls directly, has been on the side of
moderation and diplomacy.[9] Because the Department of State has
always been unwilling to take on the responsibility of running an
operational intelligence agency, the Central Intelligence Agency (CIA)
began at an early date to function clandestinely in areas where State
was carrying on normal diplomatic relations. This was generally done
with the State Department's knowledge and consent, but not always.
The intersection of the interests of these three agencies has at times

---

7. See Committee on Foreign Affairs Personnel, *Personnel for the New Diplomacy.*

8. See, e.g., John S. Odell, *U.S. International Monetary Policy* (Princeton: Princeton University Press, 1982).

9. Most recently, the chair of the Joint Chiefs of Staff, General Colin Powell, preferred
economic sanctions to military intervention as the means of dislodging Iraq from Kuwait
in late 1990. See Bob Woodward, *The Commanders* (New York: Simon and Schuster, 1991).

been so large that one would be hard put to say which was or were most responsible for the formulation and execution of foreign policy in particular cases.[10]

(2) In the early postwar years the agency responsible for European economic recovery and development, originally the ECA (Economic Cooperation Administration), was established by Congress to stand independent of the State Department. For nearly a decade thereafter the foreign-aid administrator in any country was often regarded by the host government as a more important individual than the American ambassador because the former had more resources to dispense. This conflict was eventually eased when the aid program became a semiautonomous agency within the State Department, where it has since been subjected to varying pressures, political and other, to make it sometimes more, sometimes less, responsive to the political interests of the department. And in some bureaus, especially the Bureau of Inter-American Republic Affairs, there has been a rather effective integration of the aid program within the ongoing political activities of the bureau.

(3) Since the early 1970s the international-economic position of the United States has weakened perceptibly, and its vulnerabilities have grown. As a consequence the State Department has often been preempted by the Treasury Department, especially on issues where the latter has had acknowledged expertise.[11] Other economic issues, particularly those involving the use of economic instruments for foreign-policy purposes, have divided responsibility between the State Department and other departments such as Agriculture, Energy, and Commerce.

It is important to remember here that all of the above agencies, being executive in character, share the *president's* constitutional grant of the foreign-relations power. Hence, the president is the focal point for the resolution of conflict between and among these subordinates. But because one takes up the time of the president only for the most important matters, questions of jurisdictional competition tend to simmer unresolved, or the participants themselves try to establish a modus vivendi, usually by the creation of interagency committees. Occasionally the president has to intervene, the ultimate recourse being a request for someone's resignation. To forestall these conflicts, however,

10. See, e.g., Charles W. Kegley, Jr., and Eugene R. Wittkopf, *American Foreign Policy: Pattern and Process*, 3d ed. (New York: St. Martin's Press, 1987), pp. 371–414.
11. S. B. Cohen, *The Making of United States International Economic Policy* (New York: Praeger Publishers, 1977).

and to provide some coherence and coordination to the many departments and agencies in the foreign-affairs field, presidents have relied on three different mechanisms:[12]

(a) In 1947 the National Security Act created the National Security Council (NSC) as the successor to the State-War-Navy Coordinating Committee, the body that coordinated wartime policy among these departments. The National Security Council has a legally prescribed membership, but in practice its membership is determined by the president, who may invite anyone and who may as a consequence use the council in a variety of ways. The NSC has been used as an arena for collective decision making and as an arena in which policy advice is offered as a basis for presidential decision. In either case, it becomes a device for conflict resolution among contending parties. But the NSC has also been used more or less regularly since 1960 as a foreign-policy staff for the president, with the effect of introducing still another agency and another powerful official into the competitive environment of foreign-policy making.[13]

(b) Most presidents since 1960 have also tried to dampen competition by giving a measure of organizational leadership in much of foreign policy to the State Department, to make it *primus inter pares* among agencies having foreign-policy agendas. Interesting in principle, this procedure has never worked in practice for a multiplicity of reasons: the State Department has had no experience in such overall management and little interest in it;[14] Presidents have usually demonstrated by their behavior that they themselves had reservations about the arrangement—for example, continuing to use the NSC for issues they considered important to themselves; the Defense Department has always resisted State Department leadership as a matter of principle and of law, and other agencies have not been willing to accept State Department authority when they have discerned doubts and hesitations about it at the top levels and among the most important agencies.

(c) President Reagan, more than other recent presidents, sometimes used the entire cabinet as a vehicle for policy coordination and conflict resolution; this approach recognized that the NSC as le-

---

12. These mechanisms are discussed in detail in I. M. Destler, *Presidents, Bureaucrats, and Foreign Policy: The Politics of Organizational Reform*, 2d ed. (Princeton: Princeton University Press, 1974).

13. For an interesting perspective on this problem, see Henry Kissinger, *The White House Years* (Boston: Little, Brown and Co., 1979), esp. pp. 17–42.

14. See, e.g., such typical State Department viewpoints as those reported and reflected in John Franklin Campbell, *The Foreign Affairs Fudge Factory* (New York: Basic Books, 1971).

gally defined and customarily conceived may not have the appropriate membership for foreign-policy making in an era of "interdependence."[15] But as foreign-policy issues began to grow in importance during his presidency, he seemed to have recognized the limitations of what has been called the "fixed-membership committee,"[16] albeit without finding a workable substitute.

In sum, American foreign policy, which demands at least a measure of consistency and coherence, is in fact so extensive in character and so diverse in its component parts that there is no organizational principle at hand that can give it even the appearance of unity. Policy is formulated and executed in an environment of keen competition among institutions that are juridically equals, where hierarchical authority exists (in the presidency) but for practical reasons can be exercised only sporadically. Bureaucratic responsibility becomes, in these circumstances, something like a hunting license: to bag real game, one needs ammunition, resources, allies. Much of the struggle to find those goes on inside the bureaucracy.[17] But there is unending opportunity here for individuals and groups in the public arena to get involved; to pick sides, often with the encouragement of officials wanting outside support; to seek information and to give it; to strengthen those whose interests seem most nearly like their own. The organization of American foreign-policy making, in other words, invites participation as well as support from outside.

The Organization of Dutch Foreign Policy

Because of the "competition among equals" that characterizes American foreign policy, many people would take issue with my having given precedence to the State Department in my discussion of the organization of foreign-policy making in the United States.[18] In the Netherlands, however, as I have indicated above, no one would dispute the importance of looking first to the Ministry of Foreign

15. See the arguments of Graham Allison and Peter Szanton in *Remaking Foreign Policy: The Organizational Connection* (New York: Basic Books, 1976).

16. See I. M. Destler, *Presidents, Bureaucrats, and Foreign Policy.*

17. See, e.g., Morton Halperin, *Bureaucracy and Foreign Policy* (Washington, D.C.: The Brookings Institution, 1974); Francis E. Rourke, *Bureaucracy and Foreign Policy* (Baltimore: Johns Hopkins University Press, 1972); and Francis E. Rourke, *Bureaucracy, Politics, and Public Policy,* 2d ed. (Boston: Little, Brown and Co., 1976).

18. I found it necessary, for example, to justify my having put the State Department at the center of my study: Bernard C. Cohen, *The Public's Impact on Foreign Policy* (Boston: Little, Brown and Co., 1973).

Affairs. In his introduction to his edited volume on small countries (the Netherlands among them), Ronald Barston writes, "Many small states have only a limited machinery for conducting foreign policy. . . . The foreign ministries of small states tend to have few personnel."[19] By that criterion, the Netherlands does not really belong in the company of small states. Its Foreign Ministry (including the Foreign Service) employs around 3,700 persons in all positions at home and abroad—approximately 1,670 in the home department and a bit over 2,000 in the Foreign Service. On a per-capita basis, that is three times as many as in the United States Department of State. In 1963 the Netherlands stood sixteenth among all nations in the world in the number of diplomats assigned per country with which it maintained relations, although by 1985 the Netherlands, like the United States, had cut back substantially on the personnel in its missions abroad.[20]

The organizational structure of the Foreign Ministry is also complicated beyond what one might expect of a "small country." Indeed, there is even some disagreement among informed observers as to whether it is effectively organized principally on geographical or functional lines.[21] "Line" authority runs through two directorates-

19. R. P. Barston, "Introduction," in R. P. Barston, ed., *The Other Powers: Studies in the Foreign Policies of Small Countries* (London: Geo. Allen and Unwin, 1973), p. 19.

20. See Philip P. Everts and Guido Walraven, eds., *The Politics of Persuasion* (Brookfield, Vt.: Gower Publishing Co., 1989), pp. 59–60.

21. Academic observers claim that the Dutch Foreign Ministry "tends to" or "bears the marks of" functional rather than geographical organization; see Jan Deboutte and Alfred van Staden, "High Politics in the Low Countries," in William Wallace and W. E. Paterson, eds., *Foreign Policy Making in Western Europe: A Comparative Approach* (New York: Praeger Publishers, 1978), chapter 3; Peter R. Baehr, "The Decision-Making Apparatus: the Ministry of Foreign Affairs," in Philip P. Everts, ed., *Controversies at Home* (Dordrecht: Martinus Nijhoff Publishers, 1985), p. 71; and Everts and Walraven, eds., *Politics of Persuasion*, p. 51. A former high official in the Ministry, however, described it to me as geographically organized. The difference may reflect the importance one attaches to the place of development cooperation within the ministry: if it is regarded as "in" the ministry but not "of" it—under the purview of a different minister—then one may well focus on the geographic basis for the organization of most of what remains. In any event, the director-general for political affairs has the coordinating function in the ministry, and he is *primus inter pares* among the directors-general. See Everts and Walraven, eds., *Politics of Persuasion*, p. 57; and Everts, ed., *Controversies at Home*, p. 72.

Dutch doctoral dissertations all contain a loose page with (typically) ten propositions, nine relating to the substance of the thesis itself and one thrown in for fun. The more interesting of these propositions (of both types) are periodically published in the Dutch press—for instance, the following, by F. Grünfeld (coauthor of the section on the Foreign Ministry and other ministries in Everts, ed., *Controversies at Home*), in his thesis at the University of Limburg: "The increased power position of the director-general, political

general: European Cooperation and International Cooperation. Political Affairs, oddly, has a director-general but not a directorate-general. Some of the offices in these directorates have "staff" or functional responsibilities, and others are geographically focused. In addition, other departments in the ministry outside of these directorates have staff responsibilities.

The most important and difficult organizational feature lies in the relations between the directorates-general and also between them and the top in the ministry. Since the mid-1960s there have been two persons with ministerial rank in the Foreign Ministry: one is the foreign minister, and the other is technically a minister without portfolio but actually the development cooperation minister, in charge of what in the United States is called foreign aid.[22] The latter post was created originally to meet the political needs of a specific cabinet formation—to have enough ministerial posts to meet the agreed-on division of "seats" in the cabinet for the coalition parties—but it has taken on a more or less permanent character in the Foreign Ministry because development cooperation is almost universally seen as a part of foreign policy. This ministry disposes of a budget of approximately six billion guilders (over three billion dollars) and oversees a policy arena that has over the years had few audible critics.[23] Those sections of the Directorate-General for International Cooperation that deal with development cooperation report both to the foreign minister and to the development cooperation minister. In addition, there are geographical divisions within the Directorate-General for International Cooperation that duplicate those in Political Affairs, despite the "primacy" accorded to the latter.[24] The structure requires internal "clearances," and it encourages competition, especially between Political Affairs and International Cooperation and between the two ministers, regardless of party. It also encourages the formation of informal alliances between Political Affairs and sections of other ministries that deal with international affairs.

---

affairs, of the Ministry for Foreign Affairs is in conflict with democratic control of Dutch foreign policy through the Parliament" (NRC-Handelsblad, Weekeditie, May 14, 1991).

22. There is a history of such administrative "oddities" in the Dutch Foreign Ministry: from June 1945 to July 1947 there were two ministers of foreign affairs, who rotated between themselves the designation "without portfolio" and who both dealt with the major issues of the day. See Joris J. C. Voorhoeve, Peace, Profits, and Principles (The Hague: Martinus Nijhoff, 1979), pp. 66, 70.

23. But there are more than a few private critics of an arrangement where, as one of them put it, for most nondevelopment purposes "one minister has the authority and no money, and the other has the money but no authority."

24. See Baehr, "Decision-Making Apparatus," p. 73.

The "political level" in the ministry is quite shallow: it consists of two ministers and generally only one under secretary. Everyone else, including the secretary-general (third level of the ministry) and the directors-general (fourth level), is permanent civil service. Although the bureaucracy is at least formally loyal and responsive to its political leadership, it is still an entrenched bureaucracy with its own interests, perspectives, and traditions—most of them (outside of Development Cooperation) rather conservative in character.[25] (One senior bureaucrat, contemplating the possibility of a succession of socialist-led governments a few years back, observed, "Our loyalty is theoretical.")[26] It would be difficult under any circumstances for so few political people, who are not always party allies in the first place, to move such a bureaucracy in new directions to bring about specific changes. One official estimated a minister's impact as, on the average, "ten percent," and he justified the appointment of a political adviser to the minister as a way of increasing the minister's capabilities and hence his political leverage vis-à-vis the (not always neutral) bureaucracy and vis-à-vis other ministers.

The Dutch Foreign Service has undergone substantial growth in the postwar period, from about 350 in 1950 to over 2,000 in all capacities by 1985.[27] The growth was a consequence of the emergence of the Netherlands, like the United States, from its long period of isolation and neutrality precisely at the time when the number of new countries in the world was beginning to grow and when "interdependence" and the "new diplomacy" placed new obligations on foreign relations even for countries like the Netherlands.[28] After many years of efforts, the Netherlands succeeded in 1987 in effecting a major integration of its Foreign Service and home staff in the Foreign Ministry into one Service of Foreign Affairs, such as the United States accomplished in 1954 and for some of the same reasons: to end the political "alienation" of the Foreign Service officers, to permit greater flexibility in assignments and

25. See Everts, ed., *Controversies at Home*, p. 75.

26. This concept of conditional loyalty is regarded by some observers in the Netherlands as unthinkable. Alfred van Staden has recently written: "Central to the traditional ethos of [the] Dutch civil servant is a loyalty to the minister who heads his department which is irrespective of political colour. . . . Civil servants in the Netherlands remain at their posts and pride themselves in their political neutrality." See "The Officials at the Ministry of Foreign Affairs: Recruitment, World Images, and Communications Patterns," in P. Everts, ed., *Controversies at Home*, p. 76. In any event, the prospect of a succession of socialist foreign ministers receded, so the issue remains abstract.

27. See Everts and Walraven, eds., *Politics of Persuasion*, p. 55.

28. See ibid., Chap. 4.

transfers, to give diplomatic officers experience in policy development as well as in its execution, and to give to "specialists" a footing equal to that traditionally held by diplomatic "generalists."[29] All new appointees are required (and existing employees encouraged) to serve abroad on a periodic basis.

In almost every major respect, the Dutch Foreign Service both before and after integration seems to display the same characteristics and experiences and to receive the same evaluations as its counterpart in the United States. It is an organization dominated by "generalists" who have been quite successful at containing political efforts to increase the capabilities of the service either by special-entry recruitment of specialists or by their integration.[30] It has a conservative, even aristocratic image among parliamentarians and others who have occasion to observe it, although (again like the United States Foreign Service) democratizing processes are seen to be at work in it.[31]

The ministry as a whole has not had a tradition of "openness." On the contrary, even into the 1960s foreign policy—and by inference the Foreign Ministry—was treated as more or less a private sphere. Although that began to change under the many pressures for democratization that swept the country in the late 1960s, the ministry is hardly the "leaky sieve" that the State Department is. The reasons for this have much to do with political norms and with the role of the press in the Netherlands and will be discussed in those contexts. Until 1980, the major public-information office in the minis-

29. See, e.g., the statement by the Foreign Minister at the start of the Second Chamber debate on the Foreign Ministry budget, *NRC-Handelsblad*, November 12, 1975; and Everts and Walraven, eds., *Politics of Persuasion*, pp. 57–58.

30. J. Niezing, "Diplomatie: Een organisatie in beweging (II). Enig statistisch materiaal m.b.t. de Nederlandse buitenlandse dienst" (Diplomacy: An organization in motion (II). Some statistical material with respect to the Dutch Foreign Service), *Acta Politica* 4:248–74 (1968/69). See also the postintegration criticism of J. van Bolhuis, "Amateurisme als doel, incompetentie als uitkomst: Het personeelsbeleid van Buitenlandse Zaken en de gevolgen" (Amateurism as goal, incompetence as outcome: The personnel policy of the Foreign Ministry and the consequences), *Internationale Spectator* 44(3): 159–65 (March 1990), and a reply by the secretary-general of the Foreign Ministry, B. R. Bot, "Respons" (Response), *Internationale Spectator* 44(5): 312–15 (May 1990). In fairness, however, there is ample reason to believe that the requirements of specialization simply cannot be met in any organization run by generalist standards, which are—perhaps necessarily—at the core of every Foreign Service.

31. See, e.g., Peter R. Baehr, "The Foreign Policy of the Netherlands," in J. H. Leurdijk, ed., *The Foreign Policy of the Netherlands* (Alphen aan den Rijn: Sijthoff en Noordhoff, 1978). But the weight of custom lies heavy still: "Five of us from the old Foreign Service are the ones who pick new ambassadors. Others—the integrated officers—are not interested; we'd be happy to have them involved."

try was located in the Directorate-General for International Cooperation and was chiefly in the service of the Development Cooperation sections. The rest of the ministry watched the public-relations success of Development Cooperation with awe but were little inclined to take the steps necessary to "go public" themselves. Since then, however, the public-information functions of the ministry have been somewhat more centralized as a result of a partial combination with the activities of the ministry's spokesperson, and one might expect a more visible Foreign Ministry in the future.[32] At the same time, however, international cultural affairs, which have a large public-relations component, are more in the hands of the minister of education and science and the minister of welfare, health and cultural affairs than of the minister of foreign affairs.[33] But public information, by its conception, tends to be a one-way rather than a two-way process, and it remains to be seen whether a more visible Foreign Ministry will be a more accessible Foreign Ministry, as the Information Division has promised. The public-relations needs of Development Cooperation, with its six-billion-guilder budget, will in any event continue to outstrip those of the rest of the Foreign Ministry. As one of its high officials put it, "We have the money; they don't. We need to maintain public interest in Development Cooperation, if we are to keep 1.5 percent of the net national product for foreign assistance. But our international conferences and whatever else our diplomats do would continue even if no one were interested in what the Foreign Ministry does."

The Dutch Foreign Ministry, like the U.S. State Department, had more or less unchallenged control over a narrowly defined political area until World War II; thereafter, it began to suffer the same fate as the State Department, for essentially the same reasons: its control over foreign policy began to fade when "foreign relations" began to mean many more things than one could incorporate in the traditional framework or conception of a Foreign Ministry. In the Dutch case, the fundamental developments were these:

(1) Dutch membership in NATO has created certain military obligations for the country and has led to an increased role for the Defense Ministry in international affairs, particularly in recent years. The

32. *"Macht slijt snel, gebruik haar wel," Blauwdruk voor het voorlichtingsbeleid van het Ministerie van Buitenlandse Zaken* ("Power erodes quickly, so use it," Blueprint for the information policy of the Ministry of Foreign Affairs) (The Hague: Staatsuitgeverij, November 1981).

33. This policy change follows the recommendations embodied in *Culture and Diplomacy* (The Hague: Netherlands Scientific Council for Government Policy, 1987).

NATO modernization issue since 1979 is a prime example of the kind of foreign-policy problem that has to be shared with Defense.

(2) Even more important, overall, is the deep Dutch commitment to the European Community (EC)—a central element in the set of international structures that protect the interests of the smaller European countries (and that allowed the Netherlands a measure of equanimity in the face of German reunification).[34] The European Community has already put into the "international" context an extraordinary range of issues, from agriculture to monetary and fiscal problems to traffic regulation, that are the normal province of ministries other than Foreign Affairs; these developments can be expected to intensify as the EC continues its consolidation in the 1990s.[35] Already by 1985, over 760 officials were working in ministries other than Foreign Affairs in organizational units dealing with international affairs, mostly related to the EC. By way of contrast, at the start of World War II there were only 140 people working for the Ministry of Foreign Affairs, both in the home staff and abroad in the Foreign Service.[36]

(3) The third development is more subtle and less obvious. The Dutch perspective on international relations is a mixture of hard-headed commerce and high-minded moral conviction. The Dutch are deeply involved in a world that they did not make and that they realistically understand they cannot unmake, except perhaps at the margins. Many important interests, thus, tend to be defined not so much in terms of political power or competitive national advantages as in economic and moral terms. Development cooperation, for example, is justified publicly as paying one's dues in the world—as an "engagement of the spirit," to quote a parliamentarian—and privately no doubt as perhaps having a long-term if not a near-term economic payoff, but never as a means of shaping or influencing political relations with receiving countries in ways that might further the Dutch political position in the world. In the words of a former Foreign Ministry official: "A

34. The importance of the EC in Dutch foreign policy is also evidenced in the fact that the *staatssecretaris* in the Foreign Ministry, one of the three political assignments to that ministry in the process of the government formation, is ordinarily charged with the European "portfolio" (Peter R. Baehr, "Democracy and Foreign Policy in the Netherlands," *Acta Politica* 18(1): 39 (January 1983)).

35. See Marjolein C. Groenendijk and F. Grünfeld, "The Foreign Ministry and the Other Departments," in Everts, ed., *Controversies at Home*, pp. 88–98. For the official perspective on the EC, see the annual budget document of the Ministry of Foreign Affairs, e.g., *Rijksbegroting* (National Budget 1990, Chapter 5: The Ministry of Foreign Affairs) (The Hague: SDU Uitgeverij, 1990).

36. See Everts and Walraven, eds., *Politics of Persuasion*, p. 61, and Voorhoeve, *Peace, Profits, and Principles*, p. 71.

cut in the development budget would be domestic politics, not foreign policy. Being a theological people, we don't justify aid in political terms but in moral terms. It is a domestic affair."[37] Since important policy areas such as this are not universally deemed to be *politically* instrumental, the Foreign Ministry has no unique claim to be the source of policy decision with respect to them. Indeed, the Ministry of Economic Affairs, which has jurisdiction over export permits for arms sales, was deeply concerned about the worsening economic picture at the beginning of the 1980s and successfully asserted the claim of Dutch economic interests ahead of diplomatic interests—even of such important moral interests as human rights—in the sale of submarines to Taiwan.[38]

The most striking example of the kind of conflict—and the concomitant need for policy coordination—generated by the interplay of these values comes from within the Foreign Ministry itself, where it divides the Development Cooperation sections of the ministry from the Political Affairs sections and runs from the relevant offices up to the two ministers, as I have indicated earlier. This is all made more difficult by the fact that the higher-level Development Cooperation sections report to both ministers. Baehr suggests that the differences between Political Affairs and Development Cooperation are exacerbated by ideological differences, with the former attracting more conservative individuals and the latter more progressive—those who are able to capitalize on the moral elements of foreign aid.[39] In any event, a budget of nearly six billion guilders speaks very loudly, and Development Cooperation has aspirations to make general policy toward countries in which it has invested heavily. The record of conflict between the two ministers

37. In the spring of 1990 an advertisement appeared in a Dutch newspaper (*De Volkskrant*, March 30, 1990) for Max Havelaar coffee, in which the claim was made that in September 1989 Third World coffee growers made ƒ0.62 (approximately $0.34) more on every 250-gram (8.8-oz.) pack of coffee bearing the Max Havelaar trademark than they did on other brands of coffee—the extra profit presumably supported by a price 10 percent higher than other brands. It is difficult to imagine a coffee ad in the U.S. that relied for its appeal on how much profit there is for the Third World coffee farmer in each pound sold. Anthony Bailey reports, however, that in its first year on the market Max Havelaar coffee gained a market share of 2.5 percent ("Letter from the Netherlands," *The New Yorker*, Aug. 12, 1991, p. 63).

38. See J. Colijn and P. Rusman, *Het Nederlands wapenexportbeleid, 1963–1988* (The arms-export policy of the Netherlands, 1963–1988) (The Hague: Nijgh en Van Ditmar Universitaire, 1989), and A. Timmermans and W. E. Bakema, "Conflicten in Nederlandse kabinetten" (Conflicts in Dutch cabinets), in Rudy B. Andeweg, ed., *Ministers en Ministerraad* (Ministers and Ministerial Council) (The Hague: SDU Uitgeverij, 1990), p. 179.

39. Baehr, "Decision-Making Apparatus," p. 75.

spans at least two decades, several governments, and various combinations of political parties. In the Den Uyl Cabinet (1973–1977), the two ministers were both PvdA, yet they were not on speaking terms by the time the government had run out its term.[40] In the spring of 1982, in the Second Van Agt Cabinet, the development cooperation minister (CDA) acknowledged, in answer to a parliamentary question, that political prisoners in Laos were engaged in forced labor on a development project that the Netherlands was partially financing—directly cutting across the human-rights position of the foreign minister (PvdA) and the ministry and bringing relations between the two ministries to the "moment of truth."[41] In February 1984, in the First Lubbers Cabinet, the foreign minister (CDA) suspended aid to Surinam pending the restoration of democracy and respect for human rights, while the development minister (VVD) set aside 100,000 guilders for humanitarian aid to that country.[42] In April 1990, in the Third Lubbers Cabinet, the foreign minister (CDA) and the development minister (PvdA) were again in conflict, this time over aid versus human rights in Indonesia, in a running battle reported at length in the Dutch press. The entire problem is reminiscent of the conflict between the U.S. State Department and the ECA in the early postwar period, when the ECA possessed the policy importance, the large budget, and the institutional autonomy that Development Cooperation possesses in the Netherlands. In the early 1980s a major government commission on the organization of the Dutch government service suggested—in vain—a solution to the problem in the form of a single minister for foreign affairs and development cooperation, with the latter tasks in the hands of a *staatssecretaris*.[43] In the meantime, the creation of a single public-information service for the ministry has as one of its purposes the amelioration of, if not a cure for, the problem of "two foreign offices."

40. Ibid., p. 73.

41. See the account by An Salomonson in *NRC-Handelsblad*, March 6, 1982. She stresses that the relations between the incumbent ministers in the two preceding cabinets were equally bad, pointing out that while Development Cooperation disposed of enormous sums with a free hand, Foreign Affairs had to deny urgent requests for such things as security provisions in important foreign posts for lack of funds.

42. Baehr, "Decision-Making Apparatus," pp. 73, 108.

43. *Eindadvies van de Commissie Hoofdstructuur Rijksdienst* (Final recommendations of the Commission on the Principal Structure of the Government Service), Ministerie van Binnenlandse Zaken (Ministry of Internal Affairs), 25 May 1981, pp. 15–16. A similar argument has been made more recently by J. W. M. Engels, "De minister zonder portefeuille" (The minister without portfolio), in Andeweg, ed., *Ministers en Ministerraad*, pp. 147–74.

Disputes such as these—and there are others[44]—clearly run as deep as any that have bedeviled the American government. Overall, however, there appear to be some rather effective mechanisms that serve from time to time to keep most of these conflicts from becoming so wide and so public that other interested groups outside the government get involved in them. Disagreements seem, on the whole, to be held much more closely than in the United States, although occasionally one breaks through: the Laotian affair in 1982, for example, was a matter of deep concern all over the Foreign Ministry for months before it became a public matter.[45] One could hardly imagine such reticence in the State Department, which in this respect resembles more an echo chamber, even, than a goldfish bowl. But the dispute over aid versus human rights in Indonesia in 1990, when the foreign minister was in Dublin and the development minister in Jakarta, was carried on by the two men with the help of the press.

All of these mechanisms incorporate what Graham Allison has called "negotiated environments."[46] They involve both jurisdiction and coordination, and they may be either formally or informally regulated. Formal regulation involves cabinet-level agreement, whereas informal regulation may range from well-developed practices among officials to the exchange of letters between ministers. I noted above that the Ministry of Economic Affairs has jurisdiction over export permits for arms sales; it also has coordinating responsibility for that subject. The Finance Ministry has jurisdiction over International Monetary Fund matters. The Foreign Ministry coordinates human rights and general United Nations matters, the Ministry of Education coordinates United Nations Educational, Scientific, and Cultural Organization affairs, and the Agriculture Ministry coordinates Food and Agriculture Organization matters. There are also explicit agreements between ministries to make decisions jointly on matters of equal importance to both: a good example is the formal agreement between the Foreign Ministry and the Defense Ministry to establish a steering group to reach an integrated policy on arms control and nuclear armaments, an agreement reached during the formation of the Second Van Agt Cabinet in the summer of 1981 and made public the following September.[47] These assignments of responsibility resemble international agreements among

44. See, e.g., the case studies reported in Everts, ed., *Controversies at Home*, Part 2, and the review of the Everts volume: P. 't Hart, "Beslissen over buitenlands beleid" (Determining foreign policy), *Acta Politica* 21(2): 209–24 (April 1986).
45. Salomonson, *NRC-Handelsblad*.
46. Graham Allison, *Essence of Decision* (Boston: Little, Brown and Co., 1971).
47. See *Nederlandse Staatscourant*, 23 September 1981.

sovereign powers: they may change over time, and they may even be violated, but they tend to be respected as an aspect of the autonomy of the ministers.

If officials have difficulty in establishing jurisdictional boundaries and coordinating responsibilities or in maintaining boundaries and responsibilities agreed to at an earlier period by mutual consent, their disputes may be settled by the ministers. If the ministers cannot settle them, they may be taken to the Ministerial Council for resolution. But just as cabinet secretaries in the United States hesitate to take their jurisdictional disputes to the president, there is some reluctance among ministers in the Netherlands to move these issues to the cabinet level, particularly because it is a bargaining rather than a hierarchical institution, where party as well as departmental interests are at stake.[48] And there are also differences among prime ministers in the degree to which they even want to pay attention to issues that others are supposed to decide and that may have wider political ramifications. Thus, there is more pressure on the ministers to agree among themselves.

A final word about the Foreign Ministry: the administrative autonomy of ministries makes them formally equal (like member states in the United Nations), and to a large extent that equality is formally respected. But two surveys among administrators, inquiring into the prestige of Dutch ministries, show that in fact not much prestige attaches to Foreign Affairs.[49]

Let me summarize all this in an argument that parallels the structure of my conclusions with respect to American foreign-policy-making institutions: the Dutch, like the Americans, aim at policy consistency and coherence, but with autonomous departments and a "small" foreign policy—one that is not very extensive in character or diverse in its component parts—there is no organizing principle that enables them to achieve it. Dutch foreign policy is formulated and executed in an environment of keen competition among institutions, as well as among Ministers, that are juridically equal and where *no* hierarchical authority exists. This, plus the weak position of the minister-president, has forced a "politics of accommodation" on the ministers involved, so that their conflicts tend to take place within more clearly defined boundaries or, at least until recently, to be kept

48. See Timmermans and Bakema, "Conflicten in Nederlandse kabinetten."
49. See U. Rosenthal, E. van den Gronden, L.G. Gerrichhauzen, and M. van Giessen, "Prestige van departementen" (Prestige of departments), *Acta Politica* 21(2): 133–47 (April 1986).

from public view if they could not be so contained. To the extent that there is growing public awareness of conflicts, however, one can expect to find growing opportunities for individuals and groups in the public arena to know what is going on in this bureaucratic structure and to get mobilized and involved.

The Cultural Norms of Participation

Any discussion of political culture is necessarily less concrete than a discussion of political systems or foreign-policy-making institutions. Social anthropology as applied to political behavior lacks the comforting sound of hard facts knocking on strong institutions. Yet one cannot look closely at political participation in the foreign-policy arena without being sensitive to the cultural norms that in the largest sense appear to regulate it. I am not asserting any necessary cause-and-effect relationship between the organization of political power and political institutions in a country and the norms of participation in that land. Rather, I believe that one cannot understand the invitation or inspiration to participate in foreign policy from the outside merely by looking at structural phenomena. The structures may define or create opportunities to participate, but they do not tell us how or why the opportunities may or may not be seized.

All observers of Dutch political and social life agree that what was once a profoundly stable society has been undergoing very rapid change, but there is less agreement on the causes for the change and on when it all began. The social invention that held together a religiously divided country was "pillarization" (*verzuiling*). Each major religious and secular grouping formed its own "pillar"—a more or less discrete subculture in which social, religious, and political institutions were closely interwoven, making for a life apart. The separate pillars came together at the top in a "politics of accommodation," sustained by strong norms of political and social deference to leadership and authority.[50] The essence of the change—whatever its sources—that has overtaken Dutch society was the rapid "deconfessionalization" of Dutch social and political life and the parallel erosion both of the pillars and of

50. See Arend Lijphart, *The Politics of Accommodation*, 1st ed. (Berkeley: University of California Press, 1968). There is some debate today as to whether deference and accommodation produced stability or whether stability permitted deference and accommodation. See Hans Daalder, "The Mould of Dutch Politics: Themes for Comparative Inquiry," *West European Politics* 12(1): 12–13 (January 1989). Daalder also traces the Dutch "political culture of pluralism and bargaining . . . and a preference for collegial forms of decisionmaking" back to the years of the Dutch Republic, prior to 1795. Ibid., p. 3.

the patterns of deference that supported them.[51] The process of deconfessionalization and at least the political aspects of depillarization (*ontzuiling*) are apparent in the decline in the percentage of votes cast for the three major confessional parties—the Catholic People's Party (*Katholieke Volkspartij*–KVP), the Anti-Revolutionary Party (*Anti-Revolutionaire Partij*–ARP), and the Christian-Historical Union (*Christelijk-Historische Unie*–CHU)—in the elections for the Second Chamber, prior to their merger into the Christian Democratic Appeal (CDA). Between 1946 and 1963, these parties together regularly polled between 49 and 53 percent of the total vote. By 1972, the same three parties garnered only 31.3 percent of the vote. And in the elections since the founding of the CDA, from 1977 to 1989, the figure has ranged between 29.3 and 34.6 percent.[52]

The reasons for these changes are less evident. Explanations have included such diverse phenomena as the impact of World War II, the royal crisis of the mid-1950s, the impact of the Vietnam War, the predominantly socialist government of Den Uyl from 1973 to 1977, the impact of mass education, and the substantial accomplishment of religious emancipation. No doubt each of these factors contributed something to the demise of the old order. A well-placed observer of the Dutch scene described the practical consequences of all this for the Dutch press, but his words speak to the shift in the rules of the entire political game: "Now we are more and more impertinent; there are even hostile attitudes. Those are not the rules of the game, which call for antagonism but not hostility."

But the Dutch who remember the way things used to be may be underestimating the continuities, if not exaggerating the change. Despite the ferment of recent years, there remains a substantial amount of deference in the Dutch political system, just as there remains a stable residue of traditional political values represented in the confessional

51. Although the two processes are independent, they are not unrelated. See Rudy B. Andeweg, *Dutch Voters Adrift: On Explanations of Electoral Change, 1963–1977* (University of Leiden, 1982); and W. E. Miller and Ph. C. Stouthard, "Confessional Attachment and Electoral Behavior in the Netherlands," *European Journal of Political Research* 3: 219–58 (1975).

52. Cees van der Eijk and Broer Niemöller, "Stemmen op godsdienstige partijen sinds 1967" (Voting for religious parties since 1967), in C. van der Eijk and B. Niemöller, *In het spoor van de kiezer* (On the trail of the voter) (Meppel: Uitgeverij Boom, 1983) (a special issue of *Acta Politica* 18 [2]: 169–82 [1983]); Cees van der Eijk and Philip van Praag, Jr., eds., *De strijd om de meerderheid: De verkiezing van 1986 (The struggle for a majority: The election of 1986)* (Amsterdam: CT Press, 1987), appendix, table 1, p. 142. (In the election of 1994—after this book was completed and beyond its time frame—the CDA suffered what was called a "historic" loss, winning only 22.2 percent of the vote.)

vote.[53] It is still the case in the Netherlands that the government is at a considerable social-psychological distance from the individual citizen and that individual political activity directed at the government (other than voting) is not customary behavior.[54] And what is broadly the case for the government as a whole is doubly the case for the Foreign Ministry, where civil servants have few substantive contacts with people outside of government—with the occasional exception of background discussions with the press.[55]

Through the 1970s, at least, and even through the 1980s although with less clarity, one could observe the distance, the attendant constraints, and the observance of formalities even among individuals with strong professional credentials in foreign affairs, including academics and journalists. A member of Parliament once described for me his institutionalized contacts with academic foreign-policy specialists and then added: "In Holland everyone lives in his own pillar, and there is very little contact between . . . people in these different professional groups. . . . We are very rigid." Social credentials, on the other hand,

53. G. A. Irwin and J. J. M. van Holsteyn, in "Decline of the Structured Model of Electoral Competition," *West European Politics* 12(1): 39 (January 1989), argue that the "simple structured model" (i.e., the pure pillars) once accounted for as much as 72 percent of vote choices but that the percentage had declined by 47 percent in 1986. They then point to both sides of the new reality: "Although close to half the vote is still a substantial figure, it confirms that the structured model has lost explanatory power." Arend Lijphart also argues that changes in Dutch democracy should not be exaggerated. "The overall pattern of the new Dutch politics in the 1967–88 period still looks a great deal more like the old 1946–67 Dutch politics than like British or New Zealand politics. The Netherlands has merely moved from the politics of accommodation to the politics of relatively less accommodation" ("From the Politics of Accommodation to Adversarial Politics in the Netherlands: A Reassessment," *West European Politics* 12 [1]: 151 [January 1989]).

54. The antinuclear movement of the 1980s mobilized hundreds of thousands of Dutch in opposition to government policy, but in all these activities substantial comfort was to be found in large numbers. See Bert Klandermans, ed., *Tekenen voor vrede* (Signing for peace) (Assen: Van Gorcum, 1988), and Chapter 6 below. Jacques J. A. Thomassen and Jan W. van Deth concluded that "the Netherlands still has a low level of conventional political participation compared with the United States and Germany" and that although Dutch society is extremely permissive, it has not yet developed a "participant culture" ("How New is Dutch Politics?" *West European Politics* 12 [1]: 71–73 [January 1989]).

55. In the 1970s J. H. Leurdijk referred to the often-cited difficult accessibility of policy officials in the Foreign Ministry, and Peter R. Baehr wrote that the informal Dutch elite attached relatively minor significance to the official apparatus as a channel of influence. See Peter R. Baehr et al., *Elite en buitenlandse politiek in Nederland* (Elite and foreign policy in the Netherlands) (The Hague: Staatsuitgeverij, 1978), pp. 26, 167. It is not inconsistent with this restraint, however, that some Dutch civil servants, even in the Foreign Ministry, can be quite active and prominent in their political parties, provided that "they remain clearly loyal to [their] ministers" (Daalder, "Mould of Dutch Politics," p. 8).

were long the key to access and will still open many doors that are ordinarily closed. Several people expressed it in nearly identical language: "It is necessary to adapt to their social setting—it is a small inner circle. If you have access to that—I know them from my Leiden days." As a general rule, individuals without such social credentials (in the broad sense) do not have "standing," and as a general rule they do not seek it. Participation tends to be indirect, through established institutions.[56] And one of the problems in contemporary Dutch political life is that "depillarization," which has weakened some of the old constraints and has improved access for some people, has also shaken up both public and governmental conceptions of just which institutions are "established."[57]

The differences between the Dutch and American political cultures as they apply to foreign policy are nicely juxtaposed in two comments, one from each side. A Dutch journalist reflected on the traces of "the feeling that the Minister is still 'your excellency.' That is fading now, to be sure, but you still shouldn't arrogate to yourself the right to pass judgment on them. It is still true. People don't *think* about writing in those terms. They *talk* about it all the time, but they don't write about it."[58] By contrast, one may recall Henry Kissinger's first press conference after he was appointed secretary of state in 1973. Reporters wanted to know how to address him: should they continue to call him Dr. Kissinger, or should it be Mr. Secretary? To

56. In the 1960s American respondents were three times as likely as Dutch respondents to express a preference for acting alone to prevent government action they considered harmful or unjust. See Robert A. Dahl and Edward R. Tufte, *Size and Democracy* (Stanford: Stanford University Press, 1973), table 4.7, p. 53, utilizing data from Arend Lijphart, *The Politics of Accommodation*, pp. 152–53, and from Gabriel A. Almond and Sidney Verba, *The Civic Culture* (Princeton: Princeton University Press, 1963), p. 203.

57. An example of a recently established institution is the IKV—the Interchurch Peace Council. In his study of antinuclear movements in western Europe, Thomas R. Rochon traces the range of contacts attained by IKV Secretary Mient Jan Faber by the 1980s: "ministers and members of parliament, high civil servants in the Foreign Affairs and Defense offices, and staffers in the American Embassy in The Hague and at NATO headquarters in Brussels." *Mobilizing for Peace: The Anti-Nuclear Movements in Western Europe* (Princeton: Princeton University Press, 1988), p. 181.

58. See also the description of the press conferences of J. M. A. H. Luns, Dutch Foreign Minister is seven consecutive cabinets from 1956 to 1971, by H. M. Bleich, "U moet de sigaar uit de mond nemen als U met ons spreekt" (You should take the cigar out of your mouth when you talk to us), in J. Th. J. van den Berg et al., *Tussen Nieuwspoort en Binnenhof: De jaren 60 als breuklijn in de naoorlogse ontwikkelingen in politiek en journalistiek* (Between Nieuwspoort and the Binnenhof: The 1960s as a fault line in the postwar developments in politics and journalism) (The Hague: SDU Uitgeverij, 1989), pp. 27–33.

mutual laughter he replied, "That's all right, you can just call me 'Your Excellency.' " The social-psychological distance is small in the United States not only between journalists and foreign-policy officials but also between academics and those officials, between them and ordinary citizens, and even between permanent officials and political decision makers. Permanent foreign-policy officials in the Netherlands take their "invisibility" seriously. In the United States many of them skirt the edges regularly, maintaining continuous and open contact with all sorts of "outsiders."[59] And for some time now they have had the right even to express their own personal views in institutional but nevertheless public channels.[60]

In the American political system, with its wide dispersion of political power and the inefficiency of its political parties for the communication of policy preferences, the expression of preferences by individuals directly to government officials is culturally sanctioned and even encouraged. The norm of direct individual participation in the political process is deeply embedded in the American political culture; it has its constitutional base in the First Amendment right of petition for the redress of grievances (written before the development of the party system in the United States) and its historic roots in the New England town meeting and in the self-government of frontier settlements. President Carter was widely applauded in his first days in office when he called on ordinary citizens to send him their ideas on policy questions. The president and the secretary of state together have in recent years received in the vicinity of 300,000 individual letters a year on foreign-policy matters—a small percentage of the population, to be sure, but ample evidence of the vitality of the old axiom, "Don't complain to me, write the president."[61] The "Great Decisions" programs of the Foreign Policy Association, in which many thousands of individuals across the country study a current policy issue for a week and then send their opinions to the State Department, is a contemporary national town meeting on foreign policy. In short, there may be complaints about the

59. Piet Dankert, former member of Parliament (PvdA), former chair of the European Parliament, and *staatssecretaris* in the Ministry of Foreign Affairs in the Third Lubbers Cabinet, once observed that he learned more by talking with officials in Washington for three days than he could in a whole year at the Dutch Foreign Ministry (*Elsevier*, 38 [9] March 6, 1982).

60. For example, four country-level officials from the Bureau of Near Eastern and South Asian Affairs argued in the spring of 1982 for an independent Palestinian state, in the pages of *Open Forum*, a quarterly publication in the State Department. This did not pass unnoticed in the Dutch press; see the account in *De Volkskrant*, March 10, 1982.

61. For a broad study of this subject, see James N. Rosenau, *Citizenship Between Elections: An Inquiry into the Mobilizable American* (New York: Free Press, 1974).

responsiveness of American foreign-policy officials to particular expressions of opinion by American citizens, but there is little complaint in the United States about their *accessibility*.

Some Implications of National Differences

Although we have seen some striking similarities between the political systems of the United States and the Netherlands insofar as they affect foreign relations, the differences between them are on the whole quite substantial and have had important consequences for the development of public-opinion institutions in the foreign-policy field in these two countries.

The structure of the American political system, as we have seen, provides no clear institutional routes for political preference in or control of foreign policy. Party organizations are not policy organizations, and they provide no effective party control over the exercise of the executive foreign-policy power. There is no possibility of elections except at constitutionally prescribed intervals, and there is little possibility of extracting foreign-policy mandates from elections when they are held. These structural limitations hold also for the exercise of the legislative foreign-policy power, which is considerably less than the executive foreign-policy power to begin with. In these circumstances, it is politically reasonable (as well as culturally acceptable) for politically concerned individuals to seek or to organize more direct ways of expressing preferences to foreign-policy makers in the executive and in the Congress. And it is equally reasonable for a government that wishes to be (or even just to seem) responsive to its citizens to encourage the development of these direct channels of communication. Indeed, as I noted earlier, beginning with the Second World War and the pursuit of an active "internationalist" foreign policy, the Department of State has made explicit provision for regular contact with private, nongovernmental, nonparty, public groups.[62] In short, those who share in the exercise of the foreign-relations power have to go outside the political structure of government to cultivate a public opinion, to discover what it is, to help move it along, and not infrequently to mobilize allies first for the policy struggles within the executive branch and subsequently for the political struggles between the executive and the Congress.

The Dutch political system, on the other hand, provides relatively clear channels for the expression of political preferences in foreign pol-

62. For the origins of these measures, see Dean G. Acheson, *Present at the Creation* (New York: W. W. Norton, 1969).

icy, as in all other policy areas. The existence of many political parties that have policy as well as electoral functions, that are not bound to the divergent and parochial interests of specific electoral districts, and that shape the very organization of both legislative and executive power seems to have discouraged for many years the development of other channels for the direct expression of foreign-policy views. Nor was the political culture particularly conducive to that kind of public institutional development; the "pillars" (including their parties) were themselves the appropriate and the only necessary institutions. After World War II, thus, on neither the public nor the government side did it apparently seem necessary to develop either a public following or a means of ascertaining or shaping the public's foreign-policy preferences, even though the Dutch were undergoing the same kind of "revolution" in their foreign policy as the Americans, giving up a long historical tradition of isolationism and neutrality for a policy of commitment to the anti-Soviet alliance of the West. In public administration at the local level, a process known as *inspraak* has been established in recent years whereby citizens are offered the opportunity to express their opinions on policy proposals,[63] but *inspraak* has not carved a place for itself in the foreign-policy field. The foreign-policy alternative—formal advisory bodies—has been more elite than mass.[64]

But the Dutch political parties have not always been able to contain or to satisfy significant currents of foreign-policy opinion, in large part because foreign policy has almost never been the central interest around which these parties have organized.[65] Indeed, the political changes beginning in the late 1960s reflected changes in societal values and policy preferences—both foreign *and* domestic—on too great a scale and at too rapid a tempo to be fully absorbed by the ordinary political channels, against which, as a result, some of the rebellion was directed.[66] The outcome was the rapid growth of new forms of nongovernmental, nonparty political action in foreign policy, about which I shall have more to say at a later point.[67] But accommodation at the elite

---

63. See, e.g., A. Hoogerwerf and J. A. M. Maarse, "Het overheidsbeleid en zijn effecten" (Government policy and its effects), in R. B. Anderweg, A. Hoogerwerf, and J. J. A. Thomassen, eds., *Politiek in Nederland* (Politics in the Netherlands), 3d ed. (Alphen aan den Rijn: Samsom Uitgeverij, 1989), pp. 278–79.

64. See Chapter 6.

65. See, e.g., A. P. M. Lucardie, "Politieke Partijen" (Political parties), in Andeweg, Hoogerwerf, and Thomassen, eds., *Politiek in Nederland*, pp. 60–77.

66. The Labor Party, however, was radicalized during this period, with the help of its New Left faction.

67. See Chapter 6.

level and at least the expectation of deference at the mass level still have enough vitality so that the most important of these organizations— those that attract a large number of adherents from a variety of political directions—have been *given* standing, so to speak; that is to say, they have been made a part of the established quasi-governmental institutions of public participation in foreign affairs.

The differences between these two national systems can be better understood by closer and more direct comparisons of the way their major public-opinion institutions function and interact with respect to foreign policy. To that task I now turn.

3
Public Opinion
Some General Considerations

I have up until now put the stress on public participation rather than public opinion, as if the two were wholly different subjects or concepts. In reality, however, public participation is concerned with public opinion in its concrete—and often institutionalized—manifestations. In that sense, this whole book is about public opinion. But something also needs to be said here by way of prologue or overview about public opinion in some of its more abstract manifestations, so that we have a general context within which to place the more concrete observations. I am especially interested here in comparing some dimensions and characteristics of the foreign-policy communities in the Netherlands and the United States and in exploring an elusive phenomenon within these two societies, the "foreign-policy consensus" (or absence thereof). I also want to look at the way that mass opinion on foreign policy has been approached in these two countries. I shall be looking at continuity and change in opinion over time, but I shall not try to compare anything that might be called the "current state of public opinion" in these countries; that is inherently issue-specific, and thus it is a transient phenomenon that is not worth the effort.

There are some important differences in the way that surveys of mass opinion on foreign-policy matters have been approached and used in the Netherlands and the United States. Americans—in polling agencies, in universities, in community foreign-policy organizations, even in government agencies—have been continuously interested for more than fifty years in questions that might illuminate the state of public thinking about foreign policy. Some of the reasons for that I discussed in the introductory chapter. Another reason, I believe, lies in the characteristics of the American political system that I discussed in the two immediately preceding chapters: democratization of foreign policy has far outstripped the capacity of formal political structures in the United States adequately to inform policy makers about the state of public opinion on important issues of foreign policy. Put differently, the network of political institutions that are capable of conveying public opinion to government officials is meager compared with the number of citizens who have opinions—well-informed or ill-informed—about foreign policy. The norm that encourages a one-to-one relationship between the individual and his leaders, bypassing formal political structures, also encourages the development and use of public-opinion polling as an appropriate and convenient institutional expression of that relationship.[1] It is also the case that members of Congress, who (unlike their Dutch counterparts) are directly dependent on the views of a specific geographical constituency, have an important "need to know" the opinions of those constituents, and almost all of them engage in some form of polling among them. Regular and repeated polling on foreign-policy subjects over the years has long since created more data than one knows what to do with; it has also contributed to (if it did not indeed create) the belief that there is always a specific public opinion "out there" on any subject, at any time. Even further, discussions about public opinion on foreign-policy matters are now generally assumed to refer to the state of opinion as it is (or could be) revealed through the polls.[2] Happily for my present purposes, there is an extensive body of primary and secondary analyses both of individual surveys and of large numbers of them, some of which have stood up rather well over time.[3]

In the Netherlands, over this same time period, there has been less of an urge to ask these kinds of questions in public opinion polls.

1. Discussions of the polling instrument in the United States are almost always couched in the language of progressive democracy. See, for example, George Gallup, *The Sophisticated Poll Watcher's Guide* (Princeton: Princeton Opinion Press, 1972).

2. P. E. Converse, "Changing Conceptions of Public Opinion in the Political Process," *Public Opinion Quarterly*, vol. 51, 1987.

3. For analyses of individual surveys, see, for example, A. T. Steele, *The American People and China* (New York: McGraw-Hill, 1966); John E. Rielly, ed., *American Opinion on Foreign Policy 1975* (Chicago: Chicago Council on Foreign Relations, 1975), and succeeding volumes for 1979, 1983, 1987, and 1991; for analyses of larger bodies of data, see, e.g., Gabriel A. Almond, *The American People and Foreign Policy* (New York: Harcourt Brace, 1950); John Mueller, *War, Presidents, and Public Opinion* (New York: John Wiley & Son, 1973); and Barry B. Hughes, *The Domestic Context of American Foreign Policy* (San Francisco: W. H. Freeman, 1978).

Among the reasons for that, I believe, is a different conception of public opinion—a very different view from that long current in the United States as to what is politically relevant opinion in the first place and as to the practical ways to get at that opinion, given the size of the relevant political community. The democratization of foreign policy in the Netherlands was substantially contained, until sometime in the 1970s, by the representative institutions of the political system. Foreign Office officials—along with everyone else—learned as much as they needed to know about the state of public opinion on foreign policy from debates in the Parliament and the parties and from the press. As a result, for many years there was no regular flow of public-opinion data on foreign-policy questions,[4] and discussions about public opinion on foreign-policy matters were generally assumed to refer to the opinions expressed in Parliament, the parties, and the press.[5] There was also little incentive for many years for Dutch scholars to subject the data that did exist to extensive analysis, primary or secondary.[6]

4. In 1975 the Netherlands Institute for Peace Questions published in a single volume (offset from spacious typewritten copy) all of the Dutch opinion-poll data, from national and subnational samples, from 1960 to 1975 that had anything to do with foreign policy, development assistance, European policy, and defense. The data from the period prior to 1960 were described as mostly fragmentary and some of the research after 1960 as badly kept and in danger of imminent disappearance unless it were properly stored. See Frans M. Roschar, comp., *Buitenlandse politiek in de Nederlandse publieke opinie* (Foreign policy in Dutch public opinion) (The Hague: Nederlands Instituut voor Vredesvraagstukken, June 1975).

5. Cf. the issue of *Internationale Spectator* 24(1): 1–75 (1970), which is given over to the subject of public opinion and foreign policy. There is only one article in that issue that deals with polling, and that is an argument for more of it: see Peter R. Baehr, "De waarde van de openbare mening bij de bepaling van het buitenlands beleid" (The value of public opinion in the determination of foreign policy), pp. 35–48. Baehr's line of reasoning was subsequently questioned by Cees van der Eijk and Frans N. Stokman in a commentary in *Internationale Spectator* 24(17): 1599–1611 (1970).

6. In 1970 the Netherlands Institute for Public Opinion published a summary volume on its first twenty-five years of public opinion research; the attention paid there to foreign-policy questions is minuscule—even including the Indonesia question. See Het Nederlands Instituut voor de Publieke Opinie (NIPO) en Het Marktonderzoek, *Zo zijn wij: De eerste vijfentwintig jaar NIPO-onderzoek* (The Netherlands Institute for Public Opinion [NIPO] and Market Research, This is what we are: The first twenty-five years of NIPO-research) (Amsterdam: Agon Elsevier, 1970). Philip Everts' analysis of Dutch opinion on nuclear weapons, "Wat vinden 'de mensen in het land'? Openbare mening en kernwapens" (What does "the man in the street" think? Public Opinion and nuclear weapons), *Acta Politica* 15 (3): 305–54 (July 1981), was a welcome exception, but Everts himself complained about the lack of data that would permit a comparison of changes over time. See also Everts, *Public Opinion, the Churches, and Foreign Policy* (Leiden University, Institute for International Studies, 1983), which integrates the data from this and other articles.

In the late 1970s the Dutch peace movement came to life, raising the issues of nuclear-arms policy in venues outside of Parliament, political parties, and the press;[7] at about the same time, public-opinion polling on these and related issues began to proliferate, permitting some comparisons over time that were not possible earlier.[8]

Although the opinion data that can inform us about the *structure* of foreign-policy opinion are very uneven between the two countries, there are nevertheless enough for at least a tentative comparison of the dimensions and characteristics of the foreign-policy public in each. I will be guided here by the classifications used by Almond in his analysis of American public opinion on foreign policy.[9] Dutch scholars have themselves employed Almond's framework,[10] and since it is essentially a scaling technique it does no violence to the reality of either the Dutch or the American situation.

The Structure of Public Opinion

The structure of American opinion on foreign policy, as it has emerged in countless surveys and many analyses over the years, is generally described as pyramidal, with a very large base of the disinterested and the ignorant (the general public), a small layer of interested and informed observers (the attentive public), and at the top a very thin layer

7. See Chapter 6.

8. Philip P. Everts has been a central figure in the collection and analysis of this material. He and Ch. J. Vaneker followed the earlier Roschar collection with a new volume of polls on foreign-policy questions from 1975 through 1984, this time nine years only, national samples only, and many more surveys: *Buitenlandse politiek in de Nederlandse publieke opinie: Inventaris van de in Nederland gehouden opinie-onderzoeken m.b.t. de buitenlandse politiek in de periode 1975–1984* (Foreign policy in Dutch public opinion: Inventory of the opinion surveys in the Netherlands with respect to foreign policy in the period 1975–1984) (The Hague: Netherlands Institute for International Relations "Clingendael," December 1984). See also Philip P. Everts, *The Peace Movement and Public Opinion* (Leiden: The Institute for International Studies, March 1990); Philip P. Everts, "Continuity and Change in Public Attitudes on Questions of Security in the Netherlands: The Role of the Peace Movement," in Hans Rattinger and Don Munton, eds., *Debating National Security: The Public Dimension* (Frankfurt-am-Main: Verslag Peter Lang, 1991); and Everts' annual "Ontwikkelingen in de publieke opinie" (Developments in public opinion), *Jaarboek vrede en veiligheid* (Yearbook on peace and security) (Alphen aan den Rijn: Samsom Uitgeverij, annually since 1984).

9. Gabriel A. Almond, *The American People and Foreign Policy* (New York: Harcourt Brace, 1950).

10. E.g., Peter R. Baehr, et al., *Elite en buitenlandse politiek in Nederland* (Elite and foreign policy in the Netherlands) (The Hague: Staatsuitgeverij, 1978); and Everts, "Wat vinden."

of active participants, in and out of government, who engage in foreign-policy debate, discussion, and decision (the elite).[11] The most important correlates of interest, information, and activity are education, income, and profession: the higher one's socioeconomic level, the more likely one is to be in the higher reaches of the pyramid. Sex, age, and place of residence also have some bearing on this: women, young people, and rural residents are less likely to be interested, informed, and active than are men, older people, and urban residents.[12]

Because these are all gradations, there is considerable imprecision with respect not only to the dividing lines between the major classifications but also to the personal characteristics that may be associated with each. To what extent are the people who qualify as the "attentive public" by virtue of interest, information, and activity the same when the foreign-policy issues differ? To what extent is "Don't know"—the basic index of assignment to the "general public"—evidence of lack of knowledge and interest in any particular issue or evidence of humility in the face of an excess of knowledge? Given these kinds of ambiguities, we can have only very rough estimates of the size of the groups: elites (interest, opinion, bureaucratic, political),[13] perhaps 1 percent of the adult population, or roughly 1.5 million people; the attentive public (which Almond defines as continuously interested and informed), perhaps 15–20 percent of the adult population, or approximately 25 million people;[14] all the rest, perhaps 80 percent of the adult population, or

11. See Almond, *American People*, pp. 138–39; and James N. Rosenau, *Public Opinion and Foreign Policy: An Operational Formulation* (New York: Random House, 1961), pp. 33–34.

12. Almond, *American People*, chapter 6. In the spring of 1964, the Survey Research Center at the University of Michigan found that 28 percent of a sample of adult Americans did not know that there was a Communist government in China; 54 percent of the grade school–educated did not know, compared with 3 percent of those with college degrees, and 34 percent of the women, compared with 19 percent of the men. In the same survey, 25 percent of the sample—49 percent of the grade school–educated and 4 percent of the college graduates, 29 percent of the women and 20 percent of the men—had heard nothing about the fighting that was going on in Vietnam. The survey was commissioned by the Council on Foreign Relations, New York, and appears in A. T. Steele, *The American People and China* (New York: McGraw-Hill, 1966), Appendix, pp. 252–313.

13. This is Almond's classification of elites, *American People*, chapter 7.

14. Rosenau estimates it as "probably no larger than 10 percent of the population, and probably much smaller" (*Public Opinion and Foreign Policy*, p. 40), although in a later work he argues that the attentive public is growing (*Citizenship Between Elections: An Inquiry into the Mobilizable American* [New York: Free Press, 1974]). He also quotes Elmo Roper as putting the figure in 1955 between 10 and 25 million Americans, or approximately 10–25 percent of the adult population at the time; see Roper's "Foreword" to E. Katz and P. F. Lazarsfeld, *Personal Influence* (Glencoe, Ill.: Free Press, 1955). For a more recent and more

about 120 million people, part of the mass public or general public, who usually pay no attention but who may be briefly interested from time to time in a single issue when public events take a dramatic turn.[15]

Americans have sometimes been a bit defensive whenever comparisons were made between the levels of general public knowledge of and discourse on world affairs in the United States and those in European countries. Among the factors that seemed to support a higher level in Europe were the quality of many national newspapers and periodicals there, the proximity of foreign countries and the relative ease of international travel, and the demanding preparation for and the greater selectivity of European university education. This image has often been cultivated by cosmopolitan Europeans;[16] it may even have been reinforced by the flood of young American tourists in Europe, who can see the newspapers, the journals, and the borders for themselves and who encounter highly politicized (and multilingual) university students in the bars and cafés.

The structure of Dutch opinion on foreign policy, insofar as it is discernible in the relatively limited data that are available, does not support this subjective comparison. The same pyramid is evident, but the base may perhaps be even larger and the top even smaller than in the United States.[17] A study of the Dutch "foreign-policy elite" in the

---

restrictive estimate of political attentiveness in general, see W. R. Neuman, *The Paradox of Mass Politics: Knowledge and Opinion in the American Electorate* (Cambridge: Harvard University Press, 1986).

15. The classic estimates of the size of the "general public" by James Rosenau in *Public Opinion and Foreign Policy* and by Alfred Hero in *Americans in World Affairs* (Boston: World Peace Foundation, 1959), ranging from 75 to 90 percent of the adult population, are supported regularly by the contemporary polling by the Times Mirror Center for the People and the Press. See, e.g., Times Mirror News Interest Index, March 1990: "Public Interest and Awareness of the News."

16. The remarks of a high official in the Dutch Foreign Ministry are typical: "I was in New York for three and a half years. I was horrified at the lack of foreign-policy information on the part of the American people, even educated Americans. . . . There is a lot of good work being done in the United States on foreign-policy problems, but it does not radiate out into the country." According to another Foreign Office official, who had spent some years in Washington: "The interest in foreign affairs outside Washington and New York is small compared with here."

17. In a parallel analysis, Jacques J. A. Thomassen and Jan W. van Deth argue that "the level of subjective interest [in politics in general] is remarkably low in the Netherlands" and that the proportion of people who are *not* interested in politics is much higher in the Netherlands than it is in the United States ("How New is Dutch Politics?" *Western European Politics* 12 [1]: 69 [June 1989]). These conclusions are also reflected in the judgments of Dutch members of the lower house of Parliament, who by three to one agree with the statement that "most citizens have a low interest in politics" and by seven to one disagree

late 1970s makes a distinction among the elite, opinion leaders, and the attentive public. If for purposes of comparability we compress the first two into one group of active participants, in and out of government, who engage in discussion, debate, and decision, we get an elite estimated at about fifty thousand, which is about one-half of 1 percent of the adult population in Holland.[18] A few years earlier, Van den Tempel and Van Staden made a rough estimate of the size of the Dutch "attentive public" on the basis of responses to two questions from the 1972–73 Dutch election study—an objective question getting at knowledge of international events and a subjective question describing participation in discussions of international issues. Applying their criteria, only 4 percent of the sample belonged to the attentive public; slightly more relaxed criteria brought that up to 6 percent.[19] Everts mentions estimates ranging from 5 to 10 percent of the adult Dutch population.[20] If we take the highest of these figures,[21] that would be roughly one mil-

---

with the statement that "most citizens have a good knowledge of political affairs." See M. P. C. M. van Schendelen, J. J. A. Thomassen, and H. Daudt, eds., 'Leden van de Staten-Generaal, . . .': Kamerleden over de werking van het parlement ("Members of the States-General, . . .": Members of Parliament on the workings of Parliament) (The Hague: VUGA-Uitgeverij, 1981), table 3, p. 174. And in a "political interest score" fashioned from the answers to four questions on both the 1981 and 1986 national election studies, between 8 and 10 percent were reported to have had high political interest. See C. van der Eijk, B. Niemöller, and A. Th. J. Eggen, Dutch Parliamentary Election Study 1981 (Amsterdam: Department of Political Science [FSW-A], 1981), pp. 45, 104–5, 188, 418–19; and C. van der Eijk, G. A. Irwin, and B. Niemöller, Dutch Parliamentary Election Study 1986 (Amsterdam: Steinmetz Archives, 1988), pp. 37, 222–23.

18. See Philip P. Everts, "Een onderzoek naar binnenlandse invloeden op het buitenlands beleid—een theoretische verantwoording" (An inquiry into domestic influences on foreign policy—a theoretical justification), in Baehr, et al., Elite en buitenlandse politiek in Nederland, pp. 10–11. Everts estimates the elite itself, not including opinion leaders—i.e., those in position to exercise direct influence but not those who seek indirect influence via public opinion—at eight hundred to a thousand. Several journalists estimated the group of interested and informed people who carry on the nontechnical debate about foreign policy as somewhere between fifty and two hundred people: "You know everyone who is involved." And in his farewell lecture at the University of Amsterdam in 1976, "The Relation between the Study and the Practice of Foreign Policy," Baehr noted that "even if one keeps a rather wide margin, for the Netherlands one comes to not many more than a few hundred people who are regularly and intensively occupied with problems of foreign policy."

19. C. Paulien van den Tempel and Alfred van Staden, "De burgers en de buitenlandse politiek: Profiel van 'het aandachtige publiek' in Nederland"(Citizens and foreign policy: Profile of "the attentive public" in the Netherlands), Internationale Spectator 28(11): 345–56 (1974).

20. Everts, "Wat vinden," pp. 309–10.

21. In a discussion with me in 1990, Van Staden expressed some doubts about his early figures.

lion people. And if everyone else is part of the mass or general public, that is approximately 90 percent of the Dutch population.

The correlates of information, interest, and activity (i.e., the criteria for inclusion in the Dutch attentive public) differ only slightly from those in the United States: Van den Tempel and Van Staden describe the typical member of the attentive public as "a well-educated man, with a good income, middle-aged, a city resident, and holding a white-collar job."[22] Education made less difference than it does in the United States, however, and gender made more: although the whole sample was somewhat unrepresentative at 40 percent female and 60 percent male, the small group of "attentives" was 8 percent female and 92 percent male.

Other survey data point in the same general direction, although not without some confusing signals. Repeated questions about the readership of foreign or international news ("for example, about tensions or negotiations [sometimes 'discussions'] between countries") show quite consistently that between 20 and 25 percent "always" read it[23]—or at least they say they do, though without having to indicate what or how much they read.[24] In 1971, when a Dutch national sample was asked, "In what news are you most interested?" and "least interested?" 13 percent said they were most interested in foreign news, and 53 percent said they were least interested in it.[25] Regrettably, this question was not asked in succeeding surveys. In the same survey, 62 percent agreed with the statement "Problems such as, e.g., relations between East and West, and the unity of

22. Van den Tempel and Van Staden, "De burgers" pp. 348–49.

23. This question has been regularly asked in the recent Dutch national election studies (see, e.g., *Dutch Parliamentary Election Study, 1981* and *1986*) and in the fifteen surveys commissioned between January 1972 and March 1977 by the Continuous-Survey Workgroup of the Subfaculty of General Political and Social Science, University of Amsterdam (reported by C. van der Eijk and G.C. de Vries in C. van der Eijk et al., *Longitudinaal enquête onderzoek: Mogelijkheden en problemen*, Mededelingen 6/7 van de Subfaculteit der Algemene Politieke en Sociale Wetenschappen [Longitudinal inquiry research: Possibilities and problems, Reports 6/7 of the Subfaculty of General Political and Social Sciences], Universiteit van Amsterdam, November 1980, pp. 129–32).

24. Some insight into what it might mean to "read international news" may be gleaned from what is now quite an old study by the American Institute of Public Opinion of readership of international news in fifty-one American newspapers: out of an average of 106 column inches of international news published daily at that time in those papers, the adult reader actually read an average of only 12 column inches—taking about two and one-third minutes to do so! See *The Flow of the News* (Zurich: International Press Institute, 1953).

25. R. J. Mokken and F. M. Roschar, *Dutch Parliamentary Election Study* (Ann Arbor, Michigan: ICPR 1975), pp. 44–45.

Europe, are too complicated for people like me"; 28 percent disagreed, and 10 percent did not know or gave no answer; in the 1977
parliamentary election study the question was repeated, and the
comparable figures were 64, 29, and 7 percent.[26]

Another measure of the limited interest in the Netherlands in international problems is contained in the answers to the questions repeatedly asked in the Dutch national election studies: "In your opinion,
what are the most important problems in our country?" In each case,
respondents were invited to name five successive problems. The responses were then aggregated into approximately thirty major categories, only two of them "international" in character: defense, war, and
peace (including armaments, nuclear tasks within NATO, and defense
expenditures); and foreign relations (including Europe, the EEC (European Economic Community), development assistance, and the Third
World). The 1977 election study reviewed the most frequent responses
to this question from the 1967, 1971, 1972, and 1977 election surveys and
omitted the defense and foreign-relations categories, among others, because they did not occur sufficiently often to warrant inclusion in the
comparison.[27] Some insight into just how meager the results were may
be gleaned from Table 3.1, which compares the responses from 1972
with those of 1981 and 1986—years in which public activity in foreign affairs was most visible. Clearly, it was the nuclear and defense issues that
attracted the lion's share of the limited attention paid to international
problems in the Netherlands. At no time, however, were more than 8.9
percent of the responses international in character, despite there having
been five opportunities to identify major problems.[28] Comparisons with
the United States are instructive: in 1982 and 1986 national samples in
the U.S. were asked about the "two or three biggest problems facing the
country today." With fewer opportunities than the Dutch respondents

26. Ibid., pp. 154–55, for the 1971 figures. For the 1977 data, see Alfred van Staden and
C. Paulien van den Tempel, "Buitenlands beleid en internationale politiek" (Foreign policy and international politics), in G. Irwin, J. Verhoef, and C. J. Wiebrens, eds., *De Nederlandse kiezer '77* (The Dutch Voter '77) (Voorschoten: VAM Drukkerij, 1977), p. 116.

27. See C. J. Wiebrens, "De grootste problemen in het land" (The greatest problems in
the country), in Irwin, Verhoef, and Wiebrens, eds., *De Nederlandse kiezer '77*, pp. 53–59.

28. Rochon points out that this situation was not limited to the Netherlands: "It cannot
be said that the peace movement has transformed public opinion. In every European
country, economic issues remain at the top of the agenda, and attitudes toward nuclear
disarmament remain substantially what they were before 1980. But the peace movement
did heighten public interest in nuclear weapons" (Thomas R. Rochon, *Mobilizing for
Peace: The Anitnuclear Movements in Western Europe* [Princeton: Princeton University Press,
1988], p. 207).

Table 3.1.

	Total number of problems mentioned	Percent of total responses relating to:	
		Defense	Foreign Policy
1972	3,350	1.7	1.0
1981, 1st wave	5,446	4.3	0.4
1981, 2d wave	4,412	5.0	0.4
1981, 3d wave	4,219	5.8	0.1
1986	3,469	8.5	0.4

Source: The data for 1972 are found in L. P. J. de Bruyn and J. W. Foppen, *The Dutch Voter, 1972–73*, vol. 1 (Nijmegen: Institute for Political Science, 1974), pp. 38–59; the data for 1981 are found in Van der Eijk, Niemöller, and Eggen, eds., *Dutch Parliamentary Election Study 1981*, pp. 301–16; the data for 1986 are found in Van der Eijk, Irwin, and Niemöller, eds., *Dutch Parliamentary Election Study 1986*, pp. 232–43.

to identify problems, 15.2 percent of the American responses in 1982 and 25.9 percent in 1986 were in the international areas.[29]

In the light of such findings, it is difficult to accept the views of those Americans who believe that the Dutch are especially internationally minded or of those Dutch who argue, as one Foreign Office official did, that "there is an extraordinary situation in the Netherlands, that there is a lively interest in public opinion in matters concerning foreign policy." Rather, one has to agree with the observation by members of the small Dutch foreign-policy elite that the Dutch people as a whole are little interested in foreign policy. A Foreign Ministry official: "Holland has no tradition in foreign policy, very few specialists. The public doesn't think in foreign-policy terms." A member of Parliament: "International affairs are not a real issue with the electorate. . . . We have far less public-opinion feedback here than in the United States." A journalist: "The Foreign Ministry has to operate in a climate where even NATO is not understood."

In these respects, however, the Dutch people differ marginally, if at all, from the American people. In both countries, foreign policy appears to be the province of a very few, and it was the East-West conflict, now at rest, and the attendant periodic fears of nuclear war or reprisal

29. See John E. Rielly, ed., *American Public Opinion and U.S. Foreign Policy 1991* (Chicago: Chicago Council on Foreign Relations, 1991), p. 10. However, when asked by a *New York Times*/CBS poll in October 1991, after the effective breakup of the Soviet Union, to name "the most important problem facing the country," only 1 percent identified a foreign-policy problem. See Leslie Gelb, "Throw the Bums Out," *New York Times*, October 23, 1991, p. A11.

that attracted public attention from time to time, not the ongoing political and economic issues of foreign relations.[30]

Stability and Change in Public Opinion

These structures of opinion, with their very large and usually inert bases, cannot of course be taken as evidence that there is "not much public opinion" in these two countries. Rather, they tell us other things, such as the likelihood that certain policies, relatively simple to explain and to understand, will easily get securely anchored in a large and inattentive mass public.[31] In the United States, for example, an elemental anti-Communist foreign policy took root easily in the late 1940s and became the crabgrass of the 1970s and 1980s. In the Netherlands, a similar attachment to NATO flourished in early postwar circumstances, and it maintained overwhelming support for decades[32]— even though people did not always know what it is or does[33]—and rejected many of its strategic premises.[34] Furthermore, the existence of a proportionately large mass public tells us something about the size of the population amongst which, on rare occasions, efforts at political mobilization or activation may be possible. We might hazard the proposition that the larger the proportional size of the mass public, the more politically consequential its initial mobilization is likely to be—on the premise that large increments make more of a difference than small increments in foreign-policy decision making, as in other matters. In the United States during the Vietnam War it took some time and very extensive mobilization efforts among the mass public before the policy makers recognized that new elements were participating in the political process and responded affirmatively to them. In the Netherlands, on the other hand, the first of two large demonstrations against nuclear

30. For a measure of the degree to which communication to policy makers about specific foreign-policy issues is essentially limited to "advantaged" population groups in the U.S., see S. Verba, K. L. Schlozman, H. Brady, and N. H. Nie, "Citizen Activity: Who Participates? What Do They Say?" *American Political Science Review,* 87(2): 312, table 2 (June 1993).

31. Cf. G. van Benthem van den Bergh, "Over de democratisering van de buitenlandse politiek" (On the democratization of foreign policy), *Internationale Spectator* 24 (1): 49–66 (1970).

32. As recently as summer 1989, 81 percent of the Dutch population sampled by NIPO believed that NATO should be maintained despite the changed relationship between the U.S. and the U.S.S.R. See *De Telegraaf,* October 26, 1989, pp. 1, 6.

33. See Roschar, comp., *Buitenlandse politiek in de Nederlandse publieke opinie,* polls on pp. 189 and 216.

34. See Everts, "Wat vinden," p. 349.

weapons (November 1981), which turned out between 300,000 and 400,000 people, many of whom had never taken part in a demonstration before,[35] was rather quickly reflected in statements of governmental policy.[36] Over time, however, the Dutch government was to respond negatively to these mass-mobilization efforts, carrying out its initial policy intentions. Other factors are involved, of course, in these events, and I will return to this subject in Chapter 6.

These structures of opinion also provide us with a useful context within which to look at the phenomenon of change in public opinion on foreign policy. In both the Netherlands and the United States the years from 1945 to about 1965 were marked by a large amount of agreement on certain fundamental aspects of foreign policy. In both countries the word most often used to describe that condition is *consensus*,[37] and most observers seem to agree that the consensus on foreign policy—as on other areas of public policy—broke down at least to some degree in both countries sometime after 1965. As a word, however, *consensus* is like *charisma*—it eludes precise definition. We have an intuitive sense of its meaning, but we do not know exactly what it is (or was) or what it should be. We seem to mean by it some minimum level of agreement on some minimum central policies[38]—or, alternatively, on some central belief systems[39]—but

35. *NRC-Handelsblad, Weekeditie,* December 15, 1981, p. 14, reported survey results showing that one-half of these demonstrators had never participated in a demonstration before. Van Staden, however, reports 400,000 marchers and says that only about one-third of the participants had not marched before. "To Deploy or Not do [sic] Deploy: The Case of the Cruise Missiles," chapter 6 in Everts, ed., *Controversies at Home,* p. 146.

36. Van Staden in Everts, ed., *Controversies at Home.* See also P. R. Baehr, "Democracy and Foreign Policy in the Netherlands," *Acta Politica* 18(1): 37–62 (1983).

37. Everts and Walraven, however, argue that the political climate of the period 1955–1960 is better described "as one of disinterest rather than of consensus" (Everts and Walraven, eds., *The Politics of Persuasion: Implementation of Foreign Policy by the Netherlands* [Brookfield, Vt.: Gower Publishing Co., 1989], p. 333).

38. See, e.g., the discussion of the American foreign-policy consensus in Almond, *American People,* chapter 8; J. H. Leurdijk's discussion of the Dutch foreign-policy consensus, "De buitenlands-politieke elite en het veiligheidsbeleid van Nederland" (The foreign-policy elite and the security policy of the Netherlands), in Baehr et al., *Elite en buitenlandse politiek in Nederland,* pp. 25–47; and J. G. Siccama's discussion of the Dutch security-policy consensus from 1949 to 1968, "The Netherlands Depillarized: Security Policy in a New Domestic Context," in Gregory Flynn, ed., *NATO's Northern Allies: The National Security Policies of Belgium, Denmark, the Netherlands, and Norway* (Totowa, N.J.: Rowman and Allanheld, 1985).

39. See, e.g., Ole R. Holsti and James N. Rosenau, "Vietnam, Consensus, and the Belief Systems of American Leaders," *World Politics* 32 (1): 1–56 (October 1979); and Ole R. Holsti and James N. Rosenau, *American Leadership in World Affairs: Vietnam and the Breakdown of Consensus* (Boston: Allen and Unwin, 1984).

we have no clear understanding on how much agreement, among whom, on what subjects, or how it should be measured. Do we mean substantial agreement among the general public, between the general public and the elite, within the elite itself—for example, among or between political parties—or some combination of these? And what do we mean by "substantial agreement"? The major elements of postwar Dutch foreign policy—membership in NATO and in the European Community and the deployment of American nuclear weapons on Dutch soil—were all decided with little public or parliamentary debate.[40] Does that imply "substantial agreement," disinterest, resignation, or still something else? And because we did not know what to ask, of whom, some years ago, today we have no agreed-on base point for comparing *changes* among certain groups, particularly elites, along these unknown dimensions. Furthermore, we seem to have in mind today a consensus on policy and perhaps policy beliefs, but also at work during those years were certain shared understandings—again, without specifications—about appropriate foreign-policy-making *procedures*, in which leaders and institutions were granted substantial operating autonomy. And the possible relationship between opinion on substance and opinion on process is another matter of which we have little comprehension, it being sometimes suggested in both the Netherlands and the United States that there is a relationship between the decline in the foreign-policy consensus and increased participation in foreign affairs by interest groups and by legislatures.[41]

The concern about the "breakdown" of consensus, incidentally, suggests a new dimension to the old question of the incompatibility between democracy and foreign policy. Democratic institutions are designed to deal with major disagreements in society; self-government loses its importance if nearly everyone thinks alike. (That may in fact be part of the explanation for the "consensus" on foreign-policy-making procedures in the years after World War II: so long as we agreed on the policies, it was all right to let George—or the CIA—do it!) Paradoxically, however, democratic institutions do not function well if the load of disagreement placed on them is heavy; democracy presumes a certain (unspecified) level of agreement on policy matters, as well as on

40. Everts and Walraven, eds., *Politics of Persuasion*, p. 41.
41. See, e.g., Everts, *Public Opinion, the Churches, and Foreign Policy*, chapter 8: "Foreign Policy and the Parliamentary Elections of 1981 and 1982"; and Bernard C. Cohen, "The Influence of Special-Interest Groups and Mass Media on Security Policy in the United States," in Charles W. Kegley, Jr., and Eugene R. Wittkopf, eds., *Perspectives on American Foreign Policy* (New York: St. Martin's Press, 1983).

the procedures for determining them. And foreign offices in particular do not do well under such a burden, partly because they have so few resources to devote to the domestic political problem and partly because the nation's external policies, no matter what they are, lose much of their effectiveness in these circumstances. And so, ironically, we regret the collapse of "consensus" in the abstract, even if we were not happy with the policies of consensus in the concrete, and we wish for a new "consensus" even though we cannot agree on what it should consist in and though we recognize the high cost of the political resolution of such foreign-policy conflicts.[42]

In the light of these conceptual and philosophical difficulties, I will not attempt a comparison of the *changes in the foreign-policy consensus* in the United States and the Netherlands. Rather, I shall limit myself here to discussing a few of the *changes in foreign-policy opinion* as these have been revealed by public-opinion polls during the past thirty or so years. But that in itself should give us some guidance as to where we should be looking for evidence concerning the present state of "the consensus" in foreign affairs. Public-opinion polls, of course, tell us more about the opinions of the mass and attentive publics than about the elites; because there are so few of the latter, they don't show up in representative samples in meaningful numbers.[43] Most of my observations about changes in elite opinion will be part of the chapters that follow. One word of caution, however: the implications of the collapse of Communism in Europe for the foreign policies of the Western alliance partners are not yet clearly understood. If history is any guide, it will take some time for such important changes in international relationships to be reflected in stable attitudes at the mass level.

The United States and the Netherlands differ in the degree to which there have been changes over the last two decades in the opinion that is revealed (or suggested) by the polls. In the U.S., on the one hand, the data indicate major swings in general public opinion toward national-security-policy matters between 1970 and 1990. In the Netherlands, on the other hand, the evidence suggests a greater stability and continuity of public opinion toward the major national-security issues over these years, despite the mass mobilizations by the Dutch peace movement.

42. See, e.g., James Chace, "Is a Foreign Policy Consensus Possible?" *Foreign Affairs* 57(1): 1–16 (Fall 1978), and Holsti and Rosenau, *American Leadership in World Affairs.*

43. For examples of the differences between mass and elite opinion on foreign-policy issues, see the quadrennial surveys reported by the Chicago Council on Foreign Relations, *American Public Opinion and U.S. Foreign Policy.*

"Trend questions" on national defense in the 1970s indicated a steady and striking reversal of American public opinion away from the post-Vietnam "dovishness" of the early 1970s and back to the "hawkishness" of the years that preceded the Vietnam War. In the late 1960s, approximately half of the respondents on national surveys believed that the U.S. Government was spending "too much" on defense, and about 10 percent believed the government was spending "too little." Throughout the decade of the 1970s, however, through more or less steady change, the figures were reversed: by 1980, more than half were answering "too little" and 10 to 15 percent "too much."[44] Similarly, from 1972 to 1980, the proportion of the population willing to use military force in the defense of western Europe against a Soviet military attack increased from one-half to three-quarters.[45]

Through the 1980s, however, there was a swing back toward the views of the early 1970s: an upward climb in the proportion of those who wanted to cut back on defense spending (from 12 to 32 percent), and an even sharper drop (from 60 to 12 percent) in the proportion who wanted to expand defense spending.[46] At the same time, the proportion of the population willing to use force in the defense of western Europe receded from the 1980 high back toward the 1970 level (58 percent by 1990).[47]

On the Dutch side, the visible increase in party debate on and public participation in foreign-policy issues after the mid-1960s, together with the absence at the time of a long history or a strong tradition of public-opinion polling on these issues, helped to create a widespread impression within the small foreign-policy community that there had also been substantial change in Dutch public opinion through the 1970s. Journalists and scholars alike spoke repeatedly of the collapse of the postwar consensus and of a "fundamental reorientation" of the public toward foreign policy.[48] The passage of another decade and the

44. Bruce Russett and Donald R. Deluca, " 'Don't Tread on Me': Public Opinion and Foreign Policy in the Eighties," *Political Science Quarterly* 96(3): 381–99 (Fall 1981); Rielly, ed., *American Public Opinion . . . 1991*, p. 32.

45. Russett and Deluca, " 'Don't Tread on Me,' " p. 386.

46. Rielly, ed., *American Public Opinion . . . 1991*, p. 32.

47. Ibid., p. 34.

48. See, e.g., Everts, "Wat vinden," p. 311. There were a few, however, who at the time took note of the gap between the public criticism of NATO, esp. by the Labor Party (PvdA), and the continued high levels of support for NATO in public-opinion polls. See Baehr, "De waarde van de openbare mening," *Internationale Spectator* 24(1): 40 (1970); and Joris J. C. Voorhoeve, *Peace Profits and Principles: A Study of Dutch Foreign Policy* (The Hague: Martinus Nijhoff, 1979), chapter 6.

expansion of public-opinion polling, however, have led nearly all Dutch observers in the 1990s to a more accurate view of what is really a rather remarkable *stability* in Dutch public opinion over these years.[49]

Some of the major issues in Dutch foreign and security policy for which there are now some reasonably good trend data[50] and that reveal a stable public opinion are the following: Dutch membership in NATO (for years averaging around 75 percent support); nuclear tasks for the Netherlands within the NATO alliance (more than 50 percent opposed, before as well as during the long campaign by the peace movement to remove such weapons from the Netherlands); nuclear weapons themselves (in the abstract, opinion runs very strongly against them, but in specific contexts, opinion is invariably divided evenly); levels of defense expenditure (very low support for increased defense spending);[51] levels of expenditure for development assistance to Third World countries (a nearly universally supported *moral* imperative, but support for cutting it back is at least as great as for expanding it);[52] need for a military balance, including a

49. Everts himself began to speak of "continuity rather than change" in "De openbare mening over de kernwapenproblematiek: Continuïteit of verandering?" (Public opinion on the nuclear weapons problem: Continuity or change?) in Jan G. Siccama et al., eds., *Wapens in de peiling: Opinieonderzoek over internationale veiligheid* (Taking soundings on arms: Opinion research on international security), The Hague: Staatsuitgeverij, 1984, pp. 22–37. For a more extended argument, see Ph. P. Everts, *The Peace Movement and Public Opinion* (Leiden: Institute for International Studies, 1990). See also G. A. Irwin and J. J. M. van Holsteyn, "Towards a More Open Model of Competition," *Western European Politics* 12(1): 117–18 (January 1989), and Rochon, *Mobilizing for Peace*, p. 207.

50. The best sources for these data are Vaneker and Everts, *Buitenlandse Politiek in de Nederlandse Publieke Opinie*; Everts, *The Peace Movement and Public Opinion*; and Everts, *Public Opinion, the Churches, and Foreign Policy.* See also Everts, "De openbare mening," esp. table 3.1, p. 24 (on NATO membership) and table 3.2, p. 25 (on the need for an East-West military balance).

51. In the early 1970s, when respondents were asked how they would allocate a hypothetical increase in government income among six possibilities (housing, defense, education, the fight against pollution, development aid, and lowering taxes), only 1.5 percent put defense in first place, and 59 percent put it in last place. See L. P. J. de Bruyn and J. W. Foppen, *The Dutch Voter, 1972–1973*, vol. 2 (Nijmegen: Institute for Political Science, 1974), p. 382. And in the early 1980s, when asked to choose from among twelve goals the one they preferred the most, .9 percent put "a strong defense" in first place; the figures increased inversely and almost linearly to 37 percent who put it in last place. See Van der Eijk, Niemöller, and Eggen, *Dutch Parliamentary Election Study, 1981*, pp. 252–58.

52. In the early 1970s, when respondents were asked how they would allocate a hypothetical increase in governmental income among six possibilities, only 4 percent put development aid first, 35 percent put it fifth, and 24 percent put it in sixth and last place. See de Bruyn and Foppen, *Dutch Voter, 1972–1973*, vol. 2, p. 382. In a survey taken by the Social and Cultural Planning Bureau in August 1981, nearly half of the population

nuclear balance, between East and West in Europe (approximately two-thirds see such a need); and the European Community (strong support, but equally strong opposition to any eventual transfer of political sovereignty).

I have made reference to the efforts of the Dutch peace movement to eliminate nuclear weapons from the Netherlands and especially to prevent the "modernization" of the NATO arsenal of intermediate-range nuclear missiles by the emplacement of forty-eight cruise and Pershing II missiles on Dutch soil. The very size of the mobilization efforts—a third of a million people on the streets of Amsterdam in 1981, a half million in The Hague in 1983, a "people's petition" with three and three-quarters million signatures in 1985—created the impression of great changes in public opinion on the issue of nuclear weapons in the Netherlands and on the related issues of Dutch security policy. At no point in the seven-year campaign against nuclear weapons, however, do the public-opinion polls show any change in the content of public conceptions of foreign policy or in the "traditional wisdoms about military affairs."[53] Indeed, it is even argued that the attitudes of the antinuclear activists were so far removed from those of the general public in the Netherlands that they tended "to alienate much of the public from the movement."[54] Furthermore, if there was any enlargement of the Dutch foreign-policy community as a consequence of the lengthy campaign, it would have to be measured in small numbers against a background of initially even smaller numbers. Democratization may have broken down some of the barriers to public participation in foreign policy in the Netherlands, thereby changing some of the players and the program, but it has not led to a substantive

---

thought that development cooperation was the preferred place to make budget savings; 73 percent thought that defense was the preferred place to make savings. See *De Volkskrant*, March 25, 1982.

53. Everts has addressed this issue at length in his writings; see esp. *Peace Movement*, p. 59. His conclusion is that although the *content* of public opinion did not change, there was a change in the *salience* of the issue among antinuclear activists and in the *intensity* with which they held their views. Rochon notes that the peace movement was unable to "maintain the climate of insecurity that had helped it grow so spectacularly. . . . The fear of world war . . . began to decline during 1981," just when the movement was gathering popular support (*Mobilizing for Peace*, p. 51).

54. Rochon, *Mobilizing for Peace*, p. 105. Everts points out that although there was support in the country for the peace movement in the early stages, its roots in the political left subsequently engaged the suspicions of a majority of the population ("Public Opinion on Nuclear Weapons, Defense, and Security: The Case of the Netherlands," in Gregory Flynn and Hans Rattinger, eds., *The Public and Atlantic Defense* (Totoma, N.J.: Rowman and Allenheld, 1985), p. 244.

reworking of the conception of foreign policy in the public mind or to major changes in foreign policy. To the extent that the members of the mass public are "followers" in Mueller's sense,[55] it will take major changes in the orientation of Dutch foreign policy before there are major reorientations in Dutch public opinion. That is a possible development of the 1990s, in a world without East-West tension, but as the possibility of major war recedes, it is also to be expected that public indifference to all matters of foreign affairs will grow.

In the light of the above, one additional word may be said here about "consensus." Quite clearly, what is perceived by so many people as a "breakdown of consensus" has little to do with mass public opinion on many of the major structural issues of foreign policy in either the Netherlands or the United States. In a negative sort of way, that is a helpful finding. If we wish to clarify that nebulous concept, we will have to look in other directions: at the elites themselves[56] and at the relationships among elites and between them and their (would-be) followers.

The Significance of General Public Opinion

A word, finally, about the significance of general public opinion in a study that focuses on public participation: mass opinion does not "act" in a policy-making process the way that other participants do. Indeed, I described it at the start of this chapter as providing a general context within which the participation of specific actors takes place. But I do not mean to suggest, either by the data I have included here or by the context they set, that "public opinion" is not important to foreign-policy makers. I believe it is, in both countries—even though officials do not know how to come to grips with it, how to understand it, or even what to do with it. "Public opinion" is a formless concept; I have indicated elsewhere that American officials are able to react to it only in its specific manifestations, not as a general phenomenon.[57] The same is true of Dutch officials, who ordinarily define public opinion in terms of parliamentary opinion and the views of the nonparliamentary parties, the media, and interest groups—and only rarely in more general terms involving the society as a kind of political entity (*samenleving*).

But even though general public opinion is institutionally formless,

55. John E. Mueller, *War, Presidents, and Public Opinion* (New York: John Wiley and Sons, 1973).
56. Holsti and Rosenau have made a start in *American Leadership in World Affairs*.
57. Bernard C. Cohen, *The Public's Impact on Foreign Policy* (Boston: Little, Brown and Co., 1973).

even though a careful scrutiny of the polls reinforces the sense of hopelessness in being able to deal concretely with the preferences that they suggest, there remains in both governments—and, I suspect, in governments everywhere, to a greater or lesser degree—a residual concern with it. Perhaps it is precisely *because* it is so formless that officials treat it with a mixture of disbelief and respect—like a beautiful lake that just may have alligators hiding in the weeds. Their concern is that *others* may find and stir up the alligators, mobilizing elements in the population in ways that have an adverse effect on their *own* goals and purposes. Sometimes they have to feed the alligators, but their preference is to restore calm to the lake. And so they mostly seek to shape public opinion themselves, without knowing exactly what it is they are working with or against, and sharing a common constraint against anything that resembles "propaganda." The Americans came to this position in the 1940s; the Dutch were still developing it in the 1980s.[58] It is a public-information and education function, and yet it has strong public-relations overtones. The major differences between the two efforts is that the Dutch Foreign Ministry explicitly recognizes the significance of Parliament as an intermediary between the government and the people and thus includes it as an appropriate target group, so to speak, whereas the American State Department deals with the Congress only on a political level and in political terms (i.e., through an assistant secretary for congressional liaison), restricting the public-information function to the media and to whatever other public groups with which it may have contact. Let us turn first, then, to legislatures and political parties and explore their roles both as forms and as channels of public participation in foreign policy.

58. See *"Macht slijt snel, gebruik haar wel," Blaudruk voor het voorlichtingsbeleid van het Ministerie van Buitenlandse Zaken* ("Power erodes quickly, so use it," Blueprint for the information policy of the Ministry of Foreign Affairs) (The Hague: Staatsuitgeverij, November 1981).

4
Political Parties and
Legislatures

In Chapters 1 and 2 I covered some formal, legal-constitutional aspects of the political-party system and the legislative and executive roles in foreign policy, insofar as they had some bearing on the structure of public participation in foreign-policy making in both the Netherlands and the United States. In this chapter I will pay more attention to the informal, behavioral aspects of parties and legislatures in the foreign-policy field in a further effort to uncover the actual or effective public participation in foreign policy that is accounted for by these institutions.

This subject has a complexity that is not fully obvious at first glance: political parties may be regarded both as *forms* of public or nongovernmental participation and as *channels* through which other nongovernmental individuals or groups try to reach foreign policy or foreign-policy makers. And national legislatures themselves have both formal legislative functions with respect to foreign policy that make them "official" and informal representative functions with respect to foreign policy that are essentially "unofficial" and that may differ little from the representative functions exercised by other groups in society. Furthermore, parties in a parliamentary system have institutional identities within Parliament and outside it that are quite separate yet have many overlapping members. Although these distinctions are clear analytically, they are often difficult to keep separate in concrete situations.

Political parties in democratic societies are often cast in the role of "aggregators" of interests and demands that develop within a political system, and thus the state of their "health"—their capacity to perform that assigned role—has some bearing on the character and extent of other forms of public participation in the policy process.[1] In the United States it is conventional wisdom that the major political parties are not very healthy on a national scale—that their breadth and their internal weaknesses make the Congress an inviting target for important outside pressures of every sort.[2] In the Netherlands the mythology is that a multiparty proportional-representation system without an arbitrary "threshold" for parliamentary election means that every significant viewpoint in society can have its own representation in the Second Chamber—and thus, implicitly, that the Parliament does not invite or attract important organized pressures or participation from the outside, or at least from nonparty sources.[3] These propositions relating parties, legislatures, and outside pressures are important, if imprecise (e.g., what is a "significant viewpoint" or an "important pressure"?), and I will try in this chapter to explore their accuracy and relevance for issues of foreign policy.

Political Parties and Foreign Policy

Political parties and political candidates in the United States are, most of the time, not sharply differentiated on foreign-policy matters as election day approaches. Even in the emotion-filled presidential election of 1968, at the height of the Vietnam War, the positions of the candidates were sufficiently close that the Vietnam War issue did not play a significant role in determining the electoral choices of voters.[4] There are several reasons why the foreign-policy positions of the two parties are rarely in conflict and are often not even sharply differentiated:

(1) Foreign policy is rarely the breadwinner of American politics. Popular indifference to nonthreatening issues of foreign policy is well established both in voting studies and in public-opinion surveys.[5] Can-

1. See, e.g., Samuel P. Huntington, *Political Order in Developing Societies* (New Haven: Yale University Press, 1968).
2. See Chapter 1, pp. 10–14.
3. See Chapter 1, pp. 15–18.
4. Benjamin I. Page and Richard A. Brody, "Policy Voting and the Electoral Process: The Vietnam War Issue," *American Political Science Review* 66 (3): 979–95 (September 1972).
5. See, e.g., Angus Campbell, Philip E. Converse, Warren E. Miller, and Donald E. Stokes, *The American Voter* (New York: John Wiley and Sons, 1960); and the quadrennial surveys of *American Public Opinion and U.S. Foreign Policy* (Chicago: The Chicago Council on Foreign Relations, 1975, 1979, 1983, 1987, and 1991).
John H. Aldrich, John L. Sullivan, and Eugene Borgida argue differently, however, but their analysis is more tentative than their conclusions: "Foreign Affairs and Issue Voting:

didates usually see little advantage in making large or central issues out of the foreign-policy matters on which they may not agree, many of which are matters of style in any event. To the extent that voters pay any attention to foreign policy in their choice of candidates, they are more likely to pass judgment on the perceived ability or competence of the candidates to carry on an effective foreign policy than on the merits of proposed policies.[6] Recall that Richard Nixon won the presidency in 1968, in the supercharged atmosphere of the Vietnam War, even though he specifically and repeatedly refused to give any details on how he planned to end that war.

(2) The American foreign-policy agenda is quite large, and candidates often agree on the outlines of many of the items on it. There remains a heavy layer of bipartisanship on the central issues of American foreign policy, despite some of the interesting battles of the past generation. NATO has been the symbol of the commitment of both political parties to America's active leadership in international affairs. The differences between the parties have been differences of degree and of style much oftener than they have been differences of direction or of commitment.

(3) The electoral strategy of major candidates and of the parties they lead, which is usually to move to the center rather than to the extremes to pick up the margin of victory, is for the above reasons even more pronounced in the foreign-policy area than in other policy areas. In the unusual case, where positions have been sharply differentiated—for example, the Republican Party's emphasis on spending for defense in the 1980s—the losers tend subsequently to move closer to the winners, effectively shifting the "center."

This lack of strong partisan differentiation on foreign policy holds, I repeat, most of the time—but not all of the time. In 1972 the Democratic Party moved to the left, in 1980 the Republican Party moved to the right, and in both years there were still quite sharp differences in the foreign-policy positions of the presidential candidates at election time. But even in these cases, the parties themselves were not strong and effective participants in the foreign-policy debates and in the policy-making processes that took place after the elections were over; like mayflies, once their central purpose in life was completed they fell

---

Do Presidential Candidates 'Waltz Before a Blind Audience?' " *American Political Science Review* 83(1): 123–41 (March 1989).

6. See, e.g., William Schneider on the 1980 election: "The November 4 Vote for President: What Did it Mean?" in Austin Ranney, ed., *The American Elections of 1980* (Washington, D.C.: The American Enterprise Institute, 1981), pp. 212–62.

back, lifeless, into the waters from which they had risen.[7] In virtually all cases, therefore, the parties are nonparticipants in the continuing discussions about specific questions of foreign policy, leaving the field more or less free for other forms of external foreign-policy representation to try to bring their views to bear on both the executive and the Congress.

The number and range of the Dutch political parties compel a closer look at the differences among and within them. Are they in fact so clearly and sufficiently differentiated that they can serve as the vehicles for the unambiguous representation of the views of their supporters on foreign policy? (One might reasonably assume that they were, not only by virtue of the popular mythology but also because there are more parties than there are issues of foreign policy within the body politic at any one time!) And what does the answer to this question signify for the influence of the parties themselves on the formulation of Dutch foreign policy?

Most of the major Dutch political parties have been internally strained from time to time on important foreign-policy issues, most notably (in recent years) on the issues of nuclear "modernization," or the deployment of cruise missiles and Pershing II rockets on Dutch territory, and the acceptance of nuclear tasks within NATO. The VVD has been the only important party not to have a significant "fault line" on these issues.[8] The foreign-policy cleavages between the left wing and the more moderate center within the PvdA, which continued unabated during the PvdA-dominated Den Uyl Cabinet (1973–1977),[9] sharpened even further when the party suffered big electoral losses after 1977,[10] but they moderated again in the late 1980s after the nuclear

7. And even in these cases, the losers (the Democratic Party) moved perceptibly closer to the positions of the winners (the Republican Party) after the elections; i.e., the Republicans, by their victories, defined a new "center."

8. Peter R. Baehr, "Democracy and Foreign Policy in the Netherlands," *Acta Politica* 18(1):37–62 (January 1983); see also Philip P. Everts, *Public Opinion, the Churches, and Foreign Policy* (Leiden University, Institute for International Studies, 1983), esp. Chapter 8; and Philip P. Everts, ed., *Controversies at Home: Domestic Factors in the Foreign Policy of the Netherlands* (Dordrecht: Martinus Nijhoff, 1985), esp. chapters 5 and 6.

9. See J. H. Leurdijk, " 'Option 3' in MBFR," in Philip P. Everts and Guido Walraven, eds., *The Politics of Persuasion: Implementation of Foreign Policy by the Netherlands*, (Brookfield, Vt.: Gower Publishing Co., 1989), pp. 133–34.

10. See, e.g., the public disagreements about party policy following the large antinuclear demonstration in Amsterdam in November 1981: *NRC-Handelsblad, Weekeditie,* December 15, 1981. In the Second Van Agt Cabinet (1981–1982), the PvdA was the second party in the coalition (with the CDA), and Foreign Minister Van der Stoel (PvdA) had to make some major accommodations to the more radical-left sentiment in his party, particu-

issue subsided and when the possibilities of a role in a governing coalition became more promising.[11] The CDA, an amalgam of three confessional parties, had its divisions also, and a small so-called loyalist wing within Parliament kept CDA-dominated cabinets on a knife's edge for the first half of the 1980s over the "modernization" issue, forcing repeated delays in the government's decision on the placement of the missiles.[12]

Development assistance is another issue on which the Dutch parties have had internal differences. Although the major parties have long held formally to a position favoring substantial development aid for poor countries, up to a level of 1.5 percent of the Dutch gross national product, in fact there has always been some internal party debate about it: in the left parties, debates of an ideological character concerning the true beneficiaries of aid and the merits of linking aid to other policy aims, such as human rights; in the right parties, debates of an economic character concerning the opportunity costs of development assistance.

Dutch election studies in the 1970s explored the distribution of opinions on foreign-policy issues according to party voting intentions and showed a wide distribution of attitudes on these questions even among voters of a given party. Table 4.1 shows the range of opinions on development aid among those intending to vote for three major parties and two of the more important smaller parties in 1977.

Only in the left (*Politieke Partij Radikalen* [Political Party Radicals]— PPR) and right (VVD) parties was there a clear preference at one or the other end of the scale, but even in these ideologically more distinct parties a substantial 20 to 25 percent took deviant positions. Among the

---

larly with respect to their anti-American tendencies. See the (not wholly objective) account by An Salomonson in *NRC-Handelsblad,* April 26, 1982. But in the case of Spanish accession to NATO, Van der Stoel successfully resisted the opposition even of PvdA members of Parliament and gained parliamentary support for Spanish admission. See *De Volkskrant,* April 29, 1982.

11. See Alfred van Staden, "The Changing Role of the Netherlands in the Atlantic Alliance," *Western European Politics,* 12(1): 99–111 (January 1989).

12. Ibid. See also Peter R. Baehr, "Het parlement en het buitenlands beleid" ("Parliament and foreign policy"), in Th. C. de Graaf, D. A. van der Hoeven, and P. J. Langenberg, eds., *Omtrent het Parlement: Opstellen over parlement en democratisch bestuur* (Concerning Parliament: Essays about parliament and democratic control) (Utrecht: Uitgeverij Veen, 1985), p. 211; Thomas R. Rochon, *Mobilizing for Peace: The Antinuclear Movements in Western Europe* (Princeton: Princeton University Press, 1988), pp. 169–70, 207; and Jan G. Siccama, "The Netherlands Depillarized: Security Policy in a New Domestic Context," in Gregory Flynn, ed., *NATO's Northern Allies: The National Security Policies of Belgium, Denmark, the Netherlands, and Norway* (Totowa, N.J.: Rowman and Allanheld, 1985), pp. 137, 143.

Table 4.1. Opinion about development aid according to vote intention by party (in percentages)

Party	Give much more aid ⟶ Give much less aid							Total	N
	1	2	3	4	5	6	7		
PvdA (Labor)	14	12	10	25	13	12	15	101	512
CDA (Christian Democratic)	9	10	19	29	14	12	8	100	428
VVD (Liberal)	5	6	10	35	18	14	12	100	223
D'66 (center-left)	12	24	12	20	9	10	14	100	59
PPR (left of PvdA)	28	18	3	28	8	15	3	102	40

Source: This table appears as table 14.1 in Alfred van Staden and C. Paulien van den Tempel, "Buitenlands beleid en internationale politiek," in G. A. Irwin, J. Verhoef, and C. J. Wiebrens, eds., De Nederlandse kiezer '77 (Voorschoten: VAM Drukkerij, 1977), p. 119.

adherents of the other three parties, opinions on development assistance are very widely distributed. The same kind of spread is found in answers to similarly designed questions about defense expenditures in 1977[13] and about both development assistance and the Dutch role in world politics in 1973.[14] In the election studies during the 1980s, questions explored the perceived positions of political parties on only one foreign-policy issue, that of Dutch nuclear-weapons policy. The responses to these questions (though not necessarily to questions asked elsewhere) suggest that a substantial majority of voters were able to differentiate party stances on this most salient of international issues, both during and after political campaigns.[15] But there is no evidence

13. Van Staden and Van den Tempel, "Buitenlands beleid," p. 119.

14. See table 5.1.2 in De Nederlandse kiezer '73 (Alphen aan den Rijn: Samsom Uitgeverij, 1973), p. 41.

15. C. van der Eijk, B. Niemöller, and A. Th. J. Eggen, eds., Dutch Parliamentary Election Study, 1981 (Amsterdam: Department of Political Science, University of Amsterdam, 1981), pp. 174–78; C. van der Eijk, G. A. Irwin, and B. Niemöller, eds., Dutch Parliamentary Election Study, 1986 (Amsterdam: Steinmetz Archives, 1988), pp. 142–47.

Philip P. Everts, who has written extensively about public-opinion surveys on nuclear-weapons issues, reads the evidence differently: "The available evidence suggests . . . that voters are not very well-informed about the positions of the various parties on the nuclear weapons issue." See his "Public Opinion on Nuclear Weapons, Defense, and

that people voted for their party of choice *because* of its perceived position on this issue. Quite the contrary: in both the 1981 and 1986 election studies, respondents were asked to give a first reason and then a second reason why they voted for the party they chose. In 1981 forty-nine different reasons were coded, and in 1986 eighty-seven different reasons were coded. In both years the only international-political reasons coded concerned defense and nuclear-armaments issues. In 1981, as the Dutch peace movement was moving into high gear, defense and nuclear-armaments issues were cited by 2.3 percent as their first reason and by .67 percent as their second reason. In 1986, in the close aftermath of the hard-fought and long-delayed parliamentary decision to accept new cruise missiles on Dutch soil, only 1.7 percent of the sample gave defense and nuclear-armaments issues as their first reason for choosing their party, and 1.1 percent gave these as their second reason.[16]

It seems clear from these findings that even if the Dutch parties are perceived as the bearers of distinctive positions on foreign-policy issues, the parties do not seem to shape the foreign-policy preferences of those who vote for them,[17] and they do not move even the electorate who so perceived them to choose their party on the basis of those perceptions. In the Netherlands as in the United States, foreign policy is not the breadwinner of politics. In a practical sense, then, the Dutch parties cannot be assumed to be vehicles for the expression of the foreign-policy views of their supporters.[18]

The differences *within* the political parties on foreign-policy matters may actually be greater than the differences *among* the parties, at least as they are formally expressed in party programs.[19] In a general

---

Security: The Case of the Netherlands," in Gregory Flynn and Hans Rattinger, eds., *The Public and Atlantic Defense* (Totowa, N.J.: Rowman and Allanheld, 1985), p. 272.

16. C. van der Eijk, B. Niemöller, and A. Th. J. Eggen, eds., *Dutch Parliamentary Election Study, 1981*, pp. 343–51; C. van der Eijk, G. A. Irwin, and B. Niemöller, eds., *Dutch Parliamentary Election Study, 1986*, pp. 269–77.

17. Everts' reading of the evidence suggests "that confronted with the position of the party of their preference on this issue [nuclear-weapons policy] not less than 40 percent tend to disagree with it" ("Public Opinion on Nuclear Weapons, Defense, and Security," p. 272).

18. And not only their foreign-policy views: after the provincial elections of March 1991, in which the political party D66 was the big winner (over 150 percent gain in seats), a survey revealed that half of those who voted for D66 "had no idea what the standpoints of the party were" (*NRC-Handelsblad, Weekeditie,* 26 March 1991).

19. See Guido Walraven, in Everts and Walraven, eds., *Politics of Persuasion,* p. 45: "The three largest Dutch political parties hold quite similar views on foreign policy. This is all the more remarkable since this is concluded from the election manifestos, in which

way all the major-party programs agree on NATO membership, on "Europe," and on the importance of development aid—three enduring tenets of Dutch foreign policy that are not so widely embraced either by the general population or by party rank and file. Van Staden also discovered, to his apparent surprise, that even the amount of attention devoted to foreign policy in the drafts of the 1977 election programs of the largest Dutch political parties did not differ materially—PPR, 16 percent; CDA, 15 percent; VVD, 13 percent; PvdA, 10 percent[20]—despite the general view that the left parties are much more concerned than the others with foreign policy. These findings should not be unexpected, in fact, in a political system where all except the smallest fringe parties may expect to—or wish to—find themselves governing together in a coalition.

The following remark by a Labor Party official during the Den Uyl Cabinet (1973–1977) illustrates the common pressures on parties: "The PvdA party fraction in the Second Chamber is not representative of the PvdA. But the whole election program was something written only with a view to coming into office. If it were written for a party in opposition, it would have been more leftist. They [i.e., the parliamentary fraction] behave in a governmental way." A CDA official described his own party in similar terms, adding, "That is true of all parties. Even the VVD fraction is more 'responsible' than the party members." In this respect, the pressures that drive at least the larger Dutch political parties together are not really different from the pressures that push the two American political parties toward the political center: the search for a governing majority.[21]

But it would be misleading if I were to leave the impression that foreign-policy differences among the Dutch political parties were

---

parties may be expected to stress the differences between themselves and other parties in the struggle for electoral support. This 'profiling' on foreign policy was rather more common for the smaller political parties on the Left of the political spectrum, however, but even they still supported the main policy lines to a substantial degree most of the time."

20. Alfred van Staden, "De politieke partijen en het buitenlands beleid" ("Political parties and foreign policy"), *Internationale Spectator* 31(1): 55 (January 1977). The comparable figures for the 1981 election programs were PPR, 14 percent; CDA, 18 percent; VVD, 14 percent; PvdA, 11 percent. See Everts, *Public Opinion, the Churches, and Foreign Policy,* p. 311.

21. These coalition-driven pressures are reinforced by the depillarized, deconfessionalized trend in contemporary Dutch politics, leading all major parties to pursue "a policy of wooing votes at the center of Dutch politics" (H. Daalder, "The Mould of Dutch Politics: Themes for Comparative Inquiry," *West European Politics* 12 [1]: 14 [January 1989]). See also G. A. Irwin and J. J. M. van Holsteyn, "Towards a More Open Model of Competition," *Western European Politics* 12(1): 112–13 (January 1989).

nonexistent or inconsequential. There *are* differences—of position, of emphasis, of symbolism[22]—that are perceived both by party watchers and by ordinary voters, the importance of which depends both on the ideology and on the centrality of foreign affairs in the political thinking of those who observe the differences. The foreign policy of the small Pacifist Socialist Party (*Pacifistisch Socialistische Partij*—PSP) was clearly different from that of all other parties—even from the three radical left parties, PPR, EVP (*Evangelische Volkspartij* [Evangelical People's Party]), and CPN (*Communistische Partij in Nederland* [Communist Party in the Netherlands]), with which it has joined in the new political formation called *Groen Links* (Green Left).[23] The PSP leaders in the early 1980s claimed that the Liberal Party (VVD) had no foreign policy—but the VVD had a clearer policy on nuclear-defense questions than any of the other major parties.[24] Among the voters, too, there are some observable—and comparable—differences in the foreign-policy preferences of different party supporters. Although we saw above that voters for five important parties stand at all points on the preference scale with respect to development aid and defense expenditures, the *average* positions for the followers of each party do show some interesting differences in their centers of gravity, so to speak. The differences are greater for the left and the right among these five parties, the PPR and the VVD, than for the other three parties: on the average, PPR voters favored more development aid and lower defense expenditures than the followers of any of the other parties, whereas the VVD voters on the average favored less development aid and higher defense expenditures than the followers of any of the other parties. The averages for the other three parties, however, are considerably closer together.[25] In other words, the parties at the ideological edges (though not "fringes")—those with the clearest voices, so to speak—find a greater resonance

---

22. E.g., while all parties support development aid and a strong human-rights policy, they differ in their willingness to use the former to advance the latter—and they differ also in their degree of tolerance of human-rights abuses on the part of left-wing and right-wing regimes elsewhere. The PvdA, thus, has been more exercised by claims of such abuses in Indonesia, whereas the VVD points to rights violations in Nicaragua.

23. After the formation of Groen Links, the constituent parties dissolved, in 1990. In 1991, however, PSP decided that it would reestablish itself as an independent party, without leaving Groen Links.

24. See n. 9. See also H. Wiegel, "Belofte van twee jaar terug moet worden nagekomen" (Pledge of two years ago must be fulfilled), *NRC-Handelsblad, Weekeditie*, December 29, 1981. Wiegel was formerly chairman of the parliamentary fraction of the VVD.

25. Van Staden and Van den Tempel, "Buitenlands beleid," p. 118.

in the foreign policy views of their supporters than do the parties in the large middle of Dutch politics.

In sum, Dutch parties (despite my "reasonable assumption") are not ready vehicles for the unambiguous representation of foreign-policy opinion. They display a lack of internal clarity and agreement on foreign-policy matters that is quite comparable to the American parties. That may well be a consequence, in the first instance, of the marginal position that foreign policy has in the minds of most Dutch politicians and voters; parties form and attract chiefly on the basis of their domestic policies, not their foreign policies. One consequence is that the party leadership finds it expedient on occasion to leave parliamentarians free to take divergent positions on foreign-policy issues.[26] As a result, a variety of views get presented, but they are not often put forth with vigor and clarity as *party* views.[27]

Since the parties are "weak" in the American sense, is it likely that, as in the U.S., they invite participation in other forms by those people who do not feel "represented" by the parties in foreign policy? Let's look more closely at this possibility.

There is no question that there was an increase in nonparty foreign-policy activities, including interest-group activities, and an increase in the public attention paid to these activities in the Netherlands in the 1970s and 1980s. It has been the perception of changes of this sort that have led to the many reappraisals of the Dutch foreign-policy process referred to elsewhere in this book.[28] Since the parties themselves did not change very much in their foreign-policy priorities or postures during this period, however, people have tended to look elsewhere for the sources of these other changes in political life and organization—to broad social changes such as the erosion of "pillarization" and of deference, for example. But some political activists, political observers, and

26. The CDA was unable to enforce a party position on its "loyalists" in the Second Chamber on the cruise missile issue in the early 1980s, even at the risk of the government's collapse. The relative insignificance even of nuclear-weapons policy for the political-party preference of voters is also evident in data summarized by Everts in *Public Opinion, the Churches, and Foreign Policy,* esp. chapter 8.

27. An important exception would be the PvdA's rejection of cruise missiles and rockets on Dutch soil and its expressed determination in 1981 to leave the government if it should vote to accept these missiles—but it is also significant that this position had no apparent beneficial effect on the PvdA's popularity with the electorate in the succeeding election.

28. The Dutch research program that is referred to in the Preface, n. 13, was based on the view that the formal democratic model, anchored on the role of the political parties, presented an incomplete picture of reality and that *all* elites sought other means or routes to political influence in addition to those that ran through the parties.

political scientists believe that the increase in nonparty foreign-policy activities came about at least in part *because* the political parties had not changed very much—had not adapted their processes and priorities to the changing foreign-policy interests of the attentive public and non-governmental elite in the Netherlands. They argue that because parties are organized on traditional lines (e.g., ideology, religion) and cannot deal effectively or swiftly with complex new issues that cut across these traditional organizational structures and functions, they have contributed to the rise of action groups as a form of nonparty foreign-policy activity.[29] And once these groups were in place and their activities established, most parties gave them cooperation, support, and status; in some cases this has resulted in their getting local-government subsidies. The parties, in other words, recognized their limitations in the foreign-policy field and sought to compensate by identifying—more or less closely, depending on the parties and the issues—with nonparty groups that assumed *de facto* public leadership on certain foreign-policy issues.[30]

Party officials have had varying reactions to these developments. Some thought that foreign-policy action groups have had a positive influence overall on political parties, because the parties could not afford to lag behind but had to stay competitive. But others argued that, in effect, the tail was wagging the dog. In the 1970s the international secretary of the PvdA, Harry van den Bergh, acknowledged that action groups contributed to the democratization of policy making but added that political parties ought not to become merely their parrots.[31] In the 1980s, according to a CDA functionary, PvdA officials were saying that they had come to think that action groups had changed—and confused—the character of their party.

The foreign-policy issues that caused this political turmoil subsided at the end of the 1980s, as did the significance of many of these nonparty action groups.[32] The political parties, however, have not noticeably enhanced their standing in Dutch political circles: explanations

29. See Rochon, *Mobilizing for Peace*, pp. 218–19, and A. P. M. Lucardie, "Politieke Partijen" ("Political Parties"), in R. B. Andeweg, A. Hoogerwerf, and J. J. A. Thomassen, eds., *Politiek in Nederland* (Politics in the Netherlands), 3d ed. (Alphen aan den Rijn: Samsom Uitgeverij, 1989), pp. 60–77.

30. See Everts, ed., *Controversies at Home*.

31. H. van den Bergh, "Buitenlandse politiek als functie binnen een politieke partij" (Foreign Policy as a function within a political party), paper prepared for the Politocologenetmaal (Political Scientists' meeting), Amersfoort, the Netherlands, May 13–14, 1976, pp. 2–3.

32. See Chapter 6.

of an unexpectedly low voter turnout in the Dutch local elections in the spring of 1990 elicited a similar pattern of assessments of the unresponsiveness of the traditional party organizations and even of the political system itself.[33]

One conclusion to be drawn from this—or perhaps merely restated—is that political parties do not perform a powerful intermediary function in foreign policy between the Parliament and the government, on the one hand, and interest groups, on the other.[34] In fact, it is their failure to have served as such a channel for the foreign-policy views of others that has apparently given rise to these groups in the first place. It is an open question whether the parties ever did perform an effective intermediary role; it seems unlikely. Their weakness in this respect was not noticeable or politically significant during the years when foreign-policy differences, especially differences in foreign-policy priorities, were subordinated to the strong pro-Atlantic orientation—the "consensus"—of the Dutch foreign-policy elite. But as soon as strong foreign-policy demands began to be made on the parties, their incapacities to deal with them in organized and systematic ways became manifest; the door was then open for new groups to come into being and to deal directly or indirectly with all participants in the Dutch foreign-policy process. I will have occasion in Chapter 6 to look more closely at the influence these groups have been able to exert on this process.

The important question remains: despite these limitations, do political parties have an impact on the formulation and execution of foreign policy, as an ongoing process, in the United States and the Netherlands? I put the question this way because, to the extent that parties select candidates who espouse particular foreign policies, parties always have an initial or basic impact on the direction foreign policy will take after elections. I am concerned, rather, with parties as participants in the foreign-policy-making process, and it is in the ongoing contests over policy that such participation would be both manifest and relevant.

The Dutch public in the early 1970s, when asked about three nongovernmental institutions, perceived the political parties as having more influence over "important decisions" than the media or action

33. See the article by Ivo Hartman, under the rubric "Open Forum," in *De Volkskrant*, April 19, 1990, and the report of a discussion held in the First Chamber of the Dutch Parliament (the Senate) in *NRC-Handelsblad, Weekeditie*, October 30, 1990.

34. See Frans M. Roschar, "Een structureel model van de Nederlandse buitenlandse-politieke elite" (A structural model of the Dutch foreign-policy elite), in Peter R. Baehr et al., *Elite en buitenlandse politiek in Nederland* (Elite and foreign policy in the Netherlands) (The Hague: Staatsuitgeverij, 1978), p. 191; and Everts, ed., *Controversies at Home*, p. 341.

groups. Forty-nine percent of a national sample replied that the parties had "much say" in such decisions, and only 8 percent of the sample thought that the influence of the parties was excessive.[35] A sample of the Dutch foreign-policy elite, confronted in the mid-1970s with a longer list of nongovernmental actors, estimated the influence of the parties on foreign policy as higher than all other nongovernmental actors except for the business community.[36] There are no comparable data for the United States that I am aware of; I take that lack to mean that no one has ever thought that the role of American political parties in foreign policy was important enough to try to measure with any precision. There is ample evidence to support these divergent judgments about the impact of political parties on foreign policy in these two countries.[37]

In the United States there is both a long tradition and a legal structure that have as their purpose the separation of government officials from political parties. (In some states, in fact, "reform movements" early in the twentieth century were instrumental in separating even *elected* officials from political parties by institutionalizing nonpartisan elections for state and local offices.) Federal administrative personnel in all agencies, including the foreign-policy agencies, come under the provisions of the Hatch Act, which precludes active political-party work by members of the federal civil service. Although there is more freedom for those persons who are under presidential political appointment, traditions in the foreign-policy area impose on the secretary, deputy-secretary, and assistant-secretary levels a role above (or at least separate from) party. As I mentioned earlier,[38] it is generally a demerit for any high foreign-policy official (other than the president) to "politicize" foreign policy by being actively involved with the work or the problems of a political party or even with the political as distinct from the foreign-policy problems of the administration.[39] Since the na-

35. L. P. J. de Bruyn and J. W. Foppen, *The Dutch Voter, 1972–73*, Vol. 2 (Nijmegen: Institute for Political Science, 1974), pp. 390–405.

36. Roschar, "Een structureel model." In summarizing these data, Van Staden concludes that the political parties must be considered "far and away" the most important domestic factor in the formation of foreign policy in the Netherlands ("De politieke partijen," p. 61).

37. For a comprehensive discussion of American political parties that is informed by an equally comprehensive knowledge of political parties in other Western democracies, see Leon D. Epstein, *Political Parties in the American Mold* (Madison: University of Wisconsin Press, 1986).

38. See Chapter 1.

39. Henry Kissinger was heavily criticized for some of his actions during the 1973 Arab-Israeli War, which his critics believed were designed to alleviate President Nixon's Watergate troubles. Kissinger soon came to the conclusion that Nixon should

tional political parties are themselves "holding companies" for election purposes and are not programmatic membership organizations, and since officials are by law or practice kept from having observable contact with them anyway, it is not readily possible for parties as such to have any important impact on the ongoing processes of formulation and execution of foreign policy. This does not speak to the possible importance of political *considerations* in foreign-policy making, only to the possible means of realizing them.

In the Netherlands, on the other hand, relations between political parties and foreign-policy ministries are not at arm's length, and the opportunities for parties to have an impact on the shaping of foreign policies are readily recognized and accepted.[40] Even though parties may be divided on some important foreign-policy issues, and even though they may not be so single-minded or so open as to serve as the effective voice of or the channel for the foreign-policy interests of *others* in Dutch society, it is still the case that party organizations *themselves* are important institutions of public participation in Dutch foreign policy. In a society that is fundamentally accommodative to the views of sizeable groups, especially when they are composed of people of consequence, political parties (or most of them) are seen as significant actors—as primary sources of valid foreign-policy preference—and are accepted as such by Dutch foreign-policy leaders.

Ministers, whether of foreign affairs, defense, development cooperation, or economic affairs, are formally free to exercise their own judgment and authority; they have their own responsibility (*eigen verantwoordelijkheid*).[41] In a practical way, however, ministers are party representatives of sorts in the government; they can hardly put any substantial distance between themselves and strongly held views

---

alleviate Kissinger's own difficulties in carrying out a national foreign policy by resigning! See Woodward and Bernstein, *The Final Days* (New York: Simon and Schuster, 1976). See also Henry Kissinger, *Years of Upheaval* (Boston: Little, Brown and Co., 1982).

40. See, e.g., Siccama, "Netherlands Depillarized," esp. p. 135.

This represents a bit of a historic change, however. In the last half of the nineteenth century, the electorate was small and party organization weak, and one of the lasting consequences, according to Daalder, was the assumption that ministers "had a special mandate for country rather than party, and that there should be no close daily contacts between ministers and party groups inside or outside parliament" (Daalder, "Mould of Dutch Politics," p. 7).

41. This responsibility is another of the "lasting characteristics" that Daalder ("Mould of Dutch Politics") attributes to the weakness of party organization in the nineteenth century.

within their parties.[42] On the contrary, they are likely to cultivate their parties by consulting and informing them[43] and by using them as platforms for important speeches—and to bend before them if the pressure gets too great. Max van der Stoel, who as foreign minister had a reputation for being professional and nonpolitical in his approach to foreign policy, nevertheless devoted much time and effort to cultivating his party (PvdA), using it often as the platform for important policy statements. Still, he was forced by the left wing in the party to take a pro-MPLA (People's Movement for the Liberation of Angola) stance in Angola in 1976 at a time when he thought it highly premature, he pursued a pro-guerrilla El Salvador policy in 1981 that was shaped by articulate criticism within the Labor Party, and he took a strong position against NATO nuclear modernization for the same reasons and against his own preferences. Similarly Prime Minister Lubbers bent considerably before the "loyalist" group in his party (CDA), delaying the modernization decision for four years.[44]

If good relations with his party are necessary for a minister's political survival, they may also be useful for him in his administrative struggles with his bureaucracy. The more he can point either to support or to necessity in his dealings with his party, the more leverage he has in dealing with a large (and conservative) permanent staff. The minister "determines" foreign policy—but only to the extent that he can bring his officials to implement his initiatives. He may thus have bu-

42. See R. B. Andeweg, ed., *Ministers en Ministerraad* (Ministers and the Ministerial Council) (The Hague: SDU Uitgeverij, 1990), esp. the chapters by Andeweg: "Tweeerlei Ministerraad: Besluitvorming in Nederlandse kabinetten" (Two Kinds of Ministerial Councils: Decision making in Dutch cabinets), pp. 17–41; and A. Timmermans and W. E. Bakema, "Conflicten in Nederlandse kabinetten" (Conflicts in Dutch cabinets), pp. 175–192.

43. And ministers are not alone in so doing: the *staatssecretarissen* also serve as a channel of communication between their departments and the ministers of their party when they work under the minister of a different party. See Andeweg, "Tweeerlei Ministerraad," p. 33.

44. Andeweg describes the evolution of the "political prediscussions" on Thursday evenings prior to the Friday meetings of the Cabinet, to the point where they now include not only the ministers of a given party and the leaders of that party's fractions in both houses of Parliament but also the party chairperson. He describes the consequences of these prediscussions: "Although the participants in this political prediscussion generally deny that party discipline is involved, it was sometimes seen how ministers with a deviating, often departmentally inspired conception came back in step with the political party after the discussions. By this means a proposal could sometimes get accepted for which there was originally no majority to be found in the cabinet. The ex-ministers interviewed by me named in this connection, for example, the supply of reactor vessels to South Africa" (Andeweg, "Tweeerlei Ministerraad," p. 32).

reaucratic reasons to encourage his party's participation on certain issues. This is especially pertinent because there is nothing in Dutch law or tradition that limits the political-party activities of Dutch civil servants (who hold all but a handful of the top jobs in a ministry). Whereas a minister *must* communicate with his party, his officials *may* do so as a legal right—and the parties are not necessarily the same! All the important political parties, not just those in the governing coalition, have members somewhere in the foreign-policy bureaucracy, and even the smaller left-wing parties have some followers, mostly in the Development Cooperation section of the Foreign Ministry.

If law and tradition permit partisan activity by bureaucrats, a sense of propriety and of possible conflict of interest serve to keep it under control. Foreign Ministry officials do not sign documents or identify themselves with party activities that are at odds with the positions of the foreign minister—which usually also means the positions of the minister's political party. They tend to limit their party activities to technical services, such as providing information and analysis, although they may be quite active and prominent in so doing. And they usually inform the minister of these activities. It is difficult to know how many officials in the Foreign Ministry are active members of a political party, since no figures are kept. In the 1970s there were estimates of about 10 percent; it was said to be an even more common practice in the 1980s. But even 10 percent represents a substantial channel through which the foreign-policy views of all the Dutch political parties—not merely the minister's party—get transmitted to the people who have the largest responsibility for formulating and carrying out foreign policy.

Legislatures, Legislative Parties, and Foreign Policy

I will treat national legislatures and parliamentary parties in the same framework that I used in the first part of this chapter to discuss nonparliamentary parties. As I indicated earlier, I will concentrate on the "representative" aspects of the legislatures and what these signify for participation by nonparty groups or individuals. I repeat my earlier cautionary note that it is very difficult to separate the representative functions of legislatures from their policy-making functions. Not only are the two frequently entwined; also, the representative role of the legislature in foreign policy derives a part of its weight from the existence and exercise of the official role. Despite the difficulties inherent in trying to look at legislatures as "public participants," the effort is justified by the common conception of legislatures as important devices for democratic control of foreign policy and by the further notion that they may also serve as intermediaries between outside groups and national foreign-policy decision makers.

There are, to begin with, significant differences between the Netherlands and the United States in the place that foreign policy occupies in the legislature and in legislative parties. The Second Chamber has little formal or direct impact on the foreign-policy decisions of Dutch governments—certainly less impact than the U.S. Congress has on American foreign-policy decisions and less than the Congress had even before its post-Vietnam assertiveness.

The foreign-affairs committees in the two houses of the American Congress, like all congressional committees, have a significant policy-making role: each one reviews proposed legislation in foreign affairs (and the Senate Committee reviews proposed treaties) and must approve the proposals before they can be considered by the full chamber. In addition, foreign-aid bills must be authorized by these two committees and approved by the two houses before the appropriations committees can consider them. In this structure of specialization, the committee recommendations carry great weight among the other members of Congress.

Throughout the long period of the Cold War, when foreign policy itself was regarded as a very important subject in American politics, the substantive powers of the committees attracted legislators, particularly on the Senate side, like pollen draws bees. The Senate Committee on Foreign Relations has always had higher prestige—and thus greater drawing power—than the House Committee on Foreign Affairs, although in recent years the Senate Committee has become a relatively less attractive assignment for senators than it had been, while the House Committee has improved its relative standing as a committee assignment for representatives. At the height of the Cold War, in fact, the leadership of both political parties made some effort to assign to the Committee on Foreign Relations those senators who had serious and realistic presidential ambitions.[45] Because the number of such committee assignments is limited (approximately eighteen in the Senate and forty-six in the House), some aspirants for membership are likely to be disappointed. But many other committees are available to them that impinge on foreign affairs—notably Armed Services, Intelligence, Appropriations, and increasingly Energy and Commerce—and no matter what their committee assignments, they are all free to take an active

---

45. Not since 1972, however, has a sitting senator been the presidential candidate of either party. And in the aftermath of the Vietnam War, foreign-policy knowledge or experience was no longer a requirement for a would-be President.

part in floor debate on foreign-policy subjects. For the members of all the committees that have anything to do with foreign affairs, the staff resources are extensive. This so-called in-house expertise, some of which is regularly recruited from the executive departments, is the basis for still further information acquired through hearings by sub-committees as well as by the full committees. Party itself plays no substantive role here, except at the margins of staff recruitment by party membership on committees.

The Foreign Policy Committee (and the Defense Committee) of the Dutch Second Chamber have no policy-making role equivalent to the congressional committees; they are not gatekeepers or consensus builders on matters that go to the Chamber for discussion or vote.[46] The Dutch committees are essentially consultative; they are avenues of interaction between the relevant ministers and the Parliament. Committee hearings, which take place only on Mondays and then only one at a time, are one of the means by which the ministers can inform the Parliament and be informed by it. Since the committees have no policy-making responsibilities and commission no studies, they have no assigned staffs.[47] Nor do they attract the deep interest of many members of Parliament, who may have opinions on foreign-policy issues but who do not think that the subject is of great domestic political importance. The Foreign Policy Committee has twenty members and twenty alternates. The parliamentary parties are allotted seats on these committees in proportion to their seats in the Chamber. The larger parties will have four or five members and an equal number of alternates, but only two or three of the members (and none of the alternates) play an active role. In the smaller parties, which have only a few members in the Chamber to begin with, active involvement in these committees is limited at best to one person. So only a few specialists, often from the larger parties, bear the brunt of the discussions in Parliament on foreign-policy matters, and it is the specialists who have the responsibility of advising their

46. This paragraph draws heavily on M. P. C. M. van Schendelen, "Information and Decision Making in the Dutch Parliament," *Legislative Studies Quarterly* 1(2): 231–50 (May 1976).

47. Government funds for staff have been granted only since 1965. Staff are now available for the Members themselves and for the Parliamentary parties. As of 1990, staff numbered about three hundred. An additional hundred were employed by the Office of the Clerk of the Second Chamber, and their professional services are available to members. See R. A. Koole, "Political Parties going Dutch: Party Finances in The Netherlands," *Acta Politica* 25(1): 37–65 (1990). The American Congress is less than three times as large as the Dutch Parliament, but it employs over fifty times as many professional—i.e., nonhousekeeping—staff.

fractions on how to vote.[48] But they are not called on for advice very frequently: new foreign-policy issues do not arise daily in the Dutch parliament. The business of government and of politics is largely domestic business; that is the pollen that draws the Dutch bees. In the absence of sustained and important foreign-policy business, foreign-policy expertise is limited. Van Schendelen's general findings that Dutch parliamentarians rely primarily on their own resources, on the ministers themselves, on parliamentary party sources, and on technical publications for most of their information[49] seems to be as valid in the foreign-policy field as in any other, although some foreign-policy interest groups have also earned good reputations as independent sources of information.[50]

The absence of a substantial body of parliamentary expertise in foreign affairs and the difficulty that the few foreign-policy specialists have in keeping themselves independently and well informed have some interesting consequences, which I will assess at relevant points in the remainder of this chapter. Where there are, by all accounts, only a few people "whom you can take seriously" in foreign affairs in any given parliament, patterns of attention, of influence, and of relations with and participation by others cannot help but be affected.

Congressional parties in the United States are subject to little discipline, in the political sense of the word. Although never subject to strict parliamentary-type discipline, members of Congress were for many years responsive to powerful institutional relationships that kept the members more or less in line on important matters; the leadership was at least able to know on whom it could or couldn't count on specific issues. But even in periods when party unity has been relatively high— as it was for both parties, but especially the Democrats, during the Reagan years—divisions within the parties on all matters, foreign as well as domestic, have always existed, and the leaders have always countenanced "defections" from their line that were caused by severe and unique pressures from within particular constituencies. But even

48. Van Schendelen calls the Dutch legislative committees "relatively empty structures." See M. P. C. M. van Schendelen, "Kamercommissies en fracties" (Chamber committees and fractions), in M. P. C. M. van Schendelen, J. J. A. Thomassen, and H. Daudt, eds., 'Leden van de Staten-Generaal, . . .': Kamerleden over de werking van het parlement ('Members of the States-General, . . .': Members of Parliament on the workings of Parliament) (The Hague: VUGA-Uitgeverij, 1981), chapter 3.

49. Ibid.

50. See Chapter 6. Baehr argues for the development of parliamentary foreign-affairs responsibilities and staff resources in the American model. See "Het parlement," pp. 215–16.

this kind of limited internal discipline in the Congress has been weaker since the late 1960s, a victim of the more general "crisis of authority" that overtook democratic institutions almost everywhere at that time. Both parties in both houses of Congress are so far from having common visions of foreign policy that the party leadership groups frequently have to forge a new coalition on important issues.

By comparison with the American congressional parties, the Dutch parliamentary fractions are rather less divided most of the time on both domestic and foreign issues. That is partly because the candidate lists in the major parties have been generally put together by the party leaders with one eye either to governing—supporting a coalition—or to opposing. And it is partly because the interests of a governing coalition have generally taken precedence, for those parties *in* the coalition, over divergent foreign-policy interests. As parliamentarians themselves have put it, and as I have noted before, one does not—or at least one did not in the three decades before 1980—even threaten a minister or a government on a foreign-policy matter; that was simply not important enough in Dutch political life.[51] Put another way, in a period of widespread agreement ("consensus") on the major elements of Dutch foreign policy, one could have a falling-out only on minor elements, and these were certainly not worth the life of a government.

But even in those decades there were differences both within and among some of the fractions on key foreign-policy matters.[52] And beginning in the late 1970s, fractional disagreements over foreign policy, mostly involving aspects of security policy, reached new levels for the post–World War II period, resulting in several real threats to the survival of cabinets.[53] The decline in the levels of East-West tension at the end of the 1980s, however, reduced once again the political significance of these issues in the Netherlands.

In any event, the substantial discipline of the Dutch governing parties on foreign-policy matters up to the 1980s had, paradoxically, the same apparent effect as had the disagreements within the parties themselves: it kept the governing parties from being discriminating and effective instruments for the expression of diverse foreign-policy views,

51. Baehr, "Het parlement," pp. 205–6, 215.
52. See. e.g., A. van Staden, "De politieke partijen," table 1, p. 58.
53. See K. Brants, W. Kok, and Ph. van Praag, Jr., "De verkiezingscampagne en wat daaraan vooraf ging . . ." (The election campaign and what preceded it . . .), in A. Th. J. Eggen, C. van der Eijk, and B. Niemöller, eds., *Kiezen in Nederland* (Voting in the Netherlands) (Zoetermeer: Actaboek, 1981), p. 25, and the case studies of foreign-policy issues summarized in Everts, ed., *Controversies at Home*. See also Van Staden, "Changing Role," p. 107.

except on a very few issues. In the United States there was a comparable situation in the immediate post–World War II years, when a deliberately "bipartisan" foreign policy had the effect of diminishing political and, hence, public discussion of most foreign-policy matters. But once the postwar "revolution" in U.S. foreign policy had been achieved and a new "consensus" on international involvement forged (by 1952), bipartisanship as a formal effort receded, leaving the members of the two parties free to disagree on a wide range of issues beyond the core consensus and to take whatever positions they wished on these issues. And since the turbulence of the Vietnam War period in the late 1960s, members of the American congressional parties have felt even freer to speak out on an ever wider range of foreign-policy matters, unlike many of their Dutch counterparts in the governing parties, who remain under a substantial constraint of "multipartisanship" in the form of coalition government.

Legislatures and Outside Pressures

To what extent are there more or less regular relationships in these two countries between legislatures (as distinct from parties), on the one hand, and all manner of outside groups, on the other, on matters of foreign policy? And to what extent do such relationships serve to put the legislature in the middle, so to speak, where they transmit these views to foreign-policy officials or incorporate them directly into legislation? In other words, given that in the United States the political parties are not the bearers of consistent programs and that in the Netherlands the political parties are not consistently effective as the framers or articulators of clear views on new foreign-policy issues, what are the consequences for the legislatures themselves? Do they, as I asked at the beginning of this chapter, invite or attract organized pressure or participation from outside, nonparty sources? The answer is yes in both cases, but not in identical fashion. The differences have systemic and structural causes, not the least of which is the presence or absence of significant legislative specialization or expertise in foreign affairs.[54]

In the United States, as I indicated earlier, the policy-making role of congressional committees involved in foreign affairs and the level of staff resources available to them contribute to a substantial body of

54. This discussion inescapably overlaps my subsequent discussion of interest groups, in Chapter 6. The focus here, however, is on the legislatures; there it is on the interest groups.

congressional specialization across the foreign-policy board. This specialization does not compare in technical expertise with that in the executive branch, to be sure, but it far exceeds that which is ordinarily available to a legislative body—and, in fact, it exceeds by quite a bit the levels achieved in the U.S. Congress only two decades ago.[55]

The implications of this technical specialization of the Congress have yet to be studied, but it cannot fail to have an impact on the choice of political strategies available to outside foreign-policy interests. If they wish to persuade congressmen of the substantive merits of an alternative course of action, they have to bring to bear a level of knowledge and analysis that can compete with the growing expertise of the Congress. Failing that, their alternatives are to plead for the protection or advancement of particular private interests or to challenge the Congress by arguing for their own interpretation of the public interest. The first—a debate among experts—being rather difficult to bring off, the more likely relationship between outside groups and members of Congress is one of pressure.

The targets of this legislative "lobbying" are shaped both by the choice of strategy and by the political system. Because congressional committees and subcommittees have crucial policy-making functions, efforts are directed at committee members and their professional and legislative staffs and at committee hearings. Because members of Congress represent geographically bounded constituencies, efforts are made to mobilize constituents in the districts or states of particular congressmen. And because votes in both houses must often be taken on crucial questions, efforts are directed at those members who have taken no position and especially at those whose support may have coalition-building consequences.

In the Netherlands the Second Chamber is regarded by most observers as "the proper channel," the "classic line of access" for public groups—even though it is rarely accepted any longer as the *exclusive* channel and even though it is generally acknowledged that the foreign-policy power lies substantially within the Foreign Ministry.[56] But the

55. These developments have been fostered by the 'divided government' of the 1980s and by the efforts of the Congressional Democrats to improve the institutional resources available to them in their dealings with a Republican president. See Charles O. Jones, "The Separated Presidency: Making It Work in Contemporary Politics," in Anthony S. King, ed., *The New American Political System*, 2d ed. (Washington, D.C.: American Enterprise Institute, 1990).

56. See the analysis of the intermediary function of members of Parliament between the formal and informal elites in Roschar, "Een structureel model."

For a contrary view—that the Parliament and the parties have become permanently

choice of strategies and targets is quite different from that facing their American counterparts and is at the same time more difficult and more limited. In the first place, the structure of the majority coalition and the governing accord in most cases determine how the majority of the members of Parliament will vote on the few foreign-policy issues that come up for a vote. If decisions of a different kind are going to be made on these issues, they will be the result of fundamental changes in party and fraction positions, changes that may well be influenced by broad political and opinion calculations but hardly by short-term (or even long-term) lobbying efforts by specific groups.[57]

Another problem is posed by the very nature of the Dutch electoral system: in a proportional-representation system, there are no geographical constituencies and, hence, no formal constituency-representative relationships.[58] Members of the Second Chamber represent some proportion of the electorate, very few of whom—the most active members of their party—they know and can locate. A Dutch citizen can communicate with "his" or "her" member of Parliament only if that citizen is known to have voted for a party that won only a single seat! As a general matter, the only political connections that can be identified even approximately are those between political parties and related social groups in what little remains of a "pillarized" society—for example, between some church organizations and the CDA or between labor unions and the PvdA.[59] But the party confer-

---

subordinated to the government and the departments and that outside groups now bypass the former and have direct access to the latter—see the arguments of H. D. Tjeenk Willink and W. Kok in Ruud Koole, ed., *Binnenhof binnenste buiten* (The Binnenhof inside out) (Weesp: De Haan, 1986), pp. 123–25. (The Binnenhof, literally the 'Inner Court,' is the Parliament complex in The Hague.)

57. For comments on the failure of the IKV, the leadership organization of the Dutch peace movement, to prevent the Dutch government and Parliament from accepting cruise missiles, see Rochon, *Mobilizing for Peace*, p. 168.

58. In the spring of 1990 there was a quarrel within the Liberal Party (VVD), between the party's national council and the Second Chamber fraction, involving the replacement of the fraction chair. The new chair reflected on those events in a newspaper article ten days later. Comparing the Dutch system of proportional representation with the British system of electoral districts, he observed that the British system is "unfair because small parties hardly have a chance. But it does mean that representatives have an immediate link with their voters. The Netherlands has no electoral districts. (In the Second Chamber one often talks solemnly about the 'honorable representative,' but that is nonsense because we have no representatives)" (F. Bolkestein, "Hollands Dagboek" [Dutch Diary], *NRC-Handelsblad*, May 26, 1990).

59. For a review of Dutch literature on the "normative and physical distance" between the voters and the members of Parliament, see Paul Dekker and Peter Ester, "Cognitieve

ences rather than the parliamentary fractions are the arenas for those kinds of influence relationships.

The most promising parliamentary avenues for outside groups are those that lead to the party specialists on the Foreign Policy and Defense Committees. These are the members who conduct the debates and raise questions; they function, as I noted, with limited expertise and often have to turn to extraparliamentary sources for information.[60] The outside groups that are most respected in foreign-policy circles in the Netherlands are those that have developed a reputation for providing parliamentary specialists (and others) with unassailable information, not otherwise available, to which the government is obliged to respond. The general lack of foreign-policy expertise in the Second Chamber creates a strong incentive for outsiders to work this way; however, unlike the American situation, where the expertise of outsiders has to deal with the expertise of Congress, the Dutch situation pits the expertise of outsiders ultimately against the expertise of the government, and in neither country is this often a winning battle.[61] The more common way in which Dutch groups try to make a mark on the Parliament is to strive for general and favorable publicity. By achieving media coverage in a small country with a national press, they often succeed in stimulating members of Parliament to ask questions of ministers. A person with a vantage point high in the Foreign Ministry described the process as he saw it: "Only a limited number of people are interested in these things, [but] the minister is interested in what they say because *they* set the trend for the Second Chamber. If an issue is brought up by the press or an action group, within forty-eight hours a member of Parliament takes it up and asks a question. [Parliamentarians] don't have staffs, so they depend on the press and on action groups to know what they should be concerned about." In a more general and imprecise way, also, these groups are contributing to the limited body of articulate opinion in the country on foreign-policy issues, and their contribution is in some way registered by parliamentarians and perhaps subsequently echoed by them in discussions with Foreign Ministry officials.

---

responsiviteit van de politieke elite in Nederland" (Cognitive responsiveness of the political elite in the Netherlands), *Acta Politica* 23(4): 301–36 (1988).

60. Van Schendelen, "Kamercommissies."

61. In the most notable victory of outsiders, the Angola Committee in the 1970s had more accurate information than even the government on the state of affairs in Angola, and as a result the committee achieved enormous prestige and influence.

The Public-Representation Function of Legislatures

Lastly, do the legislatures (or legislators) play any significant or effective *representative* role in the foreign-policy process in the United States and the Netherlands? Do they function as public participants, so to speak, not on behalf of specific individuals and groups but, rather, on their own behalf, as interested and well-placed representatives of the people? And are there differences in these respects that reflect any of the foregoing differences in the legislative experience in the two countries?

As I indicated at the beginning of this chapter, it is difficult to disentangle in practice the analytically clear distinction between the legislative and the representative functions of national legislatures in foreign policy. In the United States, the Congress has enlarged its legislative grip on foreign policy since the Vietnam War; after thirty years of interpreting its formal constitutional mandate in foreign affairs with caution and reserve, acceding to the will (and to the "superior knowledge and wisdom") of the executive branch, it began diligently to seize every opportunity to insert itself into the ongoing processes of foreign-policy formulation and execution.[62] In part *because* of the legislative importance of the Congress, because there are so many official legislative points of contact, it is difficult for officials to ignore their views on matters that are not the subjects of those contacts. As I have noted elsewhere,[63] references to "public opinion" by foreign-policy officials very frequently turn out to be oblique references to the Congress, which officials see as an important element in the structure of public representation on foreign affairs. But in the U.S., the president represents the largest constituency and possesses a certain (though varying) capacity to shape preferences within that constituency; consequently those officials who exercise the president's foreign-policy power can look to the president as well as to members of Congress for a representation of those preferences. This is but to say that although members of Congress are regarded by foreign-policy officials as important public participants, they are but one source of opinion among many; they can be

62. For the period of caution and reserve, see, e.g., James A. Robinson, *Congress and Foreign Policy-Making*, rev. ed. (Homewood, Ill.: Dorsey Press, 1967); for the post-Vietnam period, see Cecil V. Crabb and Pat M. Holt, *Invitation to Struggle* (Washington, D.C.: CQ Press, 1980). Jones ("Separated Presidency") argues that the "divided government" of the Reagan-Bush presidencies has been a further encouragement to the Democrats in Congress to insert the Congress into the foreign-policy process.

63. Bernard C. Cohen, *The Public's Impact on Foreign Policy* (Boston: Little, Brown and Co., 1973).

used selectively, as support for views coming from other sources. And where their views conflict with what the executive hears from others or wants to hear from them, they are likely to be ignored—as President Johnson and his foreign-policy officials long ignored the views of Congress on the Vietnam War.

The distinction between the legislative and the representative role of the Parliament in the Netherlands is somewhat easier to make than in the American case, because the formal legislative power of the Parliament in foreign affairs is so slight[64]—for reasons that have already been made clear: there is not very much in the way of Dutch foreign policy that constitutionally requires legislative authorization (a lot of it having migrated to Brussels, where it is more or less beyond the reach of the Parliament), and for that which remains—mostly the ratification of treaties and the annual budget—the majority coalition in the Second Chamber is predisposed to accept the Foreign Ministry's proposals. As a Foreign Ministry official once put it, he and his colleagues did not need to develop outside support "because we can formally legalize our policy in Parliament *every* time." There was some slight change in this formal legislative situation in the 1980s, in the direction—as in the U.S. Congress—of greater parliamentary activism, mostly on national-security-policy issues. But in 1990 the words of a Dutch scholar in 1967 did not sound out of place or out of time: he wrote that Dutch foreign policy was "almost exclusively" formed by the government, that the government was "exceptionally autonomous," and that the influence of the Parliament was "narrow."[65]

The legislative power of the Parliament remains in the shadow of its representative function. The latter has also grown a bit since the 1960s, helped in part by the recent experience in the exercise of legislative power and in part by the rhetoric of democratization that affected all Dutch institutions during these years. References to the "influence" of the Second Chamber abound in the literature and the discourse of Dutch foreign policy, but they refer almost exclusively to the significance of the Chamber as the most *authoritative* expression of Dutch public opinion. The typical formulation by knowledgeable individuals is that the Second Chamber is without influence in foreign policy, *except* in one or two areas the observers happen to

64. So slight, in fact, that the Foreign Ministry, unlike other departments, has no legislative section of its own. See Baehr, "Het parlement," p. 204.

65. E. H. van den Beugel, "Nederland in de Westelijke samenwerking: Enkele aspecten van de Nederlandse beleidsvorming" (The Netherlands and Western cooperation: Some aspects of Dutch policy making), *Internationale Spectator* 21(1): pp. 8–26 (January 1967).

know well and in which the opinions of parliamentarians were of great importance in shaping the development of government policy. Among these policy areas are European integration; security policy, with special reference to the neutron bomb and to theater nuclear forces; development cooperation; human rights; the Third World—in short, the most important areas of contemporary Dutch foreign policy. A researcher for one of the political parties once observed that "the power of the Second Chamber is implicit, psychological; it is in the mind of the foreign minister. So it is unmeasurable. But if you talk to people you get the impression that the foreign minister can move within only a very narrow margin." Not all foreign ministers feel equally constrained in this manner, of course, but it is instructive that the one minister in recent years who was openly resistant to the preferences of Parliament—Dr. C.A. van der Klaauw, a member of the Liberal Party (VVD) and a career diplomat from 1952 until his appointment in 1977—served in only one cabinet and does not enjoy the reputation of those who preceded or followed him.[66] Throughout the ministry one finds evidence that when the reaction of the Chamber is very important to the minister, it is also important to the people who serve the minister.

The apparent contradiction between a supine chamber and a potent one that is suggested by this discussion must be understood as two aspects of a single phenomenon—embodied sometimes in different people, sometimes within the same individual. Parliament can ordinarily be counted on to "come through," as it were, so there is a tendency in the Foreign Ministry to be slightly contemptuous of it—to regard the members as intellectually unfit, always concerned with marginal issues, and so uninformed that "we can say anything we want to them and they will swallow it." At the same time, the accommodationist impulses that reflect political reality in the land are so great that the Foreign Ministry does not—cannot—long act on the basis of those contemptuous inclinations. Rather, it tends to listen closely, and it learns what it can or cannot do with comfort or safety and what it may be able to do under certain circumstances, and it uses that knowledge in determining what it will actually ask the Chamber to "swallow"—which the Chamber can then do, of course, without seriously choking.

The means and points of contact between parliamentarians and

66. See, e.g., the articles by P. R. Baehr ("The United Nations Convention Against Torture") and F. Kremer and A. E. Pijpers ("South Africa and European Sanctions Policy") in Everts and Walraven, eds., *Politics of Persuasion.*

foreign-policy officials are extensive.[67] In addition to political advisers, who have been mentioned previously, the permanent officials in the Foreign Ministry join the foreign minister and the *staatssecretaris* in policy discussions with relevant members of Parliament.[68] Members, including those in opposition parties, are put on official delegations to international conferences. The Press Office of the ministry works extensively with members of Parliament in pursuit of its general mission to improve the relationship between the ministry and its public. And there are the extensive personal, private contacts between officials and parliamentarians in a small polity—contacts that are furthered by the political-party contacts discussed earlier, as well as by the fact that there is movement in both directions between the Foreign Ministry and the Second Chamber as governments come and go.

Perhaps the most important mechanism that conveys issue salience or opinions from parliamentarians to the government with force is the parliamentary question and the written interpellation that must be answered by the government. The prevailing view in the Netherlands is that the stimulus for these interrogatories from Chamber members comes from the Dutch press, although the questions, once asked, belong to the parliamentarians. The policy-planning adviser in the Foreign Ministry estimated some time ago that more than two hundred written questions per year were directed by parliamentarians to the top officials of the ministry, and he stressed the importance of these questions in strengthening the minister's "anticipatory reactions" to the representatives' views.[69] The congressional version of this is the written request by members of Congress to the State Department for answers to questions that can arise anywhere but that are most often simply passed on from constituents. One can speculate about the role of the media, one step removed, in stimulating these constituent questions. Departmental practice is to answer these so-called specials within three days, and the responses are formulated so that they can in turn be passed directly back to constituents. In the Netherlands the minister is

67. This is reflected in the measure of direct contacts among segments of the Dutch foreign-policy elite, as reported by Roschar, "Een structureel model."

68. Andeweg points out that "a minister gets to deal rather exclusively with parliamentarians who are specialized in his policy area" ("Tweeerlei Ministerraad," p. 26).

69. H. C. Posthumus Meyjes, "De totstandkoming van het Nederlands buitenlands beleid" (The making of Dutch foreign policy), *Internationale Spectator* 31(1): 40 (January 1977). The record book of the Parliament for the years 1978–79 and 1979–80 notes that "the number of written questions [on all subjects] has increased sharply in recent years" (P. Gossens and G. G. J. Thissen, *Parlement en kiezer* [Parliament and voter] [The Hague: Martinus Nijhoff, 1981], p. 133).

usually involved in the responses, even if he has had staff assistance in its preparation. In the United States the secretary of state is almost never involved in the responses, which are typically the work of the Bureau of Public Affairs with the help, where necessary, of the geographical or functional bureau concerned. In both countries, however, those who deal with the questions claim to be sensitive to the ideas and concerns that the legislature brings to bear this way on the thinking of foreign-policy officials.

Since the media of communication play a manifestly important role in the transmission—if not indeed the formulation—of these ideas and concerns, let us look now directly at those media as public participants in the foreign-policy process in these two countries.

5
The Media of Mass Communication

I have written elsewhere, at some length, about the significance of the media of mass communication—the press in particular—for the formulation of American foreign policy.[1] Central to that discussion is a two-fold premise: (1) that the media inescapably bring the world of foreign policy to the public, to "outsiders" of all kinds, shaping their knowledge as well as their incentives and opportunities for participation in the policy-making process; and (2) that the media are themselves one of the most articulate and informed outside participants in the foreign-policy-making process. Thus, the media unavoidably affect the environment in which foreign-policy decisions are made by "insiders." We have already seen enough here of the differences between the Dutch and American political systems as they function in the foreign-policy field to anticipate that the media will behave differently in the two countries and that they will affect in quite different ways the environments in which the two sets of foreign-policy officials make their decisions.

Scale and Structure of the Media

Underlying such differences in behavior and impact are important differences in scale, as well as structural differences, in the media of the two countries that need to be noted at the outset. American newspapers, particularly in urban settings, are typically quite substantial in size, with a number of sections, often totalling fifty pages or more. Most major Dutch papers (with the exception of *De Telegraaf*, which has

1. Bernard C. Cohen, *The Press and Foreign Policy* (Princeton: Princeton University Press, 1963).

an immense amount of classified advertising) have only twenty-four to thirty pages. Many, if not most, American papers publish seven days a week, with the Sunday edition being much larger than the daily, often weighing upwards of three pounds. The Dutch newspapers, like most of their European counterparts, do not publish on Sundays. As befits the relative size of the newspapers in the two countries, the reportorial staffs of American papers are much larger than those on the Dutch side. That is particularly the case with the major urban newspapers, which in the United States provide much of their own news coverage, in a few cases even worldwide, relying very little on news services. In all of The Hague, on the other hand, there are only about 150 journalists, who represent all of the print and electronic media in the Netherlands, covering the entire spectrum of political events.[2]

In the United States, until very recently, there has been a two-tiered system of mass communication. In radio and television, effective national networks have brought news and discussion to a large audience scattered over thousands of miles. The newspapers, however, have developed locally, supported by local advertising, and whatever common tendencies they display derive chiefly from reliance on news services—such as Associated Press, Knight-Ridder, New York Times News Service, Los Angeles Times News Service—which provide a large common well of news from which individual papers can draw. Only in the last decade or so has technology provided realistic possibilities for anything approaching national distribution of daily newspapers. The *Wall Street Journal*, the *New York Times*, and *USA Today* are the only daily newspapers out of some 1,700 published in the United States that might be described as national newspapers,[3] and their total circulation figures are limited: in 1991 the *Wall Street Journal* had a circulation of approximately 1,857,000; the *New York Times* had approximately 1,109,000 for its daily editions and 1,687,000 for its Sunday editions; and *USA Today* had approximately 1,348,000.[4]

In the Netherlands the physical size of the country has facilitated the development of national media in a way that has not been possible in the United States. There are today six major national newspapers in the Netherlands. The national newspapers in 1980 had a com-

2. Addy Kaiser, *Haagse journalistiek: Een empirisch onderzoek naar relatie tussen journalisten en parlementariërs* (Journalism in The Hague: An empirical study of the relation between journalists and parliamentarians) (Amsterdam: VU Uitgeverij, 1985), pp. 53–54.

3. The *Christian Science Monitor* is available nationally but lacks an effective daily national distribution system.

4. *Editor and Publisher International Yearbook* (New York: Editor and Publisher, 1991). The *Wall Street Journal* and *USA Today* do not publish on Sunday.

bined daily paid circulation of about 1,826,000; in 1985 the circulation was 1,878,000, and in 1991 it was 1,910,200. There are, in addition, over seventy-five regional newspapers, clustered in press associations and sharing editorial staffs and foreign and domestic correspondents. These regional papers had a combined daily paid circulation in 1980 of about 2,788,000 and in 1985 of about 2,600,000.[5] In a nation of about 15,000,000 people, the national press, with approximately 40 percent of the total daily newspaper circulation, has a significant impact, especially in the urban centers that dominate the political life of the country.[6]

On the electronic side there were in 1990 four television channels, one of which was commercial (and therefore technically "offshore," or international), and five radio channels, all noncommercial. All but the commercial TV station are government-owned; the broadcast hours are divided according to a complex formula among eight politically and religiously disparate private broadcast organizations that control the content of the programs they air. News broadcasts and coverage of major national events are provided to all the radio stations and television channels by a separate national broadcast organization, whereas commentary and discussion programs are in the hands of the private organizations.[7]

5. The 1980 figures are drawn from *De Nederlandse Dagbladpers, Jaarverslag 1978 en 1980* (The Dutch Daily Press, Annual report 1978 and 1980) and reported in L. P. H. Schoonderwoerd and W. P. Knulst, *Mediagebruik bij verruiming van het aanbod, Voorstudies en achtergronden mediabeleid* (Media usage when the supply is enlarged, Preparatory studies and background materials for media policy), M4 1982, Wetenschappelijke Raad voor het Regeringsbeleid, (The Hague: Staatsuitgeverij, 1982), table 8.11, p. 123. The 1985 figures are from *Compendium voor politiek en samenleving in Nederland* (Compendium for Politics and Society in the Netherlands) (Alphen aan den Rijn: Samsom Uitgeverij [no date: sections are regularly updated]), p. B 1500–20; and the 1991 figures are from *NRC-Handelsblad, Weekeditie,* June 9, 1992. Several of the regional papers—*De Gelderlander, Haagsche Courant, Nieuwsblad van het Noorden, De Limburger*—have circulations that nearly match some of the major national newspapers. See *Handboek van de Nederlandse Pers* (Handbook of the Dutch Press).

6. While the circulation figures for the national papers have been slowly climbing, those for the regional papers have been slowly declining. See *NRC-Handelsblad, Weekeditie,* June 9, 1992. This is but one example of the continuous change that is occurring in this societally sensitive and technology-dependent area. The data and the descriptions in this chapter were those that obtained during the past two decades—the period during which most of the comparisons in this book have been made.

7. The distribution of air time, the character of programming, the terms governing advertising, and so forth are all regulated in minute detail in the 1987 MediaWet (Media law). See *Compendium voor politiek en samenleving in Nederland,* pp. B 1500-72–78. For a comprehensive view of the Dutch media, see the four volumes—M1–M4, 1982—in the series "Voorstudies en achtergronden mediabeleid," prepared for and published by the

Until recently, the narrow access to channels and the limited hours of the broadcast day helped to create a broad audience for most programs, including public-affairs discussions, even where there was little sympathy with the political orientation of those discussions. The growth in the number of channels, the lengthening of the broadcast day, the advent of cable television—which has brought additional channels from surrounding countries to approximately 80 percent of Dutch households—and the growing popularity of video recorders are together providing alternative entertainment possibilities to viewers and are introducing into the Netherlands the fragmentation of the television audience that has long been characteristic of the United States, with its larger number of channels and full broadcast day.

Until the 1960s the major newspapers and broadcast organizations in the Netherlands were identified with one or another of the "pillars" in a pillarized society and thus had close ties with the parties that were the political expression of those pillars. Their "publics" were reasonably well defined and discrete.[8] With *ontzuiling,* or the breakdown of pillarization, and with a considerable measure of deconfessionalization, the media have assumed more independent positions: lacking a well-defined audience, they have had to reach out to wider publics in order to survive.[9] As a result, the Dutch media are characterized today more by ideological preference than by the partisan political identification of an earlier generation. At the same time, the search for a wider and more general audience has led some Dutch reporters, as it did American journalists at the turn of the last century, to adopt "objectivity" and "neutrality" in reporting as a formal doctrine. But to a much greater extent than those of their American counterparts, the ideologi-

---

Wetenschappelijke Raad for het Regeringsbeleid: J. M. de Meij, *Overheid en uitings vrijheid* (Government and freedom of expression), M1; E. H. Hollander, *Kleinschalige massacommunicatie: Lokale omroepvormen in West-Europa* (Small-scale mass communication: Local forms of broadcasting in Western Europe), M2; L. J. Heinsman, *De kulturele betekenis van de instroom van buitenlandse televisie-programma's in Nederland* (The cultural significance of the influx of foreign television programs in the Netherlands), M3; and Schoonderwoerd and Knulst, *Mediagebruik.* Schoonerwoerd and Knulst refer to non-Dutch studies in arguing that the growth of television has led to an increase in the regional press at the expense of the national press, because the regional press provides local news that is not provided by the nationally organized and oriented television system. See p. 110.

8. See Kaiser, *Haagse journalistiek.* Kaiser points out (pp. 33–34) that TV viewing behavior has always been less pillarized than other media exposure because the various broadcast organizations, representing different pillars, originally all had to share the one TV channel then in use, and viewers became accustomed to watching it all.

9. Ibid. Kaiser also points to the ensuing mergers and the growing concentrations among newspaper enterprises—a process that is still going on.

cal orientations and perspectives of the Dutch news organizations permeate their presentations of public affairs.[10] This important aspect of Dutch media behavior will come to the fore several times in the course of this chapter.

These divergent approaches to objectivity or to political engagement have major consequences for the ultimate "nationalization" of political discussion in these countries. Comparisons of the national "reach" of the media may suggest that where that reach is greater, national exposure to political debate will be more uniform, with obvious implications for political mobilization and participation. But the reach of the media is less than national when different audiences hear different messages. In the U.S. the major developments in the mass media in this century have had the effect of binding together a country that was spread all over the map, so to speak. The wire services, the electronic news networks, and now a few national newspapers, all operating under the strong influence of the doctrines of objectivity, have contributed to an increasingly homogeneous news product, creating a truly national news market that coexists with a strong local news orientation. The wire services in particular play a powerful role in setting a standard of international and national "news" for the hundreds of American newspapers that have no correspondents in Washington or overseas.

The Dutch media are less easy to characterize because they have changed so much over the last generation. As recently as the mid-1970s, the ideological diversity of the Dutch media had the opposite effect, reinforcing—or at least doing nothing to mitigate—the political divisions in a country that is physically so easy to encompass. Each of the national papers, in particular, had an "identity," a set of interests and perspectives—political, social, religious—that appealed to a reasonably well-defined segment of the population.[11] These identities dis-

10. The major exceptions are the Dutch wire service, ANP (Algemeen Nederlands Persbureau), which supplies hourly radio news, and the Dutch broadcast organization (Nederlandse Omroepprogramma Stichting—NOS), which provides objective news programs on all of the state TV channels.

11. Arend Lijphart cites a mid-1960s survey by the *Nederlandse Stichting voor Statistiek* (Dutch Foundation for Statistics) in which 90 percent of the readers of the (then) two Catholic national daily newspapers belong to the "Catholic pillar," 90 percent of the readers of the Protestant-Christian paper belonged to the "Protestant-Christian pillar," and 94 percent of the readers of the (then) two socialist national daily papers belonged to the "general pillar." Only the liberal papers showed a different pattern: 76 percent of those reading the (then) four liberal papers belonged to the "general pillar," and 19 percent belonged to the "Protestant-Christian pillar" (*Verzuiling, pacificatie en kentering in de Nederlandse politiek* [Pillarization, pacification, and change in Dutch politics], 7th ed.

tinguished one paper from another and resulted in a daily presentation of "reality" that differed from paper to paper. A comparison of
the lead story in pairs of the national newspapers during a comparable period of time in 1964 and 1974 revealed an enormous divergence—an overlap of only about 20 percent in the later period and
one of about 30 percent in the earlier period (when an issue involving
the Royal House drew some attention from all papers).[12] Most important, this diversity among the media was especially striking in the
area of international news, where the number of reportable events
was—and remains—high, the sources were extensive, and the space
allocation, in newspapers that are small to begin with, was restricted.
Facing hard choices in what to cover and what not to cover, the interests and perspectives of the various news organizations had enormous room in which to express themselves.[13]

The thrust toward objectivity and neutrality in the Dutch media in
the past decade and a half has moderated this pattern a bit as the news
organizations have begun more energetically to compete for wider audiences among an increasingly "depillarized" and deconfessionalized
public. Yet, as I noted above, ideological differentiation persists in the
Dutch media to a degree that is unfamiliar in the American media—
and with it a heterogeneity of "news."[14]

[Haarlem: J. J. W. Becht, 1988], pp. 54–55). The same patterns were reflected a decade
earlier in a survey that looked at regional daily papers and weekly organs of opinion as
well as national dailies: in that sample, by the *Centraal Bureau voor de Statistiek*, 87 percent
"receive[d] their news and editorial comments from only one ideological source" (Arend
Lijphart, *The Politics of Accommodation* [Berkeley and Los Angeles: University of California
Press, 1968], p. 43).

12. H. Kneepkens, *De voornaamste kop op de voorpagina's van een vijftal landelijke Nederlandse dagbladen in de eerste twee maanden van 1964 en 1974*, Scriptie voor het doctoraal
examen in de toegepaste wiskunde, met hoofdrichting mathematische statistiek (The
principal headline on the front pages of five national Dutch dailies in the first two months
of 1964 and 1974, Thesis for the final degree examination in applied mathematics, with
specialization in mathematical statistics), University of Amsterdam, July 1975.

13. In a 1969 study of Dutch reporting on West Berlin as the site of German presidential elections, Jan Wieten showed an enormous variation among the national papers in
their attention to this issue and in the use they make of foreign press services while
covering it. See Jan Wieten, *Presidentsverkiezingen in West-Berlijn. Een onderzoek naar de
invloed van de ontspanning op de berichtgeving in een aantal Nederlandse dagbladen*, Scriptie
voor het doctoraal examen in internationale betrekkingen (Presidential elections in West
Berlin. A study in the influence of detente on news reporting in a number of Dutch
dailies, Thesis for the final degree examination in international relations), University of
Amsterdam, 1969.

14. See also Kaiser, *Haagse journalistiek*, p. 62: "News organizations each have their
own norms and value patterns, and the parliamentary journalists ultimately owe respon-

The Practices of Journalists

Successful journalists thoroughly absorb the *mores* of their profession, which they subsequently reflect in their everyday behavior. By comparing the professional behavior of foreign-affairs journalists in the U.S. and the Netherlands, we can more readily grasp the significance of the media in the foreign-policy-making process in these two countries. I shall focus in this section on the more general practices and procedures of journalists and in subsequent sections on their interactions with foreign-policy officials, parliamentarians, and other public institutions.

Although there are some commonalities in the way these two groups of journalists go about their work, on the whole they are more different than alike. Language differences aside, each would have considerable difficulty performing the other's work, making the transition from one political and professional system to the other.

The similarities, being mostly structural, are perhaps obvious. Wherever the press is uncontrolled by government, journalists face the problem of defining "the news." And the foreign-affairs journalists in the Netherlands and the United States set about that task in much the same way: they do extensive reading in and listening to the media to discover what is going on, to get ideas for their own writing, and to find a "news peg" on which to hang their efforts. In the execution of their work, they comb newspapers and periodicals, they read government documents, and to a lesser extent they talk to persons in their own government and in foreign embassies.[15] Beyond these simple things, however, it is hard to find everyday practices that are the same. Even the most basic element of competition for news that pervades the American media and shapes much of the behavior of American journalists is mostly absent from the circle of Dutch foreign-policy journalists.

The differences are pervasive. They start, perhaps, with the relative position of foreign affairs in the political life of the country and hence in the professional lives of its scribes. In the United States, where foreign affairs remain of considerable importance on the national agenda even in the absence of the Cold War, journalists who write

---

sibility only to them. In general they have the same norms and value patterns as their organizations." One of the consequences is that it is not easy for these journalists to go to work for the competition.

15. See Cohen, *Press and Foreign Policy,* esp. Chapter 3, and Kees Burger, *Pers en buitenlands beleid in Nederland:* (Press and foreign policy in The Netherlands) (University of Leiden, 1983), passim.

about these things stand high in their profession. In the Netherlands, as I have noted in other contexts, foreign policy is a secondary issue area; four decades of alliance politics and European integration created a widely shared image of a country without much real choice in its foreign relations. Its accuracy aside, this image is still reflected in the interests not only of politicians but also of journalists. Dutch journalists tend to look at Dutch foreign policy from the perspective of Dutch domestic politics, rather than from the perspective of Dutch national interests.[16] So long as foreign policy, in the words of a respected newspaper editor, "can't be much different here," the media presumably can have little influence on it, and so they put their major efforts elsewhere and rely on the international wire services for basic news reporting about international events. During the Cold War years, when Dutch foreign policy was especially stagnant, there was even some skepticism among journalists about the caliber of their colleagues who chose to cover the field.[17]

A corollary of this difference in the relative status of foreign policy among journalists is the difference in the relative importance of developing a specialization in the subject matter. American reporters who cover foreign policy full time take it seriously and learn enough about it to be able to ask officials some reasonably detailed questions about specific issues as they arise. A comparable specialization among Dutch journalists hardly exists.[18] According to a Dutch "notable": "We do not have the equivalent of State Department correspondents. There are no facilities in the Foreign Ministry or in Defense, either. There are no defense correspondents in the real sense of the word. Even the newspapers hire analysts from the [military] services to write analyses of Defense papers. . . . There are no reporters who specialize in foreign policy—who do no other things. The structure of the press makes that lack of specialization necessary: the number of reporters is too small. The papers are too small." One Dutch journalist judged that "for most reporters, foreign policy is five percent of their work." A now-defunct

16. Burger, *Pers*, pp. 17–18, 59–60.
17. That skepticism may change in the post–Cold War era, however, as a more independent Europe creates a context of greater foreign-policy opportunities for the Netherlands and thus the possibility of a more inquisitive and critical Dutch journalism.
18. In his 1983 study of foreign-policy reporters in the Netherlands, Burger reports that almost all of his fourteen respondents concluded that a thorough knowledge of *domestic* political relations was very important, if not indispensable, for foreign-affairs reporting: "In general it was stated that the domestic political situation was chosen as the starting point for such reporting. One addresses oneself, in reporting, principally to those foreign-policy subjects that play a role in domestic politics" (*Pers*, pp. 17–18).

Dutch newspaper, *De Tijd*, made a readership study in 1972, in the course of which it compared its coverage of Dutch foreign policy and of international politics with that of two other national newspapers over the four-month period from September through December 1972. Collectively, these papers showed a striking disinterest in Dutch foreign-policy news, with less than one-half of 1 percent of the news articles in the samples of each paper being devoted to foreign policy, while 12 to 23 percent was devoted to international-political news.[19] But it would not be accurate to conclude from these figures that coverage of Dutch foreign-policy news is nonexistent; rather, it is episodic, with long periods sometimes passing between foreign-policy news stories. Significantly, however, the media themselves play little role in uncovering or developing these stories; the initiative invariably rests elsewhere—in the parties, in the Parliament, in the ministries, or among interest groups.[20]

Dutch journalism, however, distinguishes between reporters and editors in a manner different from American journalism. Dutch national newspapers have diplomatic or foreign "editors" (*redacteuren*) who write interpretive or analytical pieces that are not what Americans call editorials and that appear in the general news columns of the newspaper.[21] The practical consequence of this distinction—apart from the fact that one encounters some difficulty in trying to identify Dutch "foreign-affairs reporters"[22]—is that a significant part of Dutch press coverage of Dutch foreign affairs is interpretive rather than factual, written by people who are not fundamentally dependent for their information on government officials, although they do have governmental contacts and may periodically write what Americans would consider a

19. J. J. van Cuilenberg, J. de Jonge, and G. W. Noomen, *"De Tijd" in vijf dimensies* (*De Tijd* in five dimensions), pt. 2 (Amsterdam: Free University, 1973), p. 40.

20. See Burger, *Pers*, pp. 57–58.

21. And although Dutch newspapers claim that they cannot afford to invest in specialization in foreign or defense policy by reporters, they do invest in such specialization by these editors. The *NRC-Handelsblad*, which is frequently characterized as the only Dutch newspaper that is taken seriously by the Dutch foreign-policy public, had in the 1980s eight "foreign editors"—described by one of them as "unique persons entitled to have a judgment."

22. It is not only Americans who have this difficulty: Kees Burger reports a similar experience (*Pers*, pp. 11–12). Burger was also surprised to find that only one-half of his sample of foreign-affairs reporters were part of the foreign-editorial staffs of their newspapers, the other half being part of the parliamentary or "The Hague" staff: "An outsider had perhaps expected that foreign policy as part of government policy . . . would be followed by a departmental or diplomatic correspondent, as is indeed the case in most of the countries around us" (p. 14).

genuine piece of reportage. They do not pound the halls and knock on doors in the Foreign Ministry, as American journalists do. Rather, they work for the most part at home, reading, thinking, perhaps phoning an official whom they know, writing if the muse visits, and not writing if she does not. Since their output is personal and thus explicitly subjective, there is little basis among them for the competitive spirit that animates American coverage of foreign-affairs news and that results in a convergence of judgment of what that "news" is.[23] The move toward interpretive writing by reporters as well as by editors has been a progressive post-World War II development, although observers differ in their attempts to date it. But even one of the sharpest critics of this trend acknowledges that the Dutch tradition is to be concerned with the moral element in foreign affairs and thus that interpretive reporting is partly a continuing phenomenon of this tradition.

The degree of individuality and independent judgment among those who write on foreign policy in the Dutch press is striking, and it is reinforced in many ways. The foreign-affairs reporters and editors have had widely differing professional experiences, which alert them to very different kinds of "news." And they read a very wide variety of foreign newspapers and journals, which further alert them to vastly different issues. These people play different roles within their own news organizations, and there seems to be no common pattern among them or even any agreement on what they are and what they do. For example, the general editor of a national newspaper says that Correspondent A is a "diplomatic correspondent" who covers less news and more background, just like Correspondent B, who works for a different paper. Correspondent B, however, calls himself a "diplomatic editor" but describes his main job as "reporting from the Foreign Ministry and the embassies" and thus as being in competition with ANP (*Algemeen Nederlands Persbureau*—the Dutch Press Association). Yet if he doesn't find a story that interests him on any day, he asserts, "I will stay home and read, or visit the embassies, just to talk; or I might study a longer-term subject I am interested in." Correspondent C is a reporter (American style) for a national paper but functions more like a wire-service reporter, filing four or more stories a day. Yet, unlike his American counterpart(s), "if I see an important story in the morning paper that I did not get, I don't like to work on it—it is nothing; it is out." And, referring to Correspondents A and B, C says, "I do not consider myself a diplomatic correspondent, so I don't regard myself as competing with

23. For an extended discussion of these and other observations of the American foreign-affairs journalists, see Cohen, *Press and Foreign Policy*.

them." But Correspondent D, who has multiple functions in the Dutch media, says, "You should read *The Boys on the Bus*[24] [an archetypal statement of the consequences of the competitive news process in the United States]. It is very much like the way we do it here."[25] These statements suggest an individuality so great as to amount to substantial ignorance of—or indifference to—the way other journalists function in the Netherlands. And there is no evidence of wide personal acquaintanceship among these few correspondents, or even of professional interaction.[26] For example, Correspondent C says, "I'm a loner, I don't want much contact with colleagues outside." In the United States, on the other hand, the uniformity is so great that it would be difficult to find, among a considerably larger corps of foreign-affairs journalists, four such divergent self-assessments or images.

All of these differences in the character of foreign-affairs journalism are reflected in the sense of the "audience" for whom these journalists write. The Americans mostly write news stories for a general audience—for people who are not otherwise connected to the world of foreign affairs and who have little specialized knowledge of it. It is not inconsistent with this orientation, however, that American journalists may also hope to make some contribution to the public discussion of foreign-policy issues and thus to their eventual resolution. But at both the doctrinal and the practical levels, they are motivated by the conviction that "the public ultimately makes foreign policy," and thus they have a substantially undifferentiated audience in mind, variously described as "the intelligent layman" or—in the case of the wire services—"Aunt Minnie in Kenosha," "the milkman in Omaha," or their functional equivalents.

The Dutch journalist's vision of the audience is quite different from this one. Those who work for a news organization with a political or ideological "identity" have a fairly clear idea to start with of the characteristics of those for whom they write. But in a different sense this is also true for all Dutch foreign-affairs journalists, no matter their employer, and it is wholly consistent with the narrow conception of Dutch foreign policy and foreign-policy making I have described. Despite their assertions that in a "depillarized" society they are writing for the

24. Timothy Crouse, *The Boys on the Bus* (New York: Random House, 1973).
25. These contradictions and inconsistencies are reflected also in Burger, *Pers*, who sees pressures toward "pack journalism" among foreign-affairs reporters in the Netherlands even as he stresses the large measure of independence these reporters have to write what they wish.
26. Kaiser, however, reports a large degree of collegiality among parliamentary journalists in The Hague (*Haagse journalistiek*, pp. 67–68).

broadest possible public,[27] these journalists readily acknowledge that the nature of the subject matter is such that only the well-informed, the "foreign-policy elite," will respond to what they write.[28] One senior newspaper editor: "Foreign policy is *not* an important subject here. You know everybody who is involved—the fify to one hundred people who are interested, following foreign policy and writing about it. . . . We all know each other." A journalist (*redacteur*): "I write so that the average reader, if he wants, can understand, but I don't have the illusion that the average reader cares. . . . So you write for yourself—your own standards; maybe you write for your sources. . . . Sometimes you write with a specific aim, someone in the Second Chamber, perhaps." A columnist (in the American sense): "[The reader] is an intelligent, educated man, not necessarily a university graduate but interested. Also, one who, because I confront him with more questions than answers, is willing to think for himself. . . . I am not writing an in-crowd piece, but I may write with a person in mind and hope he reads it."

Journalists and Officials

When we look specifically at the relationships between journalists and foreign-policy officials in these two countries, all the general differences I have been discussing are joined by more specific differences in the way these two elements in the "foreign-policy community" behave toward each other.

To repeat some earlier observations about the foreign-policy structures of these two political systems, journalists in each country are dealing with a different universe of relevant foreign-policy officials. In the United States, there are some forty to fifty agencies of the government that have regular responsibilities that cross international boundaries. But because time constraints compel a division of labor, these agencies cannot all be within the province, or "beat," of the typical foreign-affairs reporter. He or she deals chiefly with the Department of State and beyond that with the foreign embassies in Washington, even though many of the most important foreign-policy developments involve, most obviously, the president, the National Security Council, the Department of Defense, the Department of Energy, the Agency for International Development, the Treasury Department, and the Central Intelligence Agency—not to mention various committees of both houses of the Congress. In the Netherlands, the relevant government

27. See the arguments of Kaiser, *Haagse journalistiek*, p. 93, and Burger, *Pers*, p. 33.
28. See Burger, *Pers*, p. 34.

agencies are the Foreign Ministry (which includes Development Co-operation, the Dutch equivalent of AID), the Defense Ministry, and the Foreign Economic Relations section of the Ministry of Economic Affairs; most of the foreign-affairs journalists cover them all—and sometimes NATO and European Community meetings as well.[29] The minister-president (prime minister) becomes a relevant actor only when the issue involves European institutions of which he or she is a member, when there is an individual ministerial crisis, or when the issue involves, implicitly at least, the future of the whole government—at which point the whole cabinet participates. The differences, for a journalist, are enormous. All the structural elements that might be expected to work in the journalist's favor are more circumscribed: the number of agencies is fewer, the number of individuals is fewer, the range of ideas and the sources of disagreement are fewer—all befitting the Dutch view that there is less foreign policy in the Netherlands.

The size, the character, and the importance of the foreign-policy structure combine to create a world of difference in the significance of "Washington" and "The Hague" to American and Dutch journalists. Washington is an important career assignment for an American foreign-affairs journalist—better, even, than a foreign assignment, since a foreign correspondent has to cover all kinds of news, not just foreign affairs. The Hague, on the other hand, is not considered an important assignment for a Dutch journalist who is perverse enough to want to pursue a career in foreign-affairs journalism. The major national newspapers are located in Amsterdam and Rotterdam, and the proportion of their staffs—in all fields—that is based in The Hague is very small: for example, less than one in ten for one paper that takes national politics and political life very seriously. The Hague foreign-affairs journalists are less a fraternity than their American counterparts in Washington: they cover the same stories infrequently, and they are not often in the same places at the same time. Foreign-affairs stories tend to be Dutch reactions to events abroad; not only do those events differ according to the interests of the journalists and their news organizations, but also the reactions they seek come from all quarters—the political parties, the Second Chamber, the embassies, the ministries, NATO, the European Community—and so their paths do not cross very often. The journalists thus have little occasion—and little opportunity—to get to know each other. Nieuwspoort, a government-run facility for *all* the Dutch (as well as foreign) journalists who cover *all* phases of governmental and political activity

29. Ibid., p. 14.

in The Hague, is small and clubby and, in the absence of a ministerial press conference, rarely crowded.[30]

There is an equally great world of difference in the attitudes that journalists and officials hold with respect to each other in the two countries and in the formal and informal practices that govern their interactions. In the United States these attitudes and practices are characterized generally by equality and antagonism; in the Netherlands, by inequality and cooperation.

The relations between American journalists and American foreign-policy officials are fundamentally the relations between equals. Both intellectually and socially, they meet on more or less common ground.[31] Some journalists are brighter than others, and some come from better schools, but that is equally true of officials. Some journalists with good professional reputations become well known ("famous") and are consequently admired and even sought out by officials, who tend to lead an anonymous existence. Old and strong friendships cross these professional lines, and there is some passage back and forth between the two careers: over the years, a number of journalists have moved into the higher, political levels of the foreign-policy establishment in Washington, and a number of Foreign Service officers have left the service for a life in journalism. Foreign policy is professionally important to both groups, and each side needs the other. The journalist wants to uncover good stories but needs continued good access to do so; the official is interested in "helpful" coverage, which sometimes means no coverage and sometimes means publicity for the official's point of view. The two sides thus meet in mutual hostility and in mutual dependence—a relationship that they themselves sometimes refer to as a "natural antagonism," one that reinforces their fundamental equality. It is therefore to be expected that the journalists will pursue

30. Nieuwspoort was opened in March 1962, after eleven years of effort and many years after the establishment of similar institutions in other western European countries. See H. M. Bleich, " 'U moet de sigaar uit de mond nemen als U met ons spreekt.' Journalist-politicus en Nieuwspoort" (" 'You should take the cigar out of your mouth when you talk with us.' Journalist-politician and Nieuwspoort"), in J. Th. J. van den Berg et al; eds., *Tussen Nieuwspoort en Binnenhof: De jaren 60 als breuklijn in de naoorlogse ontwikkelingen in politiek en journalistiek* (Between Nieuwspoort and the Binnenhof: The sixties as a fault line in the postwar developments in politics and journalism) (The Hague: SDU Uitgeverij, 1989).

31. Even at the highest levels: Walter Lippmann and James Reston, for example, met frequently with the top of the foreign-policy establishment, including presidents. So did the Alsop brothers, Joseph and Stewart, who were members of the Oyster Bay Roosevelt family. For an interesting biography of Lippmann, see Ronald Steele, *Walter Lippmann and the American Century* (Boston: Little, Brown and Co., 1980).

their interest in uncovering good stories with an assertiveness that is limited only by their interest in continued good access and that they will be "fed" by officials for whom timely publicity serves their own policy interests.[32]

The relations between Dutch journalists and Dutch foreign-policy officials are fundamentally the relations between *un*equals. The overwhelming majority of Dutch journalists are regarded—by both officials *and* journalists—as neither intellectually nor socially the equals of officials. The inequalities have many roots: there are the vestiges of an aristocratic past that still cling to the Foreign Ministry—in the words of a journalist, "the *style* of officials is upper-class, even when the people themselves are not"; the Queen's Birthday Honors list annually grants distinction to a large number of Foreign Ministry officials; an appointment to the Foreign Office or to the Foreign Service normally requires a university education and fluency in at least four languages—English, French, and German in addition to Dutch; and officials are better paid, as well as better educated. All of these factors draw a sharp line between the ordinary run of Dutch journalists and the permanent Foreign Office officials.

It is widely agreed that the foreign minister sets a tone for the ministry's relations with the press, and it is also agreed that foreign ministers since Luns have moved away from the latter's patronizing arrogance,[33] if not away from an implicit claim of a superior relationship.[34] But even a few committed believers in "democratization" at the top of the Foreign Ministry make only a little impact on the rest of the rather large and conservative Dutch foreign-policy establishment. It is almost un-

32. See, e.g., the coverage of so-called covert American intelligence operations in Central America during the first half of 1983. Philip Taubman writes: "Information about the plans for covert action was obtained from officials familiar with the preparations who said they oppose expanded U.S. involvement in Central America. The information was confirmed by other administration officials" (*New York Times,* July 25, 1983).

33. Bleich highlights (and exaggerates) the changes in the relationship between Dutch officials and the press after the 1960s by contrasting the imperium of Luns, foreign minister (KVP) from 1956 to 1971, with the democracy of Den Uyl, prime minister (PvdA) from 1973 to 1977: Den Uyl was giving a regular Friday evening press conference in Nieuwspoort when one of the reporters present interrupted: "Louder, I can't understand you." Den Uyl: "You should listen closer: then you can understand me." The reporter: "No, you should take the cigar out of your mouth when you talk with us." The premier "obeyed." Bleich, " 'Sigaar,' " p. 29.

34. When the Netherlands unexpectedly lost out to France as the home for the European Community's new East European Development Bank, the Dutch diplomatic and foreign-policy communities were stunned, but not a word of explanation and not many words of criticism were uttered. As the *NRC-Handelsblad redacteur* put it: "The lid is back again on the information pot" (*NRC-Handelsblad,* May 23, 1990).

thinkable that a Foreign Office official would admire a journalist or envy his notoriety (which is virtually nonexistent anyway). There are only a few exceptions: a few journalists or occasional journalists who have some social distinction, who went to the University at Leiden at the right time, or whose intellectual ability is undeniable.[35] In the words of one of them: "It is hard to reach the minister, but that is normal. But I have no difficulty seeing the others any time I want. _____ and _____ never rebuff me. I will call them at home, in the evenings, and they tell me what I want to know. But I don't do it too often, of course. It is necessary to adapt to their social setting—it is a small inner circle. If you have access to that . . ." Apart from these few exceptions, journalists and officials live in substantially separate personal and professional worlds. Another journalist: "I do not have the impression that many people in the Foreign Ministry have close relations with many reporters. Maybe I just don't know what is going on—but I think I *do*."

The lack of sustained contact and the sense of being patronized create a feeling of antagonism among the Dutch journalists toward officials, but it is more personal animus than an institutional conflict. Whether it is because the stakes are not so high—because foreign policy is not so important to the professional life of the journalist—or because open hostility is unrewarding, the antagonism is suppressed, and the inequality is expressed in the form of deference to authority, of cooperation with the ministry, and of toleration of the secrecy that is the backbone of foreign offices everywhere (but is so universally resisted and frequently broken in the United States). Dutch journalists with long memories speak of a breakdown in deferential behavior; they speak of "overreverence in the past," although they disagree on when their profession stopped being "docile to authority" and began being "impertinent" and even "hostile." Several say it took place a generation ago; another says that "only recently have the media concerned themselves with foreign policy. . . . Go to Hilversum [the home of broadcast journalism] and look: there are no archives, no background, no specialization." But others suggest, in both their words and their behavior, that journalistic deference is alive and well today—"the lid is back again on the information pot." There remains a very large gap between what journalists (and others as well) will say

35. One of these exceptions over the past generation has been J. L. Heldring, former chief editor of the *NRC*, former director of the Netherlands Institute for International Affairs, and still an occasional commentator for the *NRC-Handelsblad*. See also the comments of Burger, *Pers*, p. 31.

about public officials in private and what they will say and write about them in public.

These different attitudes on the part of journalists and foreign-affairs officials in these two countries are mirrored in the formalities of their press relations. For nearly half a century now, the U.S. State Department's press relations have been characterized by continuous and relatively free acess. Since the days of Secretary of State Cordell Hull, there has been a daily press conference in the State Department. The Office of News in the Bureau of Public Affairs and the public-affairs officers in the substantive bureaus serve as the focal points in the organization and presentation of the department's official position on issues and as sources of information of a factual kind. But journalists are expected and even encouraged to go beyond these formal contacts, to go directly to the officials who are dealing with policy matters, if they need additional information. The vast array of journalists who cover the State Department are free to approach anyone, at any time—including, for the more senior correspondents, the more senior officials. Most of the correspondents quickly develop a small stable of officials—usually from six to ten—with whom they are especially close, but they have a larger outer circle of officials whom they can tap as the need arises. The only officials who by department rules may be quoted—who may articulate policy—are those at and above the assistant secretary level. Some lower-level officials use this restriction as an excuse to avoid the press; others, knowing that they will not be quoted, feel free to be regular suppliers of information to journalists. It seems to be personality, not institutional constraint, that determines who in the bureaucracy will be active participants in the department's informal press relations.[36] One of the consequences of this pattern of activity, resting on the structure of mutual dependence and the "natural antagonism" discussed above, is that intragovernmental conflict—disagreements over developing policy, together with personality conflicts and bureaucratic quarrels—is a staple of American foreign-affairs journalism and contributes to the general perspective that the department is a "leaky sieve"—that nothing in it stays secret for very long.

The Dutch Foreign Ministry has no tradition of dealing with the press. Members of the foreign-affairs bureaucracy were apparently not even permitted to have contacts with journalists until the mid-1960s, and, as I have indicated, few have availed themselves of the opportunity since that time. The ministry's Information Service was small, and until recently even it was concerned more with how to avoid the press

36. Cohen, *Press and Foreign Policy,* pp. 154–58.

than with how to increase contact with it. In the 1970s the Development Cooperation section of the ministry developed an active Press Office, using its large budget to develop a constituency on behalf of its foreign-aid policies. A high official in the ministry: "That press divison has a lot of money, since it can use the Development Cooperation budget. They will fly reporters to UNCTAD (United Nations Commission on Trade and Development) meetings. You get a closed circle of prodevelopment people in and out of government, with lots of money, who are a pressure group on behalf of development aid." Only under the pressure of this competition did the ministry begin to revise its thinking about its Information Service. It, too, began to put journalists into the empty seats on the government plane taking the foreign minister to international conferences, in the hope of educating the media in foreign affairs and encouraging them to pay some attention to the subject.

But this formal initiative has not had a great impact either on the ministry's overall approach to the media or on the response of the media. A senior official in Development Cooperation, in 1990: "The Foreign Ministry has never caught up with Development Cooperation in public information. There is no contest. We have the money; they don't." The Information Service holds a weekly "briefing," at which one or two officials make a presentation on a subject, and periodic special briefings prior to important international meetings. Neither of these kinds of briefings normally attracts much attention from the press corps; one journalist remarked that the ministry had difficulty filling the weekly briefing with something substantial—an observation supported by the fact that there is no detectable increase in the number of articles or news about foreign-affairs issues in the twenty-four hours following these weekly events. Yet Dutch journalists who cover foreign affairs begin their inquiries at the ministry's Information Service; the official spokespersons—ordinarily career diplomats—are the initial and often the major source of information.[37] Officials will stress that their *friends* in the press will call them, usually at home, but that this is exceptional and that they hear only rarely from other re-

37. See Burger, *Pers*, p. 65: "The bulk of the foreign policy journalists seems in any case not dissatisfied with the functioning of the departmental information."

Kaiser's comments about Dutch parliamentary journalists, which describe a relatively passive newsgathering process, seem to hold for foreign-affairs journalists: "Naturally there is rivalry among 'colleagues,' [but] because newsgathering in The Hague is for a great part very uniform and routine—communiqués available for everyone at the same time, gatherings, press conferences, etc. take place at previously announced times or are announced to all at the same time—it is not often that really great scoops can be had" (*Haagse journalistiek*, p. 65).

porters. A Hague-based foreign-affairs journalist of some twenty years' standing claimed that it took him at least ten years to break through this shell and get "a good look inside the system." And a diplomatic "editor" observed that no Dutch journalist—"not even from the *NRC-Handelsblad*"—places a daily call to the Foreign Ministry. "If you need deeper knowledge [than you get at the briefing], you have to make your own appointments. That is not always possible. You can't make an appointment each week with the director-general of European Affairs; he is just too busy for that. You see these people by chance, or occasionally."[38] The practice of holding off-the-record lunch or dinner meetings with journalists, which is common in the United States, is almost nonexistent in the Netherlands; there are too few journalists with the necessary standing, for one thing. And there is still no broad view within the Foreign Ministry that the media could serve the purpose of the government's foreign policy and thus that their cultivation is worthwhile.[39]

It should be clear from all of the above that there is no clearly defined foreign-policy "beat" for Dutch journalists. Some of them write from their own knowledge, reading, and reflection, some from the security of the Foreign Ministry's Information Service; a few go further afield, consulting (in declining order of importance[40]) the foreign-affairs specialists of the larger party fractions in the Parliament, ministry officials, a few respected "action groups," and diplomats in a few of the large embassies.[41]

One major consequence of this pattern of attitudes and activity among Dutch officials and journalists is that coverage of policy development and the attendant conflicts—whether bureaucratic, policy, or

38. See also Burger, *Pers*, p. 68.

39. For a rare and unusual public criticism of the Foreign Ministry's press relations, see J. C. F. Bletz, "Pers en buitenlands beleid" (Press and foreign policy), *Internationale Spectator* 30(6): 338–42 (1976), and the subsequent exchange between Bletz and Dr. J. Sizoo, "Commentaar: Buitenlands beleid en de pers" (Comment: Foreign policy and the press), *Internationale Spectator* 30 (8): 482–88 (1976). At the time, Bletz was "diplomatic correspondent" for the newspaper *Het Parool*; Sizoo was in the Foreign Ministry.

40. Burger, *Pers*, pp. 65–68.

41. The paucity of Burger's respondents reflects the small population of Dutch foreign-affairs journalists, but his descriptions of their "consultations" suggest attitudes at considerable variance from those of their American counterparts: "A few journalists state that . . . contacts with [Ministry] officials are much more valuable than the official policy information services"; "Some reporters also intimated that they make inquiries of diplomats or other embassy personnel. This contact, however, is described by these reporters as not of the greatest interest" (*Pers*, pp. 65, 68). In the U.S., almost *all* foreign-affairs reporters make, and value, such contacts. See Cohen, *Press and Foreign Policy*, Chapter 3.

personality—among officials and ministries (which I have called a sta-ple of American foreign-affairs journalism) is rare in Dutch foreign-affairs journalism. Officials do not "leak" these things to the media; a very highly regarded official in the Foreign Ministry stated categori-cally that he had never used a particular contact with a journalist to promote a particular purpose. Junior officials do not ordinarily talk to the press, and if they do they say nothing that senior officials have not said. The journalists, on their part, do not probe for leaks or try to elicit the expression of conflicting views within the ministry: one does not intrude, and one husbands one's limited contacts for more important things. And when information about such disagreements is known among journalists, deference to authority means that it is not often treated as "news." There have been just a few stories of this sort in recent years, and they have created quite a stir,[42] but they are still re-garded as exceptional.

Journalists and Legislatures

The American Congress and the Dutch Parliament are less important than their respective governments in the formulation and execution of foreign affairs, and thus they command less attention from the media in both countries in their coverage of this subject. Yet the relationships between media and legislature in the two countries are not much alike: the legislatures differ too much, both in their political-system functions and in the particular ways in which they deal with foreign policy.

The American Congress is not, in the crunch, a match for the execu-tive branch in the foreign-policy field, even though members of both

42. I have made reference earlier to the ill-concealed disagreements between Foreign Minister Van den Broek (CDA) and Development Cooperation Minister Pronk (PvdA) over policies toward Indonesia in the Third Lubbers Cabinet, beginning in 1989. The foreign minister's quiet acceptance of the European Community's decision not to site the East European Development Bank in the Netherlands, after weeks of very public competi-tion to win the institution for Amsterdam, led one unnamed official to express his aston-ishment to a journalist, who was himself astonished because, as he put it, in the Foreign Ministry one does not readily speak ill of the minister (*NRC-Handelsblad*, May 23, 1990).

Philip P. Everts, ed., *Controversies at Home: Domestic Factors in the Foreign Policy of the Netherlands* (Dordrecht: Martinus Nijhoff, 1985) refers occasionally to policy conflicts within the government, e.g., pp. 163ff, but it is not always clear whether or how much of those conflicts were matters of public knowledge at the time. In any event, the major focus of the eleven foreign-policy case studies in that volume is on the policy conflicts that existed between the government and political parties, Parliament, and interest groups, as reported in the press, rather than on any conflicts that might have existed within the government or the Foreign Ministry.

houses have from time to time claimed superior information, if not superior wisdom.[43] But the Congress has made substantial efforts since the late 1960s to increase its importance and its assertiveness in foreign affairs.[44] The net effect of those efforts has been to create a significantly greater level of expertise in the Congress, both among the members themselves, some of whom have developed substantial reputations in particular substantive areas, and among greatly enlarged committee and personal staffs. Hearings and debates on foreign-policy issues in the House and Senate are both frequent and important occurrences, with the consequence that there are more than a few contacts on Capitol Hill who are worth a journalist's time to cultivate.[45] While the foreign-affairs "beat" in Washington is still the State Department and the embassies, the congressional journalists willy-nilly do a considerable amount of foreign-affairs reporting.

As I have indicated earlier, foreign-affairs expertise in the Dutch Parliament is severely limited and is found mainly in the Standing Commissions (Committees) on Foreign Affairs and Defense. Each political party will put its substantively most knowledgeable Second Chamber member (more than one, in the case of the larger parties) on these two committees, but "most knowledgeable" may not be very knowledgeable when the parties are not large to begin with or when the foreign-affairs or defense specialists in a particular party have decided for some reason not to stand for Parliament.[46] And because of the pervasive judgment that foreign policy is not at the center of politics in the Netherlands, there is little incentive for

43. Before World War II, for example, Senator Hiram Johnson publicly asserted that his sources of information were better than those of the secretary of state, and just prior to the Cuban missile crisis in 1962 Senator Kenneth Keating argued that he was better informed about Soviet missile emplacement in Cuba than was the administration—although his sources were apparently from *within* the administration. See Graham T. Allison, *Essence of Decision: Explaining the Cuban Missile Crisis* (Boston: Little, Brown and Co., 1971), p. 192.

44. For a good summary of these changes, see Cecil V. Crabb and Pat M. Holt, *Invitation to Struggle: Congress, the President, and Foreign Policy* (Washington, D. C.: Congressional Quarterly Press, 1980).

45. And, since policy expertise is an important component of reputation and power in the Congress among both members and staff, there are incentives for these new foreign-policy specialists to make themselves available to the press. Former representative Stephen Solarz and Senator Sam Nunn are but two examples. Richard Perle was regarded as a particularly astute congressional staff member before he was asked to join President Reagan's Department of Defense.

46. See, e.g., M. C. P. M. van Schendelen, "Het parlement" (The Parliament), in R. B. Andeweg, A. Hoogerwerf, and J. J. A. Thomassen, eds., *Politiek in Nederland* (Politics in the Netherlands), 3d ed. (Alphen aan den Rijn: Samsom Uitgeverij, 1989), pp. 189–211.

bright and ambitious politicians to concentrate on foreign policy in or out of Parliament.

On the staff side, the picture is no better: the Foreign Affairs Committee has no staff of its own. Reflecting the way that work is done in the Dutch Second Chamber, staff resources are assigned to the party fractions, to the individual members, and to the Chamber as a whole but not to its committees. There are about ten clerks for the whole Second Chamber, and all the standing and ad hoc committees, about forty in number, have to share their services.[47] One journalist mentioned three parliamentary "experts in foreign policy and defense" as news sources and, after a little reflection, added two more, complaining that "the level of education is low among Second Chamber members." Another, reflecting his own political orientation, asserted that "there are only a few whom you can take seriously, and they are especially in the Labor Party." A third was even less generous, stating categorically (if not quite fairly), "No one in the Second Chamber knows anything about foreign policy. All they know are the ideas of certain ministers."[48]

Since the Dutch parliamentary committees do not have legislative functions, their hearings serve other purposes: they are modes of access for interest groups, points of contact between parliamentarians and ministers, educational forums for the public. A very few persistent journalists will follow these hearings on special topics as another potential source of news—or, at least, of information.

In the absence of major staff support, the foreign-policy specialists in the Dutch Second Chamber have to develop their own sources of information on foreign policy. These include their own political parties, the government itself, individuals in international organizations and in foreign embassies, and public sources such as interest groups, foreign newspapers, and Dutch newspapers. I put Dutch papers last because that is the way they are generally evaluated. The few Dutch members of

47. These are mid-1980s figures. See Van Schendelen, "Het parlement," p. 195. In all, there are about 400 staff members to help a body of 150 representatives. (The First Chamber, which has 75 members and meets only one day a week, has another 41 staff members on regular service and another 12 who work only on meeting days.) By contrast, the 535 members of the U.S. House and Senate enjoy the staff assistance of about 30,000 people.

48. E. C. M. Jurgens, a former chair of NOS (the Dutch radio-TV news broadcasting organization), argues that the parliamentary journalist, who has to cover the full range of issues that come up during the day, has a much harder job than the member of Parliament, who can specialize in only a few subjects. Dutch parliamentarians, like their American counterparts, find out from the newspapers and the evening news programs on television what happened that day among their colleagues in the legislative body. See R. Koole, ed., *Binnenhof binnenste buiten* (*The Binnenhof inside out*) (Weesp: De Haan, 1986), p. 98, and Cohen, *Press and Foreign Policy*, chapter 7.

Parliament who are knowledgeable and active in the foreign-policy field have the same opinion of the Dutch media as the media have of Parliament as a whole: they believe that their quality is low and that they pay little attention to foreign affairs (and to the parliamentary debates on foreign affairs).[49] These members of Parliament assess the Dutch press in a rather singular fashion: "One Dutch paper: *NRC-Handelsblad*"; "*NRC* is the only serious one"; "*NRC* is relatively the best one."

Perhaps the most important service that newspapers (domestic and foreign) perform for Dutch members of Parliament is to bring to light matters, or details of matters, that are not public knowledge and that can then serve as the basis for questions the members can put to the ministers. This may be purposive, on either side: Dutch journalists sometimes have an interest in performing that function, since it gives *them* some publicity and brings out further information they can use in pursuing the story at issue. And it is sometimes occasioned by a member, who works with a journalist to create a story and thus a public basis for a parliamentary question.[50] Much more often, however, it is not purposive: a journalist will report on the activities or the views of an action group, for example, having come across information that has not been provided before either by the government or by the media. Parliamentarians will then react to the news story, using it as the starting point for parliamentary interrogation.[51] Whatever the source, however, and whatever the motivation, the media in this manner have at least a sporadic impact on the focusing of foreign-policy attention.

Media Impacts on the Foreign-Policy Environment

Given these many and substantial differences in the way the media cover foreign policy in the United States and the Netherlands, we

49. In Kaiser's study, nearly one-third of the sample of general parliamentarians (i.e., those not specialized in foreign policy) thought that the parliamentary journalists were superficial. See Kaiser, *Haagse journalistiek*, p. 75.

50. See Kaiser, *Haagse journalistiek*, pp. 139–40; and Burger, *Pers*, p. 54. Since this is regarded as an unnecessarily roundabout way for a parliamentarian to get information, it must be assumed that on these occasions the questions are designed for political advantage. Burger (p. 55) describes it as a way to put a subject on the political agenda and adds that the same thing is achieved when a journalist interviews a parliamentarian. Burger refers to these as interactions between "friendly" journalists and parliamentarians, but Kaiser (pp. 123–24) reports that there are very few real friendships between journalists and members. Personal relationships are limited to *een hapje en een glasje*—a bite and a drink in a cafe.

51. "Almost all parliamentarians said they had done this repeatedly, regularly to very often" (Kaiser, *Haagse journalistiek*, p. 140). For a concrete example, see *NRC-Handelsblad*, May 23, 1990.

should expect to find corresponding differences in their impact on their respective policy environments. In the Department of State, officials absorb the media that are readily available to them: the major newspapers of the major Eastern cities and the cable and network television news, with some additional specialized attention to international wire services. But the American media dominate, and within the American media, the coverage that is effectively "nationalized" commands the attention of those who pay attention and dominates their discussion. In this respect, the American media play an "agenda-setting" role, imposing on foreign-policy officials a set of priorities and perspectives that are frequently different from the priorities and perspectives that would otherwise inform their judgment.[52] Thus the media, in the ordinary exercise of their craft, become important public actors on the foreign-policy stage. What bothers *them* and what *they* think bothers the public end up bothering the foreign-policy establishment. The ordinary members of Congress share with foreign-policy officials the same set of newspapers and the same set of television newscasts. Consequently, there is a strong sense among American legislators, even those not on the foreign-affairs committees, that they know enough about what is going on to be able to mount a challenge to the administration if they see political advantage in doing so.

Dutch Foreign Ministry officials live in a substantially different media environment. Their own newspapers contain little news about Dutch foreign affairs and even less that effectively dominates national discussion. The Dutch media as a consequence only very rarely play an agenda-setting role in foreign affairs, and they make no major contribution of their own to any ongoing public debate about foreign policy.[53] Their contribution to the parliamentary interrogation of ministers is not the same as "agenda setting," because it has a limited, often accidental, random, even idiosyncratic character; it is the result not of a widespread and persistent media focus on an issue but, rather, of an individual's success in raising a flag—and it is often a minor flag at that. To the

52. See, e.g., Bernard C. Cohen, "The Influence of Special-Interest Groups and Mass Media on Security Policy in the United States," in Charles W. Kegley, Jr., and Eugene R. Wittkopf, eds., *Perspectives on American Foreign Policy* (New York: St. Martin's Press, 1983), pp. 222–41.

53. One looks in vain for evidence to the contrary. To judge from the cases discussed in Everts, ed., *Controversies at Home*, the media report on party criticism of and parliamentary debate on the government's handling of foreign-policy issues and are occasionally themselves critics of decisions (e.g., pp. 169, 175), but they do not play an active, independent role in public discussions prior to foreign-policy decisions. To the extent that there is any such discussion, it is invariably led by spokespersons for political parties.

extent that there *is* an agenda, it is set elsewhere: in the Foreign Ministry itself—and in the political parties that comprise the governing coalition and staff the ministry—if not in Washington, Brussels, or Bonn.

Foreign-policy officials and parliamentary foreign-affairs specialists in the Netherlands read a large assortment, as well as a large number, of newspapers and journals. Everyone will read upwards of two Dutch newspapers a day to know what is going on in the Dutch political community. But to know what is going on in the world of foreign affairs—for more extensive coverage—they read the foreign press: *Le Monde*, the *International Herald Tribune*, the *Frankfurter Allgemeine Zeitung*, the *Times* of London, the *Economist*, *Die Zeit*, and *Newsweek*, to name the more important.[54] To the limited extent that these media suggest any common priorities and preferences, they are foreign, or international, in character. Dutch officials and, to a lesser extent, parliamentary specialists are likely thus to be substantially better informed about the foreign-policy thinking of foreign than of domestic foreign-policy communities.[55]

Beyond the few foreign-policy specialists in the Dutch Second Chamber, however, members of Parliament in the Netherlands are not exposed to the same sources of information or to the same media as are the ministers or the officials in the Foreign Ministry. The ability of parliamentarians to read a wide range of foreign newspapers is much more limited, and their incentives to pursue other sources of foreign-affairs information are virtually nil. Consequently, their capacity to challenge the foreign minister, at least on the details of policy, is quite restricted.

Despite these very substantial differences, the media in both the U.S. and the Netherlands do contribute one thing in common: they serve as a mirror or a reflection of what officials refer to as "public opinion." In the words of a high official in the Dutch Foreign Ministry, "If the press functions correctly, it reflects what is being thought and said by well-informed public opinion on matters of public interest." But even this one common function seems to disappear as one looks more closely at it: for one thing, the *interest* of Dutch officials in that "public opinion" is different from that of their American counterparts; for another, the constituent parts of that "public opinion" differ between the

54. Burger's responses to inquiries on this subject were much like mine: see Burger, *Pers*, pp. 69–70.

55. There is another set of publications—an "elite press"—in both countries, exemplified by *Foreign Affairs* in the U.S. and by *Internationale Spectator* in the Netherlands, which I leave out of consideration here. They are important journals, but they are not mass media; hence, they serve a different function even for their policy-making readers.

two countries. Since these differences are central to our understanding of media participation in foreign policy in the two countries, it is appropriate to conclude this chapter with that closer look.

At some level of abstraction, all democratic officials—and perhaps officials in all political systems—want to know what is being thought and said by well-informed outsiders on matters of public interest. But their *reasons* for wanting to know may vary significantly, even spectacularly. American officials follow the press closely because they meet the press regularly, and they want to know what is on the minds of reporters—what questions they will be asking, what priorities they will be following. And because these officials know that all the other participants in the foreign-policy process, foreign and domestic, are also reading the American press, they want to be ready for the questions these people will be asking. And beneath it all, of course, there is the foreign-policy bureaucracy's continuing interest in what I have elsewhere called "active and reactive manipulation": preventing some fires and putting others out.[56] Officials in the White House are naturally interested in how the president is doing, how he is being perceived and evaluated; officials in the State Department have a comparable, though less vital, concern for their secretary. But in neither case does a great deal ordinarily ride on particular foreign-policy items: there is so much going on, for one thing, in both foreign and domestic policy, and there is usually a good buffer of time and circumstance before the president has to give electoral considerations top priority.

But in the Netherlands, where foreign policy resides in the Foreign Ministry and where the effectiveness and thus the political future of the minister may ride on the evaluation of his handling of particular issues, there is enormous concern among his top advisers for the way he and the ministry are discussed in the media. In this respect, the foreign minister's situation is more comparable to the American president's than to that of the secretary of state. One of the reasons the foreign minister's advisers read such a diversity of Dutch newspapers is that they never know who may be planting a land mine or where. An official in the European divison: "When I read something in the paper, even a very small mention of a Dutch citizen jailed in Country X for what the press calls 'political reasons,' it rings a bell: be on the alert! It is not yet a question of whether it will be blown up to a case. But you have to be sensitive to whether it might develop into something that will touch the foreign minister, the ministry, or even the government. . . .

56. Bernard C. Cohen, *The Public's Impact on Foreign Policy* (Boston: Little, Brown and Co., 1973), pp. 166–83.

There may be questions in the Parliament, pressure in [the party]." The minister's and the ministry's concern for public sentiment that may trigger a reaction within the minister's own political party (which may not be the same as the prime minister's party) is ever-present and has no direct parallel in the United States. But there is also a concern among Dutch officials for "active and reactive manipulation," to a degree that would make them feel at home in Washington. The weekly press briefings in The Hague are explicit attempts publicly to establish the ministry's view of policy matters.[57] These words by a high official are a good example of "reactive manipulation": "We follow the press closely, to see whether we are in touch with public opinion or whether we should do something to bring opinion back closer to us."

Finally, the ingredients of "public opinion" that one finds in the media are not the same in the Netherlands and in the U.S., and the difference reflects some of the fundamental differences in the media themselves and in politically relevant external opinion that I have discussed earlier. American newspapers are dominated by the striving for objectivity; expressions of opinion are reserved for the editorial page and for the "op-ed" page, where some balance is usually sought among the views expressed. In many newspapers, the "op-ed" page is occupied mainly by nationally syndicated columnists representing a variety of opinions. Altogether, the newspaper is the work of journalists, and the opinions expressed are mainly the opinions of journalists. The exceptions are few and not very important: letters to the editor, news stories about organizations or individuals with foreign-policy opinions, and even reports of public-opinion polls. Overall, the press in the United States represents the participation of journalists in the policy process. Beyond that, as I have argued earlier, it is difficult to know whose opinions on foreign-policy questions *are* politically relevant. Although the nation's foreign-policy leadership may have some views on that matter, there is no easy way for the press to share those views, and both the leadership and the ordinary consumer of the products of journalism in the United States have a difficult time trying to fathom the effective or important structures of public opinion on foreign-policy questions from the media themselves.

The Dutch national newspapers, as I noted earlier, operate on a smaller scale, having neither the staff nor the amount of domestic news to fill many pages. Beyond that, the traditions of Dutch journalism encourage the expressions of political opinion, contributing to the "identi-

57. Although a high official in the ministry said to me, after I attended one of these briefings, "We are not very forthcoming, are we?"

ties" of the separate papers. In keeping with these circumstances and traditions, the columns of Dutch newspapers are open to the Dutch "elite," those members of the political community who have views on topics of contemporary public and political interest and who want to express them. And the papers themselves make a special effort to report the views of social organizations and groups, particularly when these nongovernmental institutions fill gaps in the information provided by the government. Where the American newspaper is sometimes called by policy officials "a daily referendum," it is a referendum of journalists. The Dutch press, and Dutch television too, however, can be said to represent more broadly and on a continuing basis the politically articulate stratum of Dutch society. The Dutch government, as a consequence, is somewhat better served by its press than is the American government by its press, at least to the point where the Dutch government is more likely to be kept alert and less likely to be taken by surprise in terms of political reactions to foreign-policy issues. Both governments, however, need to turn to the structure of social organizations in their countries, as well as to their legislative bodies and to their media, for a broader sense of the political response to foreign-policy issues.

6
Interest Groups

Interest groups, in the largest sense of the term, are ubiquitous in both the United States and the Netherlands. American politicians from the Founding Fathers to the present day have inveighed against "the spirit of faction" and special interest. Given the problems of definition as well as the constant mutation of such organizations, no one has seriously tried to count their numbers, but handbooks of organizations in quite narrow fields frequently list them in the tens of thousands.[1] The situation is, proportionately, not greatly different in the Netherlands: one recent study says that there are approximately three thousand Dutch interest organizations representing the Dutch business community in Brussels alone.[2] I want to look here first at the place that interest groups in general occupy in the American and Dutch political systems and then more specifically at the position and the activities of foreign-policy interest groups in the two countries. Groups active in foreign affairs are a tiny fraction of the universe of political interest groups in both countries; nevertheless, they are a visible part of the political environment for the Dutch and American foreign-policy makers.

1. See, e.g., *National Trade and Professional Associations of the United States*, 20th ed. (Washington, D.C.: Columbia Books, 1993), and Susan B. Martin, ed., *Encyclopedia of Associations* (Detroit: Gale Research, 1990). Dealing only with nonprofit membership organizations, Martin covers nearly forty-eight thousand organizations.
2. See M. P. C. M. van Schendelen, ed., *Nederlandse lobby's in Europa* (*Dutch lobbies in Europe*) (The Hague: SDU Uitgeverij, 1993). And in a recent Dutch symposium on lobbying, the mayor of The Hague reported that there were about ten thousand American lobbyists living and working in Washington (A. J. E. Havermans, "Den Haag en lobby" [The Hague and lobbying] in E. Denig, T. Michels, D. Sijbrandij, and H. J. Smittenaar, eds., *Het gebeurt in Den Haag: Een open boekje over lobby* [It happens in The Hague: An open book about lobbying] [The Hague: SDU Uitgeverij, 1988], p. 34).

Organized Groups in Dutch and American Politics

In the United States, interest groups—despite the obvious clout of some and the ease of participation for all—have no formal role in the governing process and hence may be said to be on the "outside," looking in. This is reflected in the extensive literature on such groups, which focuses on their efforts to reach and to influence policy makers and hence public policy itself.[3] It is also significant that—despite (or because of) the Federalist Papers—it is the media and not interest groups that are called the "Fourth Estate" or the "Fourth Branch" of government.[4] And no one, I believe, has yet proposed that interest groups be called the "Fifth Branch."

The relationship between organized groups in American society and the policy-making institutions of government draws much of its character from the nature of constituency in the United States. The American electoral system, with single-member districts, creates a fixed and determinate constituency for every elected member of the Congress, and, of course, the president is elected by the aggregation of majorities or pluralities in fifty separate constituencies. Elected officials need to be sensitive to the wishes of groups among their constituents, and they may want the political or the financial support offered by groups located elsewhere. But except for the president they do not need and cannot use whatever votes such groups may claim to "control" outside their districts. Two consequences flow from this: first, interest groups base their political strategies on where they find themselves within this network of geographic constituency and political and financial dependence; second, where elected officials are insulated from the importuning of interest groups—and most of the time they are—they can safely ignore them. It is this structural conflict between interest groups and electoral constituencies that puts the interest groups in the position of outsiders looking in.[5]

The relationship between interest groups and nonelected officials is shaped by the constituency factor mostly when the president's political interests are engaged; otherwise, it tends to be shaped by the varying needs of the officials for support within the bureaucracy or for spe-

---

3. See, e.g., V.O. Key, *Politics, Parties and Pressure Groups*, 5th ed. (New York: Crowell, 1964), and Lester W. Milbrath, "Interest Groups and Foreign Policy," in James N. Rosenau, ed., *Domestic Sources of Foreign Policy* (New York: Free Press, 1967), pp. 231–51.

4. See, e.g., Douglass Cater, *The Fourth Branch of Government* (Boston: Houghton Mifflin Co., 1959).

5. It also accounts for interest-group strategies that focus on electoral constituencies as a means of reaching elected officials.

cialized information or contacts, or even by individual conceptions of responsiveness to the public. These relationships may on occasion be quite close, as, for example, in cases where interest-group representatives have been brought into an administration in key positions or in good numbers.[6] And I have referred in an earlier chapter to the structural and historical factors that drove the State Department into establishing a bureau to develop and manage a continuing relationship with nongovernmental groups interested in foreign policy.[7]

Interest groups in the Netherlands have a position that is formally rather closer to the policy-making authority than is that of their American counterparts: while many Dutch groups are outside looking in and longing for the kind of access others enjoy, a few are very well ensconced inside—more comfortably so even than the most favored American interest groups. A Dutch news journal has recently referred to Dutch interest groups collectively as the "Third Chamber," following the upper (First) and lower (Second) chambers of the Dutch parliament[8]—an attribution of power more significant than that inherent in the placing of American interest groups somewhere below the "Fourth Branch."

The nature of "constituency" is as important a part of the Dutch setting for interest groups as it is for the American, but in a very different way. I have discussed earlier the Dutch system of proportional representation.[9] The Dutch parliamentarians represent a share of the national vote for their party, but they would be hard put to identify any of their supporters other than the party activists. In principle this system favors the political parties as the organized expression of public views, and it has been defended, as I have noted, as a way to maximize the representation of diverse views. In practice, however, there has historically been a competing practical definition of constituency in Dutch politics—a recognition that while parties are a tested means of public

6. The Reagan administration was well staffed by members of the Committee on the Present Danger, an interest group pressing for a stronger military posture vis-à-vis the Soviet Union. The Carter administration was also home to many members of the Trilateral Commission, a private international group seeking to redirect thinking on international economic policy away from the unilateralism of the Nixon administration. See Bernard C. Cohen, "The Influence of Special-Interest Groups and Mass Media on Security Policy in the United States," in Charles W. Kegley, Jr., and Eugene R. Wittkopf, eds., *Perspectives on American Foreign Policy* (New York: St. Martin's Press, 1983), pp. 222–41.

7. See Chapter 2.

8. Eric Vrijsen, "De Derde Kamer: Nederlands machtigste college bestuurt in stilte" (The Third Chamber: The Netherland's most powerful board governs secretly), *Elsevier*, January 11, 1992, pp. 10–15.

9. See Chapter 1 and Chapter 4.

choice in a democracy, there are still important interests in society that are not always well represented by political parties and that sometimes need to organize to represent themselves. The political strength of interest groups varies from time to time, as social circumstances or the strength of parties changes.[10] But in the ordinary course interest groups are sufficiently important that parliamentarians as well as ministers have to pay attention to them.[11]

Dutch culture, history, and tradition all help to shape an environment in which interest groups can flourish. I have noted earlier[12] the historical pervasiveness of the various "pillars" in Dutch society and the apparent influence they have had in discouraging individual in favor of group political action. Although the pillars have largely crumbled over the last generation, the constraints on individual-level activity seem to be still in place. A recent analysis of Dutch politics observes that though Dutch society may be extremely permissive politically, it has not developed a "participant culture."[13]

World War II gave added impetus to the heritage of pillarization

10. Throughout the 1970s and 1980s, when parties were losing their hold on Dutch voters, interest groups were unusually successful in their public campaigns; they frequently showed their independence from the parties, sometimes refusing them permission to participate in forthcoming events. After the large peace demonstration in Amsterdam in November 1981, the Secretary of the Interchurch Peace Council (IKV), which organized the demonstration, told reporters, "It is the task of the peace movement to turn into political currency the skepticism of the people with respect to the politicians." Similarly independent attitudes were reflected in the positions of the Angola Committee after its successes in the mid-1970s.

The party perspective is well revealed in an essay by Theo Brinkel, of the Scientific Institute of the CDA: Brinkel is exceedingly critical of Pax Christi for its adoption of a pressure-group model in the peace movement, presuming (in his view) that it knew better than a large and principled political party ("Beginselpartij en pressiegroep" [A party of principle and a pressure group], in B. Schennink, M. Becker, H. Bos, and C. Arends, eds., *In Beweging voor de Vrede: Veertig jaar Pax Christi: Geschiedenis, werkwijze, achterban en invloed* [In movement for peace: Pax Christi's forty years: History, methods, supporters, and influence] [Nijmegen: Studiecentrum voor Vredesvraagstukken, Katholieke Universiteit Nijmegen, 1988], pp. 137–46).

11. Peter R. Baehr writes that "close and regular contact with private organizations and with the most concerned departmental officials is essential for the effective functioning of a member of parliament" ("Het parlement en het buitenlands beleid" [The parliament and foreign policy], in Th. C. de Graaf, D. A. van der Hoeven, and P. J. Langenberg, eds., *Omtrent het Parlement: Opstellen over parlement en democratisch bestuur* [Concerning Parliament: Essays about parliament and democratic control] [Utrecht: Uitgeverij Veen, 1985], p. 214).

12. See Chapter 2.

13. Jacques J. A. Thomassen and Jan W. van Deth, "How New Is Dutch Politics?" *West European Politics* 12 (1): 70–73 (January 1989).

and to "ancient pluralist traditions" as the sources both of the "exceedingly dense network of groups"[14] and of the high degree of corporatism that characterizes Dutch society and politics, whereby interest groups representing important elements in the divided polity participate in the formulation of core policies. Long before the war, each of the pillars had developed its own pressure groups to ensure that its interests were adequately represented, ordinarily through its own political party.[15] After the war, the needs of reconstruction were so great that special efforts were made to secure the participation of a broad range of elite groups in major decisions, mostly of an economic and social character.[16] The governments of the day—and since—used a new phrase, *negotiating partners*, to describe the groups they worked with officially in the creation of policy. The Social-Economic Council, on which labor unions and employers' groups sat with government officials, became a model of sorts for the subsequent discussion of major issues in the Netherlands, including foreign-policy issues.[17] The pillars have crumbled and the postwar reconstruction has long since been accomplished, but groups that are thought to be politically "important" still find the door open for them. Oddly enough, the processes of depillarization allowed for the creation of still more organizations, attracting people to new issues from old pillars and old parties.[18] And the challenge for all sorts of groups, especially newer ones, is to be regarded as sufficiently important politically to acquire some sort of entrée, official or unofficial. I will take up the question of how this works in the foreign-policy field later in this chapter.

The official justification for the close contact between ministries and interest groups is that "social organizations can contribute importantly to the executability of the political decisions which are taken in

14. H. Daalder, "The Mould of Dutch Politics: Themes for Comparative Inquiry," *West European Politics* 12 (1): 15 (January 1989).

15. See, for example, H. van Goor, "Politieke participatie van collectiviteiten: pressiegroepen" (Political participation of collectivities: pressure groups), in R. B. Andeweg, A. Hoogerwerf, and J. J. A. Thomassen, *Politiek in Nederland* (Politics in the Netherlands), 3d ed. (Alphen aan den Rijn: Samsom Uitgeverij, 1989), p. 104.

16. See Vrijsen, "De Derde Kamer."

17. See, for example, Thomas R. Rochon, *Mobilizing for Peace: The Antinuclear Movements in Western Europe* (Princeton: Princeton University Press, 1988), p. 164.

18. See J. G. Siccama, "The Netherlands Depillarized: Security Policy in a New Domestic Context," in Gregory Flynn, ed., *NATO's Northern Allies: The National Security Policies of Belgium, Denmark, the Netherlands, and Norway* (Totowa, N. J.: Rowman and Allanheld, 1985), esp. p. 135, and R. A. Koole, "Political Parties Going Dutch: Party Finances in the Netherlands," *Acta Politica* 25 (1): 37–65 (1990).

The Hague."[19] Although that is undoubtedly true, there are other reasons for government ministries to support the existing contacts, reasons that have contributed to a growing dissatisfaction with the way the system works. So long as the government could point to extensive contacts with a particular set of important groups—such as trade unions, Amnesty International, or advisory groups of its own creation, to name just a few—which share its basic view of the world, it could safely ignore the views of those who had contrary interests.[20] And there can be no doubt that the pattern of government interaction with social organizations heavily favored the Dutch elite for many years, taking place as it did within "closed circuits."[21] It was not at all uncommon in the Netherlands over the last generation to find individuals who were simultaneously active in a wide variety of leading institutions—research organizations, the media, universities, business, political parties, church or other prominent social groups—and who also sat on governmental advisory boards.[22] Although the circuits have become more open, or at least less closed, in recent years, the Dutch elite, both informal and formal, is still considerably less permeable than the American elite. Furthermore, individuals within the circuits are widely seen by those outside—and increasingly by colleagues within—as having been co-opted: as one of them put it, "It is very difficult to challenge policy from the outside when some part of you is on the inside." Not only is criticism muted in these circumstances; issues are also depoliticized—a matter of concern for discerning parliamentarians, who see their own role being adversely affected.[23]

19. P. C. de Man, "Hoe open is een department?" (How open is a department?), in Denig et al., eds., *Het gebeurt in Den Haag*, p. 75. At the time in which he participated in this symposium on lobbying, de Man was the secretary-general of the Ministry of Defense.

20. See Van Goor, "Politieke participatie," p. 105, and Rochon, *Mobilizing for Peace*, p. 217.

21. See J. Th. J. van den Berg and H. A. A. Molleman, *Crisis in de Nederlandse politiek* (Crisis in Dutch politics) (Alphen aan den Rijn: Samsom Uitgeverij, 1974). See also A. Th. van Delden, "Externe adviesorganen van de centrale overheid" (External advisory organs of the central government), in Andeweg, Hoogerwerf, and Thomassen, eds., *Politiek in Nederland*, pp. 146–66.

22. See, for example, Frans M. Roschar, "Een structureel model van de Nederlands buitenlands-politieke elite" (A structural model of the Dutch foreign-policy elite), in Peter R. Baehr et al., *Elite en buitenlandse politiek in Nederland* (Elites and foreign policy in the Netherlands) (The Hague: Staatsuitgeverij, 1978), esp. table 8.9 and pp. 181–82.

23. See the report of a wide-ranging discussion in the Senate (First Chamber) about low voter turnout in recent Dutch elections, in *NRC-Handelsblad, Weekeditie*, October 30, 1990.

I have referred elsewhere to a concept important in the Netherlands that is unknown in the United States: *eigen verantwoordelijkheid,* "one's own responsibility."[24] By this is meant that individuals and organizations, once they are given authority or responsibility, have the freedom to do and say what they think is best, no matter whether there is a relationship of dependence involved. A minister, for example, will naturally temper his or her disposition to exercise that freedom if it means violating the governing accord or otherwise putting the governing coalition in jeopardy, but such constraints are self-imposed rather than structurally imposed. This concept is applied to societal organizations and interest groups as well as to ministers and others, and it has a major bearing on the role of interest groups in the Dutch political system.

In the United States, to receive government financial support—from the State or Defense Department, the CIA, or the NSC, for example—has been regarded especially since the 1960s as the kiss of death for any institution in the foreign-policy field that values a reputation for independent judgment. Such an organization might in fact be objective in judgment and candid in criticism of government policies, but no one would believe it. In the Netherlands, to illustrate the contrary, the Netherlands Institute for International Relations "Clingendael" describes itself as an independent institute wholly subsidized by the national government through the ministries of Foreign Affairs, Defense, and Education and Science. "Its activities and views are, nevertheless, in no way dependent on any public or private bodies and it is not tied to any political party or to any denominational or ideological movement."[25] It is testimony to the real meaning of *eigen verantwoordelijkheid* that Clingendael is indeed accepted as an independent international-relations institute, on a par with the Council on Foreign Relations or with university research institutes in the U.S.

The Dutch government supports not only research and educational institutes but also a variety of interest groups in the foreign-affairs field and expects that each will exercise its freedom to do as it sees fit and to say what it thinks. There can be little doubt that in deciding to subsidize these groups, the government hopes that it will co-opt the more important sources of "public opinion." A former official in Development Cooperation, within the Foreign Ministry, once de-

24. See Chapter 4.
25. The Institute publishes the journal *Internationale Spectator,* and it is from the front papers of a special English-language issue (vol. 44, no. 11, November 1990) that this self-description is taken.

scribed a two-part strategy toward pressure groups: those that were not important were ignored, and those that could be troublesome and dangerous were—literally—bought off and "encapsulated," or co-opted. The purpose was to keep the government substantially free to determine its own development policy and to ensure the continuity of that policy. In practice, however, by allowing the interest groups a free hand, the government subsidizes activities that sometimes contravene official policy and are thought to undermine good relations with other countries[26] and that often include efforts to lobby the Second Chamber and government officials on behalf of views that may or may not be identical with official policy.[27] Although the American government covertly subsidized private organizations worldwide during the coldest years of the Cold War, it would be difficult to imagine the government doing that publicly, then or now. And it would be equally unimaginable for government departments to subsidize interest groups that lobbied the Congress! The Congress is unwilling to allow the State Department even to engage in public-opinion polling because the department might use the information thus acquired to lobby the Congress.

Finally, there is a difference in the organizational structure of interest groups in the U.S. and the Netherlands that derives not from their respective political systems but from differences in the physical sizes of the two countries. In the U.S., interest groups that wish to keep a close watch on national policy need to have a Washington "presence." The country is too big for geographically decentralized groups to expect to keep politically informed and to mobilize their efforts when representation is needed in Washington. As a consequence, a very large interest-group community resides in the nation's capital, most of it composed of professional staff leadership. The representativeness even of the elected leadership of large organizations in a large country is sometimes an issue in policy debate in Washington; interest-group activity carried on on a daily basis by professional staff members is subject to additional questions of that sort. In the Netherlands, on the other hand, distance poses no such need for a presence in The Hague—nor

26. See report of a discussion in the Second Chamber concerning the channeling of Dutch development assistance to the Communist in the Philippines by interest groups financed by the Dutch government. *NRC-Handelsblad*, May 23, 1990.

27. See, for example, Marjolein C. Groenendijk, *Nederland en de rechten van de mens in Chili en Argentinië* (The Netherlands and human rights in Chile and Argentina) (Leiden: Institute for International Studies, 1984). See also Hans Daalder, "Parlement tussen politieke partijen en actiegroepen" (Parliament between political parties and action groups), *Acta Politica* 16 (4): 485 (1981): "Would there indeed be many countries where government ministries helped out their harassers with subsidies?"

does the volume of political activity require it.[28] Interest groups are often small, especially in the foreign-policy field—indeed, we will encounter one rather visible foreign-policy group composed of only two people. Staffs, where they are even necessary, are small and often part-time, and the organizations are located wherever the leaders live. There is often no "grass-roots" component to this dispersed form of organization; indeed, given the often small numbers, there is no need even to debate the question of representativeness! To have an impact in these circumstances calls for skills other than political clout.

Foreign-Policy Interest Groups

Foreign-policy interest groups in both the United States and the Netherlands are not like the typical large-scale social organizations that dominate the domestic economic scene in both countries. They are ordinarily smaller and more specific in their interests, even though they sometimes manage to foment mass movements. In the context of the universe of interest groups and the universe of policy issues, they are usually on the fringe—outliers, so to speak. As a result, generalizations about interest groups such as those I have made above sometimes need refinement. I shall begin this discussion of foreign-policy interest groups with a description of the major types and then take up more focused questions of their access to foreign-policy-making processes, their strategies, and their impact—keeping in mind that though access of one sort or another is important if not essential to influence or effectiveness, it is not to be equated with influence.

There is no satisfactory classification of interest groups in either the United States or the Netherlands.[29] In both countries, groups are classified by criteria that are not mutually exclusive: by membership (women's groups, ethnic groups, veterans' organizations, church groups), by economic activity (business, labor, importers, manufacturers), by type (general-interest groups, special-interest groups, permanent organizations, ad hoc groups, umbrella organizations, coalitions of organizations), by subject matter (civil rights, human rights, disarmament, or rearmament), by political coloration (radical left, radical right,

28. See A. J. E. Havermans, "Den Haag en lobby" p. 34. Recall, also, from Chapter 5 that assignment to The Hague offers no important career advantages to a journalist in the Netherlands.

29. See Robert H. Salisbury, "Interest Groups," in Fred I. Greenstein and Nelson W. Polsby, eds., *Handbook of Political Science*, vol. 4 (Reading, Mass.: Addison-Wesley Publishing Co., 1975).

progressive), or by function (advisory bodies, information providers, consciousness raisers). And in both countries a distinction is made between groups whose members share common interests ("interest groups") and groups whose members lobby decision makers on behalf of those interests ("pressure groups"), but whereas Americans regard most interest groups as potential pressure groups, Dutch usage suggests that the terms are characteristics of organizations rather than of their behaviors.

There is one additional type of organization that is a common feature of the Dutch foreign-policy interest-group landscape, however, but that appears only rarely in the U.S. This is the *actiegroep*, or "action group," a single-issue organization formed for the purpose of shaping foreign policies that bear on that issue.[30] Recent examples of such action groups in the Netherlands include *Stop de Neutronenbom*, which carried on a campaign against Dutch and European acceptance of the proposed neutron bomb during the Carter Administration; *Samenwerkingsverband "Stop de Wapenwedloop,"* a general disarmament organization; and *Komitee Kruisraketten Nee*, which led a massive signature drive in 1985 to dissuade the Dutch government from accepting cruise missiles. In the U.S. the closest parallel would be the Nuclear Weapons Freeze Campaign in 1982.[31] Many of the Dutch action groups concentrate on a particular country or geographic region, and many of them manage to attract parliamentarians—and in some instances even political parties—as members.[32] Examples of these *landencomités* (country committees), which have proliferated over the last two decades, abound: *Solidariteits Comité Argentinië Nederland* (Argentine Dutch Solidarity Committee), *Komitee Indonesië* (Indonesia Committee), *Angola Comité* (which later became the *Komitee Zuidelijk Afrika*, or South Africa Committee), to name only a few from a very rich roster dealing mainly

30. For a discussion of single-issue groups, see Philip E. Everts, ed., *Controversies at Home: Domestic Factors in the Foreign Policy of the Netherlands* (Dordrecht: Martinus Nijhoff, 1985), pp. 62–64.

31. See David S. Meyer, *A Winter of Discontent* (New York: Praeger, 1990).

32. For example, the organization *Stop de neutronenbom* was originally organized and supported (politically and, it subsequently appeared, financially) by the Dutch Communist Party; the PPR then joined the organization specifically to broaden its support base beyond the CPN. See P. J. J. Maessen, "The Introduction of the Neutron Bomb, 1977–1978," in Everts, ed., *Controversies at Home*, p. 126. In another example, most of the Dutch political parties were members of *"Vrij Griekenland"* (Free Greece), which was a larger, mainstream, ad hoc organization established in 1967 in reaction to the Colonels' Regime in Greece. Again, the purpose was to keep the political parties on the left from monopolizing the issue. See N. Aukes, *Nederland en het Griekse Kolonelsregime* (The Netherlands and the Greek Colonels' Regime) (Leiden: Institute for International Studies, 1984), p. 20.

with Third World countries.[33] The explosive growth of action groups in the 1970s and 1980s led many observers to regard them as a development of the political upheavals of the 1960s, but Daalder has pointed out that they have been around for over a century and that they are to be found in the background of almost all of the present-day Dutch political parties.[34]

I have mentioned advisory groups earlier, but more should be said about those in the foreign-affairs field. By their very nature, these groups blend what I have elsewhere termed "notables"[35] (including former officials) and subject-matter specialists into an informed "focus group," to use the current language, for the purpose of testing reactions, getting advice, and of course mobilizing support.[36] Governmental advisory groups in foreign affairs in the U.S. have an on-again–off-again, but mostly off-again, character. Periodically encouraged by top leadership, especially when there is little public resonance for major foreign policies, State Department bureaus rarely take them seriously, and they attract little public attention.[37] There are three major (and additional minor) Dutch advisory groups in the foreign-affairs field, established, as all such groups are in the Netherlands, by law with the cooperation of the Parliament (and evaluated every three to six years): one for Peace and Security (which in 1985 subsumed two advisory councils, one for the Foreign Ministry and one for the Defense Ministry),[38]

33. For a longer list from an earlier period, see *Vademekum van het politiek vormingswerk* (Manual of political education), 2d ed. (Amersfoort: De Horstink, 1974).

34. Hans Daalder, "Parlement tussen politieke partijen en actiegroepen" (Parliament between political parties and action groups), *Acta Politica* 16 (4): 481 (1981). Van Staden cites figures documenting the growth of the country committees from 24 in 1950 to 32 in 1960, 64 in 1970, and 174 in 1982; see Everts, ed., *Controversies at Home*, p. 62. See also A. van Staden, "The Changing Role of the Netherlands in the Atlantic Alliance," *Western European Politics* 12 (1): 105. (January 1989).

35. See Bernard C. Cohen, *The Public's Impact on Foreign Policy* (Boston: Little, Brown and Co., 1973), chapter 3.

36. In a 1977 study of the Dutch foreign-affairs advisory boards, the authors concluded (1) that the officials and the advisers shared the same "worldview," and hence their function was more to strengthen official ideas than to bring in critical ideas and alternatives; and (2) that the views of the members of these boards were "not representative of the ideas that live in the different sectors of the society (Ph. P. Everts, J. Colijn, J. Keessen, and H. van Wirdum, "Samenstelling, functioneren en opvattingen van de Adviescolleges voor Buitenlandse Politiek, Ontwikkelingssamenwerking en Defensie" [Composition, functioning, and conceptions of the Advisory Boards for Foreign Policy, Development Cooperation, and Defense] [Leiden: Institute for International Studies, October 1977], p. 23).

37. See, e.g., Cohen, *Public's Impact*, pp. 92–95.

38. A member of this new Advisory Council described the reorganization as a deliberate move by the Foreign Ministry to restore consensus among the informal elite after the long and divisive cruise missile debate in the Netherlands—the same kind of impetus

one for Human Rights and Foreign Policy, and one for Development Cooperation; all have some stature. There were five permanent external advisory organs in the Foreign Ministry in 1988.[39] They are empowered to give advice, solicited or unsolicited—though there is general agreement among participants that if the minister hasn't asked for advice he isn't going to be very interested in what he hears.[40] A measure of the general importance of advisory groups in the firmament of Dutch organizations is to be found, perversely, in the recurring criticisms of their costs and their unrepresentativeness, as well as in the frequently expressed concern that parliamentary democracy may be gradually being eroded by "countless advisory bodies that themselves take no political responsibility."[41]

Interest groups often participate in foreign-policy processes from a distance, so to speak: they engage in activities and make their positions clear without having any direct access to policy makers, counting on the media or on their members or even indirectly on various other publics both to communicate their concerns and perhaps even to suggest their muscle. Direct accessibility to decision makers, nevertheless, is an additional and a more reliable form of policy communication, especially where there can be no guarantee that indirect forms are available or will work. In addition, direct access to officials is generally regarded by interest groups as prima facie evidence of their importance or their "success" (regardless of the actual policy consequences),[42] and hence the conditions that govern such access merit our attention.

---

that propelled several U.S. advisory groups in and after the Vietnam debate. For a broad introduction to Dutch advisory groups, see Wetenschappelijke Raad voor het Regerings-beleid, *Externe adviesorganen van de centrale overheid: Beschriving, ontwikkelingen, aanbeve-lingen* (Scientific Council for Government Policy, External Advisory Organs of the Central Government: Description, developments, recommendations), 12th Report to the Government (The Hague: Staatsuitgeverij, 1977).

39. Van Delden, "Externe adviesorganen," p. 151.

40. Conversely, when advice is requested, it is not likely to be rejected. Ibid., pp. 154–55.

41. B. C. L. Waanders, "Parlement" (Parliament), commentary in *NRC-Handelsblad*, May 23, 1990; Van Delden, "Externe adviesorganen," p. 163.

42. An official of the leading American Jewish lobbying organization was recently forced to resign after claiming to have unparalleled access to the executive branch—despite all the evidence that such access has had little direct impact on executive-branch decisions on Arab-Israeli issues. See, e.g., Robert H. Trice, "Foreign Policy Interest Groups, Mass Public Opinion, and the Arab-Israeli Dispute," *The Western Political Quarterly* 31 (2): 238–52 (June 1978); and M. van Leeuwen, *Lobby's in actie: Achtergronden bij het Amerikaanse Midden-Oosten beleid* (Lobbies in action: Background of the American Middle-East policy) (The Hague: Netherlands Institute of International Relations "Clingendael," November 1986).

In the United States, foreign-policy processes are relatively permeable to all kinds of public participants, even when great efforts are invested in maintaining secrecy.[43] The media are in the very thick of most issues from the beginning, given their institutionalized presence wherever foreign policies are being made, and leaks by official participants are an ever-present part of the process.[44] A substantial layer of policy experts in the bureaucracy, in the Congress, among congressional staff members, in universities, and in Washington-based "think tanks," fed by their own knowledge of the issues or by the media's coverage, ensures that issues are publicly discussed and debated very early in the process. Groups whose interests are affected by these issues have to be either deaf or on holiday not to hear the debate and get involved early on, also. They are able thus to exploit all possible avenues to get to officials while policy is still being developed.

In the Netherlands, foreign policy and the Foreign Ministry are widely regarded as having been the "last bastion" of private policy making.[45] A good part of the unrest in the Netherlands after the 1960s, in fact, was aimed at the democratization of foreign policy. Some slight progress was made toward that end during the 1970s and 1980s,[46] but from the perspective of time and distance the emphasis should be on "slight." The Foreign Ministry is accessible to a select few who have either a principal's interest in a specific matter of foreign relations or a formal advisory role in general. But it is relatively impermeable to most of the groups attempting to be heard. Issue after issue in foreign policy is described as taking shape behind closed doors, where conflict, if indeed there is any, is limited to the insiders. And by the time the decisions are made public, activities by interest groups serve mostly to vent steam: the government is usually committed in a way that even the Parliament is unwilling to disturb.[47] B. J. van Eenennaam, a top official in the Foreign Ministry and an active participant in the discussions on the NATO modernization issue, has let us know what they were like. Be-

43. See, in general, Cohen, *Public's Impact*.

44. See Bernard C. Cohen, *The Press and Foreign Policy* (Princeton: Princeton University Press, 1963). Periodic efforts to limit the access of journalists to officials generally fail: mutual dependence overcomes momentary pique.

45. See, e.g., Siccama, "Netherlands Depillarized."

46. During the Den Uyl Cabinet, 1973–1977, with a socialist premier and a socialist foreign minister, some action groups were received by the foreign minister, thus gaining a legitimacy they had not earlier possessed. In the words of one official in the ministry at that time, "It was not possible thereafter to deny that they existed."

47. See the extensive case studies reported in Everts, ed., *Controversies at Home*. The case studies, some of which I have cited, were published in Dutch by the Institute for International Studies, University of Leiden, in 1984.

cause the group of decision makers was small, he felt it was necessary for them to maintain contact with all concerned, "and that was something that those in the official structure in these ministries were not accustomed to. . . . The involvement of the 'outside world' is less direct in our system, because policy preparation in general takes place behind the scenes. Cooperation as in the U.S., between the ministries and members of Parliament and their staff associates, or scientific researchers, let alone journalists, is out of the question in the Netherlands."[48]

American officials, subject to pressures from all sides, tend to the view that too many public cooks spoil the policy broth—that life in the Dutch system has to be better. If silence means consent, Dutch officials by and large must agree with that judgment: it is a rare Dutch foreign-policy official who believes, with Van Eenennaam, that the chances of finding good cooks are better in a system, like the American one, where so many participate that the quality of every contribution has to be high if it is to be heard.[49]

Strategies of Foreign-Policy Interest Groups

Among the most important strategic choices confronting interest groups are those of targets and of messages: whom should they try to reach, and what should they say to them? I shall discuss targets first and then messages.

The fact that the American political system is relatively permeable to outsiders, including interest groups, should not carry with it the presumption that these groups have an easy time of it. On the contrary, because the foreign-policy power in the U.S. is so dispersed, it is exceedingly difficult for interest groups to have much leverage.[50] There are so

48. B. J. van Eenennaam, *Achtenveertig kruisraketten: Hoogspanning in de lage landen* (Forty-eight cruise missiles: High tension in the low countries) (The Hague: SDU Uitgeverij, 1988), pp. 39, 43. Van Eenennaam's credentials are first-rate: he was detached from the Foreign Ministry for some months to write his book, which was read prior to publication by a former foreign minister and bears a foreword by the then prime minister. One presumes that they did not find his observations on the wild side.

49. Ibid., pp. 42–43.

50. The parallel with the student rebellions of the late 1960s is apt: because the American system of higher education is so decentralized, the student movement had to reinvent itself on campus after campus to make any progress, and on many of the campuses educational policy itself had so many guardians that the students were repeatedly frustrated in their efforts to change it. In the Netherlands, on the other hand, where the university system is controlled by the national Ministry of Education, the students were able with much less effort to bring about significant change in the governance of all universities.

many people to get to, so many minds that may need to be changed, in both the executive and the legislative branches, that group representatives have to work very hard or be very smart (and usually both) to reach and to convince enough of the right people. The president and the secretary of state, of course, are the two most "right people," but they are the hardest to reach. And when they are reached on issues of any contention, they are obviously subject to so many conflicting and competing pulls that they are typically free to balance them off and to pick and choose among them, making their decisions in their customary ways. Although the Congress is a relatively open institution, it is also a relatively unresponsive one, for reasons I have already discussed: not only the nature of the member's constituency but also the large number of "safe" districts and states; the overlapping and, in the case of the Senate, the lengthy terms of office; the predominance of local or parochial issues on the electoral agenda; the lack of real interest of many members of Congress in foreign affairs; and the same coalitional character of the local and state parties that we noted in the national parties. There are few political-party resources in this system to lighten the burden on these interest groups, to make it easier for them to reach crucial players. And since foreign-policy decisions are rarely made in a strictly partisan manner anyway, it even helps for the groups to be nonpartisan, so that their access is not arbitrarily limited to only a portion of those whose judgment or votes may be essential.

Although the Dutch political system is less permeable to interest groups, the nature of the system makes it somewhat easier for some of them to find points of leverage on foreign-policy issues. Since the foreign-policy process is substantially centralized, the task for interest groups is to try to find places where it may be vulnerable to external pressure. And those places tend to be found not so much among the officials who exercise the foreign-policy power as within the political parties and especially within the political fractions in the Second Chamber, on issues where ministers may have to find some support.[51] The groups go after these politicians directly and also

---

51. See Baehr, "Het parlement," p. 213. Rochon, on the other hand, cites "the openness of the Dutch political system" and "the extent to which prominent people tend to know each other in a small country" as the explanation for the very wide range of IKV Secretary Mient Jan Faber's contacts, which included "ministers and members of parliament, high civil servants in the Foreign Affairs and Defense offices, and staffers in the American Embassy in The Hague and at NATO headquarters in Brussels" (*Mobilizing for Peace*, p. 181). Faber's range was unusual, however, even for a prominent person in a small country.

indirectly, through the media that are of particular importance to them.[52]

Interest groups in the Netherlands direct much of their efforts toward the parties and fractions with which they have an ideological sympathy and to which they have (as a consequence) relatively easy access.[53] Often, in fact, an organization's contact with the Second Chamber is through its own members who are also members of the Chamber; contact for an organization lacking that kind of access runs through one or a few members who are particularly receptive.[54] In its first eight years or so, the CDA fraction was an uneasy coalition of confessional parties, frequently at the mercy of ten members who had favored a governing coalition with the socialists (PvdA) rather than with the liberals (VVD). This internal weakness offered opportunities especially to the church-related peace organizations such as the Interchurch Peace Council (*Interkerkelijk Vredesberaad*—IKV) and Pax Christi to try to tip the balance of party opinion against NATO modernization and the cruise missiles.[55] Similarly, left-oriented action groups cultivated the PvdA and especially the smaller and more radical left parties.[56] If the parties thus targeted happen to be governing parties, then there is the hope of getting indirectly to the ministers through their fractions; if they are opposition parties, then the object is frequently to get members to ask questions that ministers must then answer in Parliament.[57] And since the ministers have to be prepared for questions in the Chamber, they tend to be sensitive to the agendas

52. See, e.g., Groenendijk, *Nederland en de rechten van de mens*, and P. J. J. Maesssen, *De kwestie van de Neutronenbom* (The question of the neutron bomb) (Leiden: Institute for International Studies, 1984).

53. See, e.g., W. C. I. M. van Haalen, *De Kwestie van een olie-embargo tegen Zuid-Afrika* (The question of an oil embargo against South Africa) (Leiden: Institute of International Studies, 1984), p. 47; and Maessen, p. 49.

54. See, for example, Groenendijk, *Nederland en de rechten van de mens*.

55. See, inter alia, Van Staden, "Changing Role," p. 107, and "Managing Threat and Dependence in the Netherlands: The Strategy of Alignment," paper prepared for the annual meeting of the International Studies Association, April 10–14, 1990; Van Eenennaam, *Achtenveertig kruisraketten*, pp. 13, 65–68; and Rochon, *Mobilizing for Peace*, p. 175.

56. A prominent member of the PvdA told me that when action groups are formed, "they usually involve members of the PvdA. . . . In the budget of the PvdA there is an item to support actions initiated by others."

57. Cf. Groenendijk, *Nederland en de rechten van de mens:* "That the Boskalis transaction [government reinsurance of a contract won by a Dutch concern to build a gas pipeline in Argentina] was put on the agenda in the Chamber only in March 1980 had, according to the PSP, to do with the fact that, on questions of this sort, political parties are after all dependent on groups in society that react alertly here" (p. 112).

of the groups. In the words of a former high Defense Ministry official, "the ministry has to go deeply into the train of thought of action groups, because otherwise it would not be prepared" for eventual questions from the Chamber.

There are risks in these approaches to the parties and the fractions, however. Interest groups may get in trouble even with ideologically compatible parties if they seem to be asking the parties to violate their own programs[58] or if they appear to be taking on too much of the role of the parties themselves. Both Pax Christi and the IKV, the major church-related peace groups, antagonized the CDA by their behavior as leaders of the peace movement—the IKV because it tried to influence voters directly.[59] And the ultimate identification of the peace movement (and most other action groups) with the ideology of the political left meant that those organizations eventually lost their credibility with the church-related parties and with the liberal party (VVD), with whom the CDA governed for over a decade after 1977.[60]

Interest-group access to the Second Chamber is thought by many in the Netherlands—especially in the Foreign Ministry—to be the proper channel for the exercise of such pressure. In Massachusetts it was once said that the Lowells spoke only to Cabots and the Cabots spoke only to God. In the Dutch Foreign Ministry it has been said that interest groups speak only to parliamentarians and parliamentarians speak only to the minister and the *staatssecretaris*. There are some people in the ministry who claim never to have seen an interest-group representative in their halls. But there are also some who spoke proudly of their minister's discussions with action groups. One high official even referred to the *Komitee Zuidelijk-Afrika* as a member of the family in the Foreign Ministry, and Amnesty International seems to find open doors throughout that ministry and in many other ministries as well. And there is considerable evidence that economic groups in particular, but many others as well, follow a strategy on foreign-economic questions that is aimed as much at the Foreign Ministry as at the Second Chamber.[61]

58. See, e.g., Jan Pronk's answer to a question, in Denig et al., eds., *Het Gebeurt in Den Haag*, p. 82.

59. See Philip P. Everts and Guido Walraven, eds., *In actie voor een vredesklimaat: Twintig jaar IKV* (In action for a climate of peace: Twenty years of the IKV) (Amersfoort: De Horstink, 1987), pp. 60–61.

60. See Schennink et al., eds., *Veertig jaar Pax Christi*, pp. 137–46, and Everts and Walraven, eds. *In actie voor een vredesklimaat*, pp. 142–43.

61. See Van Haalen, *Olie-embargo*. On the issue of the neutron bomb, Maessen writes that the Ministry of Foreign Affairs was "overwhelmed" by a few hundred letters from

Choice of target is not the only question confronting foreign-policy interest groups; equally important is the choice of a substantive political strategy: what kind of message is best calculated to serve their purposes? And once again there are significant differences in the behavior of these groups that are shaped by both systemic and structural differences between the two countries. As a general proposition, the behavior of interest groups is substantially determined by the consequences of the scale both of the organizations themselves and of the political institutions they are dealing with as well as by the relationship of the political institutions to the citizenry.

The executive branch of the American government has enormous staff and intelligence resources, with a capability for gathering and analyzing more information relevant to foreign affairs than can effectively be used by the intended recipients. I have also noted earlier that the U.S. Congress is very well staffed, both individually and in committee; that is true in the foreign-affairs areas as well as in all others. Furthermore, the Congress has a significant foreign-policy role, offering some scope to individual members who choose to specialize in this area. In these circumstances, American foreign-policy interest groups cannot ordinarily expect to compete with either the executive branch or the Congress as a source of new policy-relevant information—although in unusual circumstances they may provide the Congress and the media with information that the executive branch has been unwilling to proffer.[62] Confronting this inequality, interest groups tend to favor a *politically relevant information strategy*, seeking to shape the electoral perceptions of their target audiences. And to that end, they stress explicitly the weight of numbers—the number of members, the number of associated groups—but implicitly they are stressing the number that can be politically mobilized in specific contingencies. Given the dependence of members of Congress on generally small and well-defined constituencies, the Congress appears to offer a more promising arena for such electorally based interest-group strategies than does the executive

---

community councils, churches, other institutions, and individuals (*Neutronenbom*, p. 51). And as I have noted earlier, the Development Cooperation section of the Foreign Ministry, with its own minister, has long encouraged direct relationships with interest and action groups, many of which it supports financially.

62. See, e.g., Bernard C. Cohen, "The Influence of Special-Interest Groups and Mass Media on Security Policy in the United States," in Charles W. Kegley, Jr. and Eugene R. Wittkopf, *Perspectives on American Foreign Policy* (New York: St. Martin's Press, 1983), pp. 235–36. "Elite" institutions like the Council on Foreign Relations or university research institutes will sometimes win a hearing with a persuasive argument or a new analysis, but such institutions do not usually fit the definition of interest groups.

branch, where the one elected official, the president, is generally able to balance off competing opinions and thus neutralize them. But if an interest group seeks to define itself as a relevant part of a representative's constituency, it needs a visible and compelling presence in his or her district or state; that is certainly possible, particularly for specialized economic interests or specific ethnic aggregations, but for the large run of foreign-policy issues that has not been very common. More typically, foreign-policy issues have had a larger impact, cutting across many electoral districts and generally ignoring party lines.[63]

The situation in the Netherlands is almost wholly different, compelling a wholly different political strategy: for one thing, foreign-policy interest groups are relatively small in size, with memberships that are often fewer than a hundred and sometimes fewer than ten[64] and staffed by one or two people, sometimes with a little part-time assistance. In fact, several of the more visible and well-regarded groups—the *Indonesië Komitee Hengelo* and the *Angola Comité*, for example—were literally the creatures of the one or two people who organized them and who carried on most of their activities by themselves. Not only do these groups represent opinions that are often different from those held by the government of the day; they also confront a government and a parliament both of which have strong ties to political parties that themselves have strong opinions, and thus these groups have immense difficulty competing with either the government or the parties as credible representatives of public opinion in Dutch society.

Although the Dutch government has good (though necessarily limited) information resources in the foreign-policy field, it has a proprietary attitude toward that information—befitting its long tradition of exclusive control over foreign affairs—and shares it only reluctantly even with the Parliament. The Second Chamber, however, having a bare-bones staff, has no significant foreign-policy information resources of its own. And although foreign affairs are not a route to prominence in the Dutch Parliament as they can be in the U.S. Congress, the Dutch parliamentary fractions, especially the smaller ones and those in opposition, are nevertheless quite receptive to reliable information

63. It is possible, however, that this situation may change as security-policy interests lose their primacy in American foreign policy and as more and more "interdependency" issues, like international trade agreements which affect very specific populations and interests, come to the fore. See my argument in "Influence of Special-Interest Groups," pp. 237–38.

64. See, e.g., Groenendijk, *Nederland en de rechten van de mens;* G. Walraven and J. Colijn, *Wapenleveranties-I: Korvetten aan Indonesië (Arms Supplies-I: Corvettes to Indonesia)* (Leiden: Institute of International Studies, 1984).

from any knowledgeable source, including the action groups and the country committees that focus on specific issues and specific countries.

As a consequence of all these factors, these interests groups are more or less driven to a *policy-relevant information strategy*,[65] seeking in their limited areas of concern to provide parliamentarians, especially, with significant information that has eluded the media and sometimes even the ordinary reporting networks of the diplomatic establishment. Since the Dutch government has invested heavily in both its European relationships and its economic relationships worldwide, important information in these areas is unlikely to escape either media or official attention; hence it is in the more remote regions and areas of foreign policy that such interest groups are able to make their mark. The *Angola Comité*, which began as a simple boycott effort, was almost universally regarded in the end as having a monopoly of relevant information about affairs in that country. The Dutch branch of Amnesty International, through its specialized knowledge of human-rights issues, made important contributions to Dutch policy on these subjects.[66] The *Indonesië Komitee Hengelo*, "a two-man affair" that nonetheless had close connections with one of the smallest left parties, the PSP, was the source of a lawsuit against the Dutch State that sought (unsuccessfully) to reverse a government decision to sell corvettes to Indonesia.[67]

There is one important exception to the pursuit of a policy-relevant information strategy by Dutch foreign-policy interest groups. In the Netherlands as in the United States, the foreign-policy interest-group scene has been dominated from time to time by efforts at mass mobilization designed to bring the weight of public opinion to bear on foreign policy. Led by specific interest groups, these mobilization efforts have acquired the character of social movements—the anti–Vietnam War movement in the U.S., the peace movement in the Netherlands—and have even been analyzed as such, rather than as political organizations.[68] Like forest fires they develop rather quickly and rage for some time without control, fanned by the winds of media attention; then almost as suddenly they are over, no longer "news," the passion of their followers spent either by the success or the failure of their policy goals. Mass-mobilization efforts thus merit our attention as foreign-

65. See Everts, ed., *Controversies at Home*, p. 266.

66. Peter R. Baehr, in Philip P. Everts and Guido Walraven, eds., *The Politics of Persuasion: Implementation of Foreign Policy by the Netherlands* (Brookfield, Vt.: Gower Publishing Co., 1989), p. 306; Groenendijk, *Nederland en de rechten van de mens*, p. 49.

67. Everts, ed., *Controversies at Home*, p. 261.

68. See, e.g., Rochon, *Mobilizing for Peace*, and Bert Klaandermans, ed., *Tekenen voor vrede: Het volkspetitionnement tegen de kruisraketten* (Signing for peace: The people's petition against cruise missiles) (Assen: Van Gorcum, 1988).

policy interest-group activity, even though they are exceptional activity in both countries.

It is not easy to mobilize masses of people in pursuit of foreign-policy issues, since most people attach a low priority to them. The only foreign-policy matters that have succeeded in attracting the attention of very large numbers of people in both the U.S. and the Netherlands over the last half century and in persuading them to take to the streets have been issues of war and peace. It is especially the fear of war or antipathy to war that is the catalyst of mass mobilization. In the U.S., prior to the Second World War, the American First Committee and the Committee to Defend America by Aiding the Allies brought out tens of thousands of people in their competitive efforts to define the road to peace for the United States.[69] In the post–World War II era the National Coordinating Committee to End the War in Vietnam organized demonstrations nationwide, and in the early 1980s the Nuclear Freeze Campaign, though not as massive, evoked one of the largest demonstrations in U.S. history, in New York. There were countless other mass actions in the U.S. in the postwar period, to be sure, but they were organized around civil rights and other domestic- rather than foreign-policy issues.

The Vietnam War had its reverberations in the streets of the Netherlands also, but the largest foreign-policy mass actions in that country took place in the 1980s, stimulated by the NATO proposal to modernize its theater nuclear weapons and to base cruise and Pershing II missiles on Dutch soil. I have referred on earlier occasions to the very large demonstrations in Amsterdam in 1981 and the The Hague in 1983, organized largely by the IKV, an organization of the Dutch Protestant churches. In addition to these, a signature campaign in 1978, organized by *Stop de Neutronenbom*, got 1,200,000 signatures[70], and another in 1985, organized by *Komitee Kruisraketten Nee*,, got 3,750,000 signatures against the missile emplacements on Dutch territory—"the most massive demonstration of resistance to a government proposal in the post-war period".[71]

69. See, e.g., Walter Johnson, *The Battle against Isolation* (Chicago: University of Chicago Press, 1944); Wayne S. Cole, *America First: The Battle against Intervention, 1940–41* (Madison: University of Wisconsin Press, 1953); and Selig Adler, *The Isolationist Impulse: Its Twentieth-Century Reaction* (London: Abelard-Schuman, 1957).

70. See Maessen, *Neutronenbom*.

71. Klandermans, ed., *Tekenen voor Vrede*, p. 2. Outside the foreign-policy area, however, the environmental movement has also enjoyed a substantial mobilization potential, unlike other new social movements, including the anti-nuclear energy movement. See Hanspeter Kriesi, *Political Mobilization in the Netherlands* (Brookfield, Vt.: Gower Publishing Co., 1993).

The anti-war movements in the U.S., both before and after World War II, were for the most part nonpartisan in character. Supporters of both political parties were found among both the prewar "isolationists" and "interventionists." The anti–Vietnam War movement began on the left in the U.S., but it spread across the political spectrum before it was finished. It made governing so difficult for Democrat President Johnson that he declined to run for a second term, and it helped to shape Republican President Nixon's decisions to extricate the U.S. from its military involvement in Vietnam. The Nuclear Freeze Campaign, however, attracted predominantly Democrats, who were more likely than Republicans to oppose President Reagan's military policies; it had no discernible effect on Reagan's policies.

The Dutch peace movement and most of the organizations that led it were heavily leftist in political color and antigovernment. The IKV, despite its churchly origins, had a polarizing effect on both the churches and the CDA, the major confessional political party, and as a consequence had limited access to both.[72] The demonstrations they organized attracted supporters of the left parties in disproportionate numbers.[73] *Stop de Neutronenbom*, as I noted earlier, was supported initially by the Communist Party but got the support of the PSP and other left-wing groups in order to dilute its communist connection and make it more acceptable to the public. The *Komitee Kruisraketten Nee* and the *volkspetitionnement* were run by members of left parties, in open opposition to the governing parties (CDA and VVD), and as a result the adherents of the latter hardly signed the petition.[74] The 3.75 million signatures against the missile emplacement were handed to Prime Minister Lubbers (CDA) on October 26, 1985; six days later the government made its long-postponed decision to go ahead with the emplacement anyway, and in national elections six months later the coalition parties (CDA and VVD) were given a new mandate to govern.

When the masses have been mobilized, there is always talk of a new kind of politics being born, replacing the old institutions and the old politics that presumably do not work. But one needs to be cautious in generalizing from a very small number of not very comparable

72. See, e.g., Jan van Putten, *Toekomst voor de vredesbeweging* (The future of the peace movement) (Amersfoort: De Horstink, 1986), p. 19.

73. B. Schennink, T. Bertrand, and H. Fun, *De 21 november demonstranten, wie zijn ze en wat willen ze?* (The demonstrators of November 21: Who are they and what do they want?), Soest, 1982, pp. 39ff; cited in Van Putten, *Toekomst* p. 88.

74. Everts and Walraven, eds. *In actie voor een vredesklimaat*, pp. 62, 76. See also Klandermans, ed., *Tekenen voor vrede*.

events in either the Netherlands or the U.S. Two factors, however, do seem to be to be working in these circumstances. On the one hand, an unusual amount of public interest in foreign affairs was aroused— caused, as I said earlier, by palpable fears of war. And on the other hand, the mainstream political parties, which were not and are not organized primarily for the representation of foreign-policy interests, found it difficult to be responsive almost overnight to a highly specific set of demands, such as the freezing of nuclear weapons or their total abolition, that have no well-established base of support among their members. Similarly, governments have their ongoing commitments to their political supporters and to other governments, and they cannot change their policies—for example, the American military buildup in Vietnam or the Dutch acceptance of nuclear tasks within NATO— easily or quickly. This leaves the field to interest and action groups, which find it easy to mobilize support in these circumstances. Small and highly ideological political parties, such as those on the fringes of Dutch politics, have been responsive to such foreign-policy demands, but they have always remained on the fringe. The mass mobilizations resulting from this lack of responsiveness by governments and major parties have often given a jolt to these conventional parties and to political systems generally,[75] but time and inertia are usually on the side of the latter. People tire; governments temporize, as the Dutch government did in the 1980s,[76] or they accommodate slowly, as the American government did in the 1960s and 1970s. If war breaks out, as it did in 1941 for the U.S., public support invariably swings back to the establishment; if war does not break out, as in the 1970s and 1980s, the fear of war recedes sooner or later, and when it does an effective balance is reestablished between the level of public interest in foreign affairs and the capacity of conventional and governing parties to cope with it.

Effectiveness of Foreign-Policy Interest Groups

Finally, what can—or should—we say about the effectiveness of foreign-policy interest groups in these two countries, in this period of their history? I have written elsewhere about the complexities of

75. Rochon takes too deterministic a position when he argues that governmental rigidity in a period of rapid change "requires [sic] that established political practices be subject to periodic jolts that originate independently of entrenched political institutions" (*Mobilizing for Peace*, pp. 218–19).

76. See, e.g., Steven B. Wolinetz, "A Quarter Century of Dutch Politics: A Changing Political System or *le plus que change . . . ?" Acta Politica* 25 (4): 422 (1990).

trying to assess the impact of such interest groups in the United States.[77] The opportunities for interest-group influence in the Netherlands are different and in recent years may have been more extensive than in the U.S.,[78] but in general the difficulties of assessment are the same.

One sees in much of the Dutch literature concerning foreign-policy interest groups the prevalence of the "pressure-group model"—the notion that effectiveness means success in changing government policy. A more accurate assessment of the impact of interest groups, however, can be made only in the context of a wider view of their relationships with the institutions of government, one in which the outsiders do not simply take initiatives and insiders do not simply resist or cave in. Interest groups do much more than that—and so do governments. In the classic pressure-group model, interest groups are *petitioners*, attempting to get particular interests protected or grievances redressed. But interest groups may also act as *competitors* of government or of political parties, endeavoring to determine the "national interest" or to set national priorities. Or they may serve as *allies* of government departments or of political parties in getting shared values reflected in foreign policy—or be used by officials as counterweights to other organizations opposing government policies. Or they may be negotiators or *bargainers*, exchanging support on some issues for help with other issues.[79] Interest groups can usually be found on all sides of issues, some "winning" and others "losing," meaning that interest groups are likely to be both "effective" and "ineffective" at the same time.

There is, thus, no single or simple measure of "success" in evaluating the efforts of interest groups, since there is more involved than simply persuading the government, by direct or indirect means, to do their bidding. Governments themselves are multidimensional: they are committed to certain goals or policies, divided on others, unwilling to get involved with some, needful of external support on others. And opportunities for outside groups to be effective vary with issues, levels of political "attention," the relative autonomy of officials, and, perhaps most important, with the larger political setting: in the United States, as

77. See esp. Cohen, *Public's Impact*, and "Influence of Special-Interest Groups," pp. 222–41.

78. See, e.g., H. Daalder, "The Mould of Dutch Politics," *West European Politics* 12 (1): 16–17 (January 1989).

79. See, e.g., David H. Davis, *How the Bureaucracy Makes Foreign Policy* (Lexington, Mass.: Heath, 1972); and Morton H. Halperin, *Bureaucratic Politics and Foreign Policy* (Washington, D.C.: Brookings Institution, 1974).

I have argued elsewhere,[80] the prevailing hypotheses about interest-group effectiveness may be time- and situation-bound. For over forty years the requirements of the Cold War gave foreign-policy officials the leverage to turn aside the claims of special-interest groups. The end of the Cold War, however, and the demise of a dominant foreign-policy paradigm marked a watershed, creating the conditions in which foreign-policy interest groups can move more freely in the continuing struggle to define the national interest and to gain support for their definition of it. In the Netherlands the most extensive analysis of cases involving interest groups concluded that a necessary condition for their success is parliamentary support.[81] Apart from the fact that there is some evidence even in the material for these cases that foreign-policy interest groups were sometimes effective in working directly with government officials, the dominant circumstance of the period studied was the political division within the CDA and its need to listen to outside groups that were capable of tearing the party and its successive governments apart. But when the CDA finally acquired the broad political support that allowed it to resolve its internal problems, it was able in 1985 to stare down even the 3,750,000 signatures collected by the *Komitee Kruisraketten Nee* and vote to emplace the NATO cruise missiles. And by 1990 the foreign-policy interest-group scene in the Netherlands was quiescent—a sea change from the generation that went before.

80. Cohen, "Influence of Special-Interest Groups," and *The Influence of Non-Governmental Groups on Foreign Policy-Making*, Studies in Citizen Participation in International Relations, vol. 2 (Boston: World Peace Foundation, 1959).

81. Everts, ed., *Controversies at Home*.

7
Conclusion

The detailed comparisons of the patterns of public participation in foreign policy in the Netherlands and the United States that have occupied the preceding six chapters do not lend themselves to conventional or concise summary here; there is simply too much to consider. Rather, and more selectively, I will try to draw some conclusions about the similarities and the differences between the two countries that have some bearing on the larger question of how democratic institutions deal with the world beyond their borders.

One cross-national comparison such as this can of course provide only a limited capacity to generalize about democracy and foreign-policy making, but even a limited capacity is better than the myopia that characterizes our present efforts. Looking at only one country, we tend to see only what is there and what we have become accustomed to seeing there. A focused comparison of the working of the public institutions of public-policy making in two countries forces each of us to look at our own national institutions from a new perspective, inquiring about the things that aren't there, as well as those that are, and about the things they don't do, as well as those they do, and asking what their presence or absence may signify for other participants in the process. A defining characteristic of a political system, after all, is the patterned interaction of its participants, and performance or nonperformance by one participant has consequences for the others.[1]

For the same reason—which is to say, because the participants in-

1. See Bernard C. Cohen, "Citizen Participation in Foreign Policy: A Comparative Perspective," in Sidney Verba and Lucian W. Pye, eds., *The Citizen and Politics: A Comparative Perspective* (Stamford, Conn.: Greylock, 1978), esp. pp. 224–28.

teract in patterned ways—it does not matter very much precisely where one cuts into the pattern. No matter where one starts, in very short order one will encounter the major participants in any system. In trying to get at the heart of the differences and similarities in public participation in foreign policy between the Netherlands and the United States, I will arbitrarily start with political parties. Before I do, however, there is one important point that needs to be made as an ever-present backdrop to the assessment of public participation.

There are, quite obviously, great variations in the character, the volume, and even the rhythm of public participation, over time, in the foreign-policy processes of these two countries. What is so clear in these two countries (and, I suspect, in most countries) with respect to public interest in foreign policy is that, most of the time, the issues of a nation's foreign policy are crushingly boring to most of its citizens and of no concern to them. The normal rhythm is very limited participation by knowledgeable principals, who often change with the issues. It is hard to define (without being tautological) precisely what it is that, on rare occasions, shakes up the routine of policy making and enlarges public participation. It is not just the presence of security issues: a major threat to the rhythm and routine of life itself will usually have such consequences, but there are times when issues of war and peace are defined in moral rather than security terms, with the same consequences. And there are other times when major foreign-economic issues—the Maastricht Treaty or NAFTA, for example—evoke the interest that we associate with security issues. Patterns of participation seem to change when the foreign-policy issues are no longer boring— or are less boring than other aspects of daily life! And that may have as much to do with the circumstances of the lives and with the content of the values of a given population at a given moment in history as it does with the character of particular "issues."

Political Parties

Dutch political parties are policy organizations. As I have noted often in the preceding chapters, they are bodies within which policy ideas develop, and they serve as focal points for debate among their followers about those ideas and as advocates for the policy recommendations that result. That remains true even though Dutch political parties are politically and organizationally weaker than they were a generation ago and even though foreign-policy issues are not the most important agenda items for most parties. Because the parties articulate the policy views of the most active and interested of their members, the parties are part of what we can call the government's daily referendum on foreign policy: although governments in democracies are granted some room for maneuver in foreign policy, as in other realms, by the "rules" of the political system and by the specific political constellations that have put them in power, they need constantly to determine the size of that room and especially its outer boundaries—that is, their freedom to act on relatively new issues—by sampling the politically relevant environment on a frequent and regular basis. Dutch parties and party members are the most important elements of this daily referendum, precisely because they are among the most outspoken participants in the ongoing policy debates.

American political parties are not policy organizations, and they are essentially nonparticipants in debates on foreign policy. The foreign-policy positions of the two major parties are rarely in conflict and are often not even sharply differentiated. The parties have little reason to quarrel over issues that have little political resonance with the voters. In these circumstances, there is no occasion whatever for American foreign-policy officials to include political-party leaders in *their* daily referendum.

The striking similarity between the major Dutch and American political parties is that they are driven to the political center by the same pressure—the desire for (participation in) a governing majority. Since Dutch cabinet government is coalition government, parties can participate in governing coalitions only by narrowing the policy distance between themselves and their opponents. The results are interesting: it is very difficult for the major parties in either country to deal with strong foreign-policy demands from groups within their society, because they are not organized around those issues and because they have submerged their differences with respect to them. Furthermore, since foreign-policy issues are, most of the time, not very important to most people, those issues are rather easily wrapped up in the "consensus" that is created when the parties do move toward each other. It doesn't matter, then, that Dutch parties are not well organized around foreign-policy matters or that American parties are not well organized around *any* policy matters, so long as there is no *need* for parties to take significant positions on foreign-policy matters—that is, so long as foreign-policy matters do not become domestic political issues. There is always some divergence of opinion on foreign-policy matters, but they are not usually contested issues. It takes powerful motivation for others to contest such issues when the parties or candidates have not done so—to move those issues from the margins of politics toward the center and even into the streets as happened in the U.S. in the spring of 1970, for instance, and in the Netherlands in 1981 and 1983. It is not an everyday—or even an every-decade—event. How and why this happens and under what circumstances are questions worthy of further research. But when it happens, the parties are not able to deal with it constructively. Rather than providing leadership, they typically follow, looking elsewhere for cues and implicitly inviting participation by non-party organizations such as interest groups, which are usually more than happy to oblige.

Media

The media of mass communication in the United States have a distinctive, though by no means exclusive, agenda-setting capability in foreign affairs. When well-respected journalists converge on a particular problem and keep it in the news for some days, they are sounding a "wake-up call" to the portion of the public that is attentive to that subject, and it virtually compels the foreign-policy establishment to pay attention and to respond. This "power of the press" (in the largest sense) carries with it an additional element of power: since the political parties are not useful as part of a daily referendum for American foreign-policy officials, those officials turn readily to the media for politically relevant reactions.

That does not happen in the same way in the Netherlands. Foreign-affairs journalists are few, they lack cachet, and they converge on a foreign-affairs subject only rarely, mostly when the Foreign Ministry leads them to it. When they do get the reluctant attention of officials, it is usually roundabout, by one journalist writing about a subject in a way that provides a member of the Second Chamber with a question to ask of the minister. Foreign Ministry officials *do* pay attention to the media, but not as part of a significant daily *policy* referendum of journalists. Rather, they are looking nervously over their shoulders at significant points to check on the *political* standing of the minister's party and on the standing of the minister within the party as these are reported in the media. In other words, even in this respect it is the parties, not the media, that provide the politically relevant opinion in Dutch foreign affairs.

Despite the differences in the way they deal with foreign policy, however, journalists in both countries share special sensitivities to the dramatic and the unusual. This has had a special impact on interest groups in recent years. As interest groups assumed the task of organizing and speaking for the anti–Vietnam War movement in the United States and as they replaced political parties as activists for the antinuclear movement in the Netherlands, the media in both countries found something dramatic and unusual to report, not so much a political conflict over an aspect of foreign policy as a public challenge to the authority of the government. The result was a quite different public issue—and a continuing flood of publicity for the activities and the goals of the organizations that the groups could never have organized, or afforded, on their own. In the end, the achievements of the interest groups in both countries in this period surely owed as much to the fascination of the media with their unusual activities as to their own political efforts.

Legislatures

Members of the American Congress have an important hold on foreign policy through their legislative powers. Though much foreign policy does not have a congressional component, enough of it does that the institution and its members have to be taken seriously at all times. A large number of committees and subcommittees deal with aspects of foreign policy, and all members have a vote on such issues. In the absence of significant political-party voices on foreign-policy matters, members of Congress are vocal and important bearers of politically relevant opinion on these matters; the rumbles, the questions, and the outbursts from the Hill are as significant to American foreign-policy officials as the debates in party meetings are to Dutch officials. And the function is the same: part of their daily referendum, provided by people who have extensive contacts with voters, and a ready set of reactions as to what will or will not be acceptable to them at any particular moment.

The Dutch *Kamerleden*, the members of the Second Chamber, are much less important to Dutch foreign-policy officials than their American counterparts are to theirs, because the foreign-policy powers of the Chamber and its committees are so much less, because only a few members specialize in foreign affairs, and because the government can ordinarily count on a majority within the governing parties on the few occasions when such issues come to a vote. The separate party fractions within the Second Chamber are important parts of their own political parties, however, and it is in that context that they—and especially their leaders—merit the attention of officials. In addition, Foreign Ministry officials pay special attention to the views of the Foreign and Defense Committee members, but not because they are institutionally strategic (which they are not) or because they have good connections with constituent groups (which they do not). Rather, they are part of the

Dutch officials' daily referendum because they are their political parties' specialists in foreign affairs and have more than ordinary leverage over the direction their parties will take on developing issues.

In both the U.S. and the Netherlands, there are from time to time similar relationships of mutual need between individual members of the national legislature and representatives of interest groups. These relationships flourish only when there is an identity of views between the two sides on a particular issue. For an interest group, it is a way to amplify its voice: having a member on its side, or in its pocket, means being taken more seriously by officials, especially if the member carries some weight to begin with. For the members, it is a way to gain some scarce political resources: information, or reputation, or financial support, or even electoral support.

Interest Groups

Dutch foreign-policy interest groups—especially those that have a specific policy agenda—share, as organizations, the fate of male praying mantises: to the extent that they concentrate their efforts on the parties in the Second Chamber, they are doomed by success. If they have acquired sufficient support among the parties, they become irrelevant, for their agenda has become the agenda of the parties or the party fractions. But if they pursue this strategy and fail to persuade, then they are doomed by failure: they are deemed irrelevant by those in the ministry who are watching. This fate may account for what appears to be an increased willingness on the part of a number of these groups to look to the ministry rather than the Second Chamber to accomplish their goals; although the strategy may not be any more promising, at least it does not so clearly put the political future of an organization at risk. The organizations that escape these dangers are predominantly those that have acquired a reputation as sources of information, allowing the data to inform policy and the reputation to secure the future.

It is the relative unresponsiveness of the American Congress that breathes life into American foreign-policy interest groups. The reasons for that unresponsiveness are many and have been discussed earlier. One is of special interest here, however: members of Congress are attuned to their constituencies much more than to their parties, and these geographic constituencies do not—at least in the short term—adequately capture the common interest of people who are dispersed across many constituencies but who may be a relatively small minority in most of them. Without the help of parties—and facing the need to be persuasive to individual representatives, senators, and members of the Federal bureaucracy—these people find interest groups to be an important vehicle for the aggregation of their interests and for their representation to the institutions of government.

In both the United States and the Netherlands, the relative importance of foreign-policy interest groups will fluctuate as other institutions of public representation do their job. When the Dutch parties are in the forefront on developing policy, for example, or when the American president himself articulates a growing national interest, the significance of and the opportunities available to interest groups diminish. When other institutions fail, however, people can be counted on to organize independently in defense or in pursuit of what they perceive as their interests.

Interest groups in either country obviously have more clout when they are united on a particular issue. But when that happens, it is usually the case that all other policy-making institutions and public participants share the same convictions, and policy is in no doubt. However, when interest groups are all over the map, so to speak, on foreign-policy issues, their multiplicity and their dispersion make them less than significant politically for policy-making officials, who are then in a position to pick and choose among the groups they wish to hear. Although this is true in both countries, it happens more often in the U.S. only because there are more issues and more groups.

In the Preface I quoted Verba and Nie on the heart of the matter about democracy: "The more participation there is in decisions, the more democracy there is."[2] Much of the social struggle in the Netherlands from the 1960s on had as its purpose the enlargement of democracy in a wide range of public institutions and endeavors, from the management of universities to the formulation of foreign policy. Quite clearly, that struggle has had major successes: the Dutch domestic political environment of the 1990s is considerably more open and responsive than it was a quarter of a century earlier. But equally clearly, the foreign-policy-making process has not so conspicuously shared in that success. The democratization of foreign policy has not come as far in the Netherlands as it has in the United States—indeed, it is still quite a long way behind the level achieved in the United States over fifty years ago. The Second Chamber, the media of communication, and the citizenry are all less involved and less active in a routine way in foreign affairs than their American counterparts, whereas the political parties

2. Sidney Verba and Norman H. Nie, *Participation in America: Political Democracy and Social Equality* (New York: Harper and Row, 1972), p. 1.

are more active and involved. Except for the emotions unleashed by the peace movement, foreign-policy interest groups do not draw much attention; many of the same people provide the thin support for the large network of *landencomités*, for example. There are deep rumblings under the surface of the Dutch political system: the political parties are losing their attraction for citizens; national commissions have paid serious attention to such proposals as holding national referenda on major issues and increasing the powers of the prime minister. But custom and history have not (yet) broken before these pressures; the Foreign Ministry remains a substantially private reserve, beyond the ordinary reach even of the prime minister.[3]

The democratization of foreign policy may have come farther in the United States, but the distance is not enormous. The Department of State shares the leadership of American foreign policy with a number of other agencies of the government, creating a porous structure. Only the intelligence agencies remain truly private reserves, and the challenge to them is mounting. The need for public support especially for foreign policies requiring congressional approval has, in the absence of a programmatic party system, long ago created an institutionalized need for public participation and a corresponding need to deal in some fashion with the messages the public provides. The latter often takes the form of what I have elsewhere called active public relations—or manipulation—in an effort to secure the consent of the governed,[4] and it is not greatly different in kind from the behavior of Dutch Foreign Ministry officials confronting public messages they have not asked for. But American foreign-policy officials seem to me to be more sensitive than the Dutch to signals from public participants precisely because the political institutions do not routinely satisfy their needs for politically relevant information about opinions.

Having said all this, however, I would repeat my earlier caution that increasing the amount of "democracy" in foreign policy is a value in its own right and is not necessarily the same as increasing the wis-

3. It is revealing that in an issue of *Acta Politica* devoted entirely to the analysis of a spate of national commission proposals for political change in the Netherlands, foreign-policy making plays no part. Much of what has been proposed by way of democratic renewal has a potential (though unexamined) impact on foreign-policy making, but problems with the inaccessibility of foreign policy are not once adduced as a reason to consider (or not consider) proposed changes. See W. Hout and R. B. Andeweg, eds., "De Nederlandse politiek: Sleutelen aan het systeem" (The Dutch polity: Keys to the system), *Acta Politica* 28 (3): 241–398 (1993).

4. Bernard C. Cohen, *The Public's Impact on Foreign Policy* (Boston: Little, Brown and Co., 1973), chapter 5.

dom of decisions taken. *Wisdom* in foreign policy is generally interpreted to mean choosing the most efficient means to reach national goals within the international political system. But it could also mean the most thoroughly representative process of deciding what those goals ought to be. There is some significance in this distinction, as well as in the findings in this study, for the discipline of international relations. The capacity of any government to respond to the choices that the international system has seemingly imposed on it has deep roots in its domestic political system, for it is the system, as we have seen, that shapes the character and manner of public participation and hence the responses that are politically permissible. Over the past generation both the United States and the Netherlands have tried to keep international-system "needs" first, defining *wisdom* as the choice of the most efficient means to reach the goals of containing Soviet/Communist power, and both countries went through internal political and social turmoil in their efforts to keep those choices politically acceptable at home. The Dutch were, in the end, better able than the Americans to understand and cope with the demands from their public and still be steadfast in their international endeavors. While Dutch governments ducked and weaved but maintained their footing, American governments yielded to important demands as early as the 1960s, in Vietnam, and have been trying ever since to balance these two frequently conflicting definitions of *wisdom*. These different national outcomes, unpredictable from considerations of "national power" and place in the international system, were largely shaped by the structures of public participation in each country, and those structures were shaped, in turn, by the domestic political system.

Glossary
Index

Glossary

ANP	General Dutch Press Association (*Algemeen Nederlands Persbureau*)
ARP	Anti-Revolutionary Party (*Anti-Revolutionaire Partij*)
CDA	Christian Democratic Appeal (*Christen Democratisch Appel*)
CHU	Christian-Historical Union (*Christelijk-Historische Unie*)
CIA	Central Intelligence Agency
CPN	Communist Party in the Netherlands (*Communistische Partij in Nederland*)
D'66	(later D66) Democrats '66 (*Democraten '66*)
DS'70	Democratic Socialists '70 (*Democratisch Socialisten '70*)
EC	European Community
ECA	Economic Cooperation Administration
EEC	European Economic Community
EVP	Evangelical People's Party (*Evangelische Volkspartij*)
IKV	Interchurch Peace Council (*Interkerkelijk Vredesberaad*)
KVP	Catholic People's Party (*Katholieke Volkspartij*)
MBFR	Mutual and Balanced Force Reduction
MPLA	People's Movement for the Liberation of Angola (*Movimento Popular de Libertacao de Angola*)
NOS	Netherlands Broadcast Program Foundation (*Nederlandse Omroepprogramma Stichting*)
NSC	National Security Council
PPR	Political Party Radicals (*Politieke Partij Radikalen*)
PSP	Pacifist Socialist Party (*Pacifistisch Socialistische Partij*)
PvdA	Labor Party (*Partij van der Arbeid*)
UNCTAD	United Nations Commission on Trade and Development
VVD	People's Party for Freedom and Democracy [Liberal Party] (*Volkspartij voor Vrijheid en Democratie*)

Index